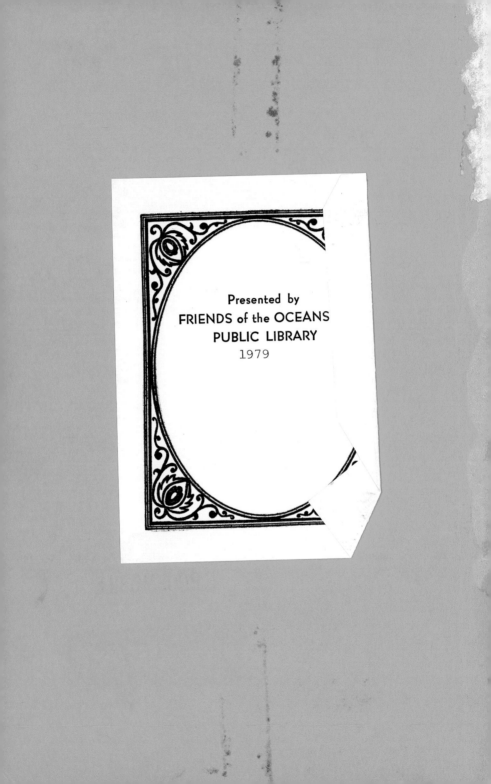

# Rickenbacker's Luck

Frank Lloyd Wright: A Biography
Black Champion: The Life and Times of Jack Johnson
Margaret Mitchell of Atlanta
The Elephant Valley
FDR: A Political Biography
Chicago: A Personal History
O'Hara
Fair Enough: The Life of Westbrook Pegler

# Rickenbacker's Luck

*An American Life*

## FINIS FARR

Illustrated with photographs

Houghton Mifflin Company *Boston*

1979

*Library of Congress Cataloging in Publication Data*

Farr, Finis.
  Rickenbacker's luck.

  Bibliography: p.
  Includes index.
  1. Rickenbacker, Edward Vernon, 1890–1973.
2. Aeronautics — United States — Biography.  I. Title.
TL540.R54F37      629.13′092′4 [B]      79-377
  ISBN 0-395-27102-9

Printed in the United States of America

V  10  9  8  7  6  5  4  3  2  1

To Rosemary Dyer

# Preface

MY OBJECT is to make readers feel the sturdy and invigorating presence of a remarkable American. In his long, crowded life Captain Edward V. Rickenbacker was a dauntless fighter pilot, a spellbinding orator, an international agent, a pioneer of commercial aviation and spokesman for all the airlines, a self-improver to rival Benjamin Franklin, a master salesman, and the moral representative of an embattled wing of the American public. In addition to this extraordinary variety of distinctions, Rickenbacker was the only accepted tribal chief in our history who once performed as a professional daredevil risking his life before excited crowds. He survived those hazards of the racetrack and for sixty years continued to evade death. And when at last they buried Rick, they found that something indestructible remained — his courage and skill which he left like Mr. Valiant-for-Truth "to him that can get it." His marks and scars he carried with him.

Admitting that Rick was a hero many times over, we ask precise definition and find that the *Encyclopaedia Britannica* has this to say: "HERO (Gr. ἥρως), a term specially applied to warriors of extraordinary strength and courage, and generally to all who were distinguished from their fellows by superior mental, physical or intellectual qualities." Rick showed that he was made of heroic stuff in two wars, and in each he had the protection of luck that has become legendary. During his first war he dealt in time, periods of time too small for measurement when he flew the Spad between bullets that came so quickly they formed almost a solid stream. The next war placed Rick in the jeopardy of space. He floated with seven companions for three weeks in the Pacific Ocean and owed his life to the fact that a pilot on regular patrol, not searching for castaways, looked again at some dots in the sea. This was an example of the luck that nourishes a hero's legend as the gods take a hand to help him on his way.

Born in 1890, Rick lived from the age of money into the age of energy. He was the child of Swiss immigrants, who told him money was the essential force of life. But before he died, Rick saw that money was going to disappear and that some form of counting energy would replace it. He himself had conjured up an incalculable amount of energy by exploding vapor to lift the airplanes for millions of flights that took place during Rick's control of Eastern Airlines. It is evident that Rick represented many things for his countrymen, and also changed many things.

The performance by Rickenbacker as the type of forceful American made itself felt not only in life but in literature. Rick was well known in Indianapolis, and the Indiana novelist Booth Tarkington might well have had him in mind for the motor manufacturer of *The Magnificent Ambersons,* the "new man" who brings a new noise — and a new danger — to the streets. Another fictional motor manufacturer is Charley Anderson in *USA.* Here, John Dos Passos presents a decorated aviator from the First World War who joins Detroit associates in exploiting his name, drinks hard, and drives into a wreck similar to one that Rick experienced while drinking, but Rick came out alive.

Many friends noticed how closely Rick resembled people who spoke for the author in Ring Lardner's stories. Rick had the same deadpan humor and calm acceptance of human folly. But of all characters in American fiction, Rick most resembled the protagonist of *The Great Gatsby*. Immigrant midwestern parentage, illustrious war record, altered name, and rise through social ranks appear in Rick's life almost exactly as they do in Scott Fitzgerald's novel. Gatsby's systematic self-improvement fits the program of young Rickenbacker as though Gatsby's creator had been given access to Rick's diaries. Although Fitzgerald did not have those materials and did not know Rick, Fitzgerald knew him generically, for E. V. Rickenbacker typified his times, a symbol more of emotion than of rational thought, and at his best he lifted the heart and made one proud to be an American.

The examination of materials on Rickenbacker's life took me around the country for more than a year. Rick had emulated the mound builders of his native Ohio by leaving cairns of documents, notably at the Manuscript Room in the Library of Congress, the National Air and Space Museum of the Smithsonian Institution, the Library of The Ohio State University, the Indianapolis Motor Speedway Museum, and the Air Force Museum at the Wright-Patterson Air Force Base in Dayton.

Equally important was the testimony, in both letter and conversation, of people who had been close to Rickenbacker, beginning with members of the family. I had the privilege of talking with Mrs. Edward V. Rickenbacker at Key Biscayne, and in Los Angeles I interviewed the Captain's brothers Louis and Albert Rickenbacker, who loaned me family albums and other memorabilia. David E. Rickenbacker, one of Captain Eddie's sons, and his wife told me of Rick's last days and kindly provided letters and pictures. My friend Rick's other son William F. Rickenbacker, himself a writer, gave patiently of time and memory during my three years of work on this book. I should like to record heartfelt thanks to Miss Marguerite H. Shepherd, the Captain's aide and confidential secretary, who graciously answered questions and furnished me with an indispensable written guide to the archives.

Robert Cowley suggested the subject and contributed much good counsel, placing me under obligation that I am happy to acknowledge. Others whom I must mention with gratitude are Walter Baker, Al Bloemker, Douglas Campbell, General Mark W. Clark, Lieutenant General James W. Doolittle, Lieutenant General Ira C. Eaker, Royal D. Frey, Charles Froesch, J. J. George, Peter Grimm, Robert H. Hinckley, Ivan S. Jones, Sr., James L. Kilgallen, Karl Kizer, Cindy Lando, John C. Leslie, Mary K. Lockhart, William Loeb, Arthur H. Motley, Charles J. V. Murphy, Brigadier General William P. Nuckols, Larry Pabst, Wayne W. Parrish, Warren Lee Pierson, John C. Ray, Sam Roshon, Joel Sayre, Gene Tunney, Helen Wada, Herbert Watt, Charles G. Worman, and Cole J. Younger. Finally, I should like to record my thanks to the reference staffs at the libraries I made use of in Miami, Washington, Atlanta, Indianapolis, Columbus, Dayton, New York City, Los Angeles, and Sioux City, Iowa.

F.F.

South Waterford, Maine

# Contents

# Illustrations

# Rickenbacker's Luck

# One Summer in Columbus

EDWARD VERNON RICKENBACKER was born on October 8, 1890, in Columbus, Ohio. His parents christened him Edward Rickenbacher, and he later added the middle name and altered the spelling of the last. But he answered to "Rick," even after he rose to such eminence that people usually addressed him with a respectful "Captain" or an affectionate "Captain Eddie." In the prime of life he had a chance to become the Honorable Mr. Rickenbacker, Secretary for Air, and during this period the two stars of a major general might have come to rest on his shoulders. Rick had an instinct for the right note, and, although at one time a reserve colonel, he remained socially a captain. It was a young man's rank, and Rick was always young in heart.

His parents were members of the hard-working immigrant class known as the respectable poor, fighting daily battles for survival, with no time for dreams of wealth and fame. They lived in a cottage at 1334 East Livingstone Avenue, near the city limits. Travelers peering at such neighborhoods from train windows knew that in a few minutes they would reach the station downtown. The visual effect was grim, because railroads and factories dominated the landscape and also made their presence felt by applications of soot; Mrs. Rickenbacher passed her time dusting and scrubbing when she had no other household task.

Rick's father William Rickenbacher had come to Columbus from Switzerland in 1879. Three years later Elizabeth Basler arrived in town, speaking the Swiss brand of German, to find work as housemaid under a cousin's guidance. In 1885, Elizabeth and William got married, the bride twenty-one years of age, the groom seven years older. The Columbus City Directory printed "lab" after William's name, denoting "laborer," but he was skilled, and when work in the contracting line was available, he had a job. But if things got slow, the Rickenbachers saw hard times. This makes it all the more remarkable that the couple managed to buy the Livingstone Avenue lot and put up a four-room house, which they later enlarged. Politicians hit them with a rise in taxes, supposedly to pave Livingstone Avenue, and William's discouragement became so great that he was ready to go back into lodgings, but Elizabeth said she would stay and somehow find the money to keep solvent. This she did by taking in nine weekly loads of laundry.*

Rick's early memories went back to when he was almost four years old, in 1893, and the family moved to East Livingstone Avenue. He recalled the house from the first as "a busy little place," and one thing that kept them busy was the raising of nearly all their food on the home lot, which measured 50 by 200 feet. The kitchen garden was feeding seven children by the time the last one was born, in 1900. A baby sister named Louisa had died in September 1896, failing to survive a seige of the child-killing sickness called summer complaint. The eldest was Mary, who was born on July 11, 1886. Then came William on August 30, 1887; Edward on October 8, 1890; Emma on November 22, 1892; little short-lived Louisa on March 16, 1894; Louis on September 17, 1896; Dewey on June 2, 1898; and Albert on April 17, 1900.

* A detailed account of the family's early days in the United States is given by Marian Pflaum Darby in *The Inspiration and Lives of Elizabeth Basler Rickenbacker and William Rickenbacker* (Columbus, 1963).

Rick was a tough kid although he didn't look strong, and because of his frail appearance bullies from other parts of town sometimes made the mistake of crowding him. He was a fearless street fighter and an accomplished thief of such portable hardware as could be fenced with a Fagin of his acquaintance. The stern Swiss Calvinist mother said more than once that he was heading for reform school, but the possibility of landing in jail didn't seem to impress Rick as it should have, and he continued to cultivate the toughness that made him leader of the Horse Head gang, ranging around the racetrack a few blocks east, where open country began.

Rick always said he had good luck during childhood, just to survive it. He carried memories of near disasters on Livingstone Avenue that are evidence of his having undergone danger. Some of the perils arose because of Rick's adventurous disposition, but from time to time the accidents of normal boyhood threatened serious results, and "the Grim Reaper reached out."* He never forgot a morning in 1894, after the move to Livingstone Avenue, when he accompanied his mother across the street to a peddler's cart. Suddenly, Rick dashed back and ran into the side of a horse-drawn streetcar. The luck came when he bounced away instead of under the wheels. He jumped up, ran around the car and into the house, up the stairs, and under his parents' bed. Elizabeth came running after; Rick was so scared that he refused to come out until his mother convinced him it was safe. He had a lump on his head and two black eyes, but, like a game little rooster after a barnyard fight, he bore no permanent harm.

Another time, he came close to burial alive when he was inspecting the hole that workmen had dug for a cistern. The edge collapsed, and he fell in, landing on his head. Rick re-

---

*Material between quotation marks attributed to Rickenbacker comes from conversation, public speeches, contemporary news columns, or dictated accounts of episodes in his life.

corded that he "lay there, limp as a broken toy." Passersby pulled Rick out before the dirt collapsed on him, and thought he was dead when they carried him home. He lay unconscious for two hours but was all right by supper time.

The New York Central Railroad running across Livingstone Avenue seven blocks to the east was dangerous anywhere along its length. Rick used to go there with his brother Bill to pick up coal beside the tracks. One summer afternoon in 1896, a locomotive came rolling slowly, and Rick jumped on the rear platform of the coal car. The engine picked up speed, then stopped with a jolt. Rick fell off on his back between the tracks. With a clank of driving levers, the engine began to back up. Bill came running and dragged Rick off the roadbed. And the locomotive trundled away, the engineer with his arm in the window looking down at them calmly under the peak of his striped cotton cap while the fireman tolled his bell.

Those who grew up around engines and freight cars can remember how no one could ever account for their stops and starts in the environs of a city's loading yards. W. T. Stead, the British journalist who visited North America during this period, told his readers that he noticed in Chicago a great number of people on crutches minus one leg or both or without an arm. They were victims of locomotives on tracks that crossed city streets, and Rick was lucky not to join the ranks of such cripples in Columbus. However, the scare he got from the reversing engine did not cure him of scavenging for railroad coal. Another time, he ran across the tracks and caught his foot in an open switch as a yard engine bore down on him. Rick yelled for help, Bill grabbed him around the waist, and they went over backward when Rick's foot came out of the shoe and the engine thundered by. That fall, when the boys went on an expedition to gather walnuts, Rick got too far out on a limb and fell. He woke up after Bill loaded him in their cart and pulled him all the way home.

What is interesting about all these risks and injuries is that Rick was not a husky boy, yet his small frame had in it elements of resilience that kept his bones from breaking as he fell from trees or tumbled into cisterns. Perhaps there are biological genes of physical and emotional survival. Whatever these factors may be, it was evident that Rick had them bred into him. Then there was the moral example of his mother's integrity, constantly before him. And in their total sum, the qualities that make for survival stood by Rick in the winter of 1898, when fire broke out in the school building. The alarm rang at two o'clock, and the children marched out. Rick recalled that when he reached the yard, an awful thought struck him. He had left his coat and cap inside, and clothes cost money. He ran into the schoolhouse, dashed to the coatroom, grabbed his coat and cap, and jumped through the hall, where flames sniged his hair. Rick came leaping down the outside steps and ran all the way home, until he felt his mother's arms, and told her, "I saved my cap and coat."

One experience at school stayed in Rick's memory throughout life, although it was so painful he might have pushed it below the level of consciousness, as we are said to do with episodes that have especially shamed us. From his first-grade days on, children called him "Whitey," for his tow-colored hair, or "Dutchy," because of the accent he had learned at home. The children also noticed shortcomings in Rick's clothes. He might have escaped mockery for jackets inherited from his older brother, but a certain pair of shoes caused humiliation. William Rickenbacher repaired the family's shoes at home, attaching soles and heels when needed, and adding patches here and there. This was not scandalously below the standards of the East Main Street School, whose parents knew that growing children wore out shoes at a rapid rate. But somehow in his piecing out of leather William sent Eddie to school in a pair of shoes that didn't match. One was pale tan, the other so dark that it appeared to be black. Mismatched colors were bad enough, but what made the shoes a matter for hilarity was the difference in shape. The left shoe, the dark one, had a conventional outline; the tan shoe projected in front with a toe that turned up like a medieval slipper. When the children saw this, they screamed, "Look at those *feet!*" They danced around Rick, mad with joy. He fought his way into the schoolhouse, fought at recess time, and at the end of the day fought his way home. Learned men tell us that experiences of this sort have something to do with making juvenile delinquents, and there may be something in it. But Rick mingled such recollections with pleasanter memories when he said, "What a wonderful childhood that was! Of far greater value than mere riches was the opportunity to work together, play together, and produce together, all under the loving yet strict Old World guidance of our parents."

Rick talked away the anguish of the grotesque feet, after more than fifty years had passed, in conversation with a friend named Hans Adamson. But in his written records of what had happened in his life, Rick left out the episode of the shoes and found something in the same period more worthy of recollection, when he gave an account of his first efforts to fly.

During the years of Rick's boyhood, the notion of flying through the use of artificial wings was under consideration by such experimenters as Otto Lilienthal of Germany and William Langley at the Smithsonian Institution. There were other theorists in the field, but all wished to become aeronauts or navigators of the sky, and all heeded the instructions of eminent authority to behold the fowls of the air. As they observed birds in flight, they nourished the hope of designing fixed wings for gliding surface, combined with moving wings for motive power. In Paris, an inventor strapped on leather wings and launched himself from the Eiffel Tower. A horrifying early newsreel recorded how he went straight down and several feet into the ground. Nevertheless, the man-into-bird approach continued to hold attention here and abroad, while boys in backyards and barn lots were happy to follow the fascinating lines of adult aerial experiment. As far back as 1867, a popular author for young people named John Townsend Trowbridge had reflected the juvenile concern with aviation in *Darius Green and His Flying Machine.* The fourteen-year-old hero of this mock epic reasoned:

> Birds kin fly
> So why can't I?

Thinking along the same lines, Rick added canvas wings to a discarded bicycle, and took off down the roof of a neighboring barn. He crashed in a sandpile he had prudently prepared. "Thanks to the sand and the good Lord," Rick recalled, he was only stunned. He added, "The bike was demolished, and so ended my first flight."

Some said the twentieth century came in on January 1, 1900. It was no use pointing out that this was the last year of the nineteenth century. But however you wanted to label the year, Rick turned ten on October 8, and he was a healthy, active boy. Around the house he had plenty of chores, which he didn't much care for, and he did odd jobs in the neighborhood for pocket money. The family spoke German at home, and Elizabeth read from the German Bible every night.

Rick remembered himself in those days as one who always wanted to be the boss among other children. The parents were strict; punishment was prompt and could be severe. Sometimes it wasn't fair. In September 1901, Rick fell into a fit of depression because of the killing of President McKinley. In a nightmare he had a glimpse of what he took to be eternity, and found it an emptiness too bleak to bear. When Rick told his father about this, William gave him a whipping, and said, "You let *me* worry about such things." Rick held no grudge against his father, who may have been taking out on the boy his own frightened bewilderment about eternity.

William, as it happened, was due to learn the incommunicable answer to the riddle in 1904. He had work that summer and went out on July 22 to lay cement sidewalks at Linwood Avenue and Mound Street, seven blocks from his home. Damp heat weighed on central Ohio; the discomfort made people edgy and hard to handle, spreading a harvest of violence over the pages of the Columbus *Dispatch* and other papers. During the noon interval, a scuffle broke out at the sidewalk job, and a Negro named William Gaines knocked William unconscious with the spirit level used in truing the squares of cement. At the hospital, William recognized Elizabeth, then went into a coma, which the doctors said soon would deepen into death. Neighbors organized a benefit picnic for the Rickenbachers at the racetrack, and newspapers reported donations of food and clothing, along with "large amounts of money." The assailant, a drifter from the South, waited in jail for the grand jury.* Rickenbacher's strength kept him breathing for a while, but on the night of August 4 they called Elizabeth to the hospital, and she saw her husband die at two o'clock in the morning. He was forty-five years old.

They brought the body home, and after the funeral Elizabeth faced reality. A widow with seven children and little money, she might well have had terrifying visions of furniture on the street, children carried to desolate orphanages, and for herself, work at scrub buckets or laundry tubs with a bunk in the poorhouse waiting when she could work no more. The brave woman was determined to keep the family together, and decided it would be better for Eddie to quit school and start earning wages than to run the risk of landing in an institution. Accordingly, he started at once to look for a place in the child-

---

*Convicted of manslaughter, Gaines served ten years in the Ohio penitentiary.

labor force, an accepted part of industry in those days. Under this system, no child needed to be without work, but the hours were long and wages low.

Rick's first job was carrying molten glass for glassblowers. He walked to and from work, a total of four miles a day, to save ten cents in carfare. At fourteen, he had not yet begun to fill out, and it looked as though the labor might stunt his growth. Stunted children and stoop-shouldered undersized men were common enough. Rick went on the night shift, did chores in the daytime, and was continuously tired. He changed jobs, putting in three months at a steel-casting plant, and then three months in a brewery, at the bottle-capping machine. After supper he set up pins in a bowling alley. His next job was at the Zenker Monument Company, where he carved a headstone for William's grave, FATHER in block letters, with the dates below.

While working for the monument maker, Rick carved a small angel, which he gave to his mother. The angel has disappeared, along with an open book that Rick cut from white marble, with HOLY BIBLE carved on the front. These activities show Rick's artistic leanings, which he had expressed in school. He had given evidence there that he could draw and paint by making delicate watercolor panels of the wildflowers he had observed in his dooryard, or while exploring open fields beyond the racetrack. He was finding artistic expression at Zenker's, but started coughing at night, and one evening he heard his mother remark, "That boy won't live if he keeps on breathing monument dust." Rick quit the following day.

# CHAPTER I

# The New Noise

AUTOMOBILES were now to be seen in Columbus, and they fascinated Rick. He thought the new two-passenger Ford a splendid thing, and kept the machine in mind through a succession of drudging jobs, including six months at the Pennsylvania Railroad shops. Here the realization came to Rick that more than anything else, he wanted to work around automobiles. He got a job in the Evans garage and learned to drive customers' cars. These horseless carriages of 1905 looked like buggies, were steered with tillers, and had two-cylinder engines under the seats.

Every Sunday Rick hung around the Frayer-Miller plant where Lee Frayer, a pioneer auto builder, was working on a car to enter in the Vanderbilt Cup Race. Frayer hired Rick as a janitor, then promoted him to the engineering department. In September 1906, Rick went with Frayer, as a mechanic's helper, to the Vanderbilt racecourse among the potato fields of Long Island. A few days before the race, Frayer made Rick his riding mechanic. On the first practice run, at seventy miles an hour, "the sensation of speed brought intense exhilaration." They went off the road, escaped without injury, but later ploughed into a flock of guinea fowl and came near turning over. On race day, Frayer and Rick started out in good style, but a piston expanded too far and stuck to the cylinder wall. Frayer said to Rick, "We're through." At this time Rick began to formulate his doctrine that failure does not necessarily mean disaster and may even be a good thing.

Even after this failure in the Cup race, Frayer's reputation as an automotive engineer remained so high that he got an offer to join the Columbus Buggy Company, now making automobiles, as chief engineer and general manager. He took Rick along with him, "a skinny 17-year-old kid who didn't look even that old." Clinton D. Firestone joined the company, and they started production of the Firestone-Columbus, one of the hundreds of brands competing for public acceptance. Rick took the car to Atlantic City and lined the clutch with an old brake band, for a demonstration of driving on sand dunes that other cars had not been able to negotiate. He drove 250 miles from Columbus to introduce the car at the Chicago Auto Show of 1909. Rick acted as floor representative and took prospective customers for rides around Chicago. Returned to Columbus, he made a favorable impression by rescuing his employer when Mr. Firestone's car broke down and he waited by the roadside until Rick could get there on emergency call. It was a scene of American folklore — the industrialist in a pickle helped by a poor but modest and efficient lad who is cheerfully working his way up. Somewhere ahead lies Easy Street, with or without the boss's daughter.

It was here that Rick made the first important organizing move of his life, out of engineering, where his lack of technical education would be a considerable handicap, into sales, where energy and personality were bound to make him a star. Something had gone wrong with three cars at the Dallas agency. Firestone sent Rick down there to straighten things out. It was Rick's first road assignment, with expense money and authority to act as he saw fit. He took care of the trouble, then got word from Firestone to travel over Texas, calling on dealers. Fire-

stone gave Eddie the hard prospects, old ranchers who suspected anyone with something to sell. He got around them with
his youth, good manners, and knowledge of the car, closing
sales with an instinct like that of the matador who knows just
when to sink the sword in the bull. The results delighted Firestone, who put Rick on salary at $125 a month, instructing him
to set up dealerships wherever he could find an undertaker,
hardware merchant, or dry goods–store owner who was good
at the bank and willing to represent Firestone-Columbus.

Rick shot up in height from five feet nine inches to six feet
two. The next time his mother saw him, she said, "They grow
them big in Texas." He was slim but well proportioned and
strong, at 165 pounds. He looked good in photographs and
had already learned how to give the papers entertaining
stories, as he did when he drove William Jennings Bryan in a
street parade. Rick now had money to entertain girls. He
brought Blanche Calhoun, of Columbus, a ring from Texas. It
went all over the neighborhood that Rick and Blanche were
engaged, but Rick couldn't see how such an idea got started.
Couldn't a man give a girl a ring without a lot of talk?

Then the F-C front office sent Rick to the north-central territory, with headquarters in Omaha, and raised his pay to $150 a
month. This established Rick as an executive in charge of a
branch office, although he was only in his twentieth year.
Omaha was a good place for the young sales manager. The city
felt its importance as an agricultural center, and at the Corn
Palace it held an autumn festival called Ak-Sar-Ben, a rite of
fertility. Red meat and red whiskey came from the corn and
traveled to consumers on nine railroads running into Omaha.
There was cash in the pockets of grain men and stock men,
which made the city one of the liveliest automobile markets in
the country. But a salesman needed stamina to keep pace beside a German farmer with a garter-sized rubber band on his
bankroll, or a wholesale butcher from Council Bluffs who

wanted company in a night of dissipation before putting down money for a motor car.

Omaha also was an obvious turning point in Rick's social career, as he went from the life of a minor employee to the spacious existence of a well-paid man beyond the indignity of poverty and the anxiety of debt. He often risked that position but never lost it.

Although now enjoying a front-office job, Rick was young enough to take an interest in the racing that had developed as part of sales promotion. He started to drive his company's car at county fairs in competition with other makes, which often had salesmen or even the manufacturers driving them. Henry Ford had set the example as a racing driver only a few years earlier. By the summer of 1912, Rick found that he was spending more time at the races than behind his executive desk. And he was earning extra money. The winner's purse at a county fair would be at least $200, sometimes as much as $500. In the summer of 1912, Rick joined Fred Duesenberg, the motor car designer, and devoted his full time to the racing of automobiles.

Rick soon built a reputation for hard going, and the experts agreed there was no more daring driver in the game. During the year 1913, he wrecked five cars at races in Texas, Nebraska, and Ohio. Each time he walked away unharmed, although metal crumpled and gasoline caught fire. It looked as though an especially watchful angel had Rick in charge. And at the end of June 1914, there came his chance to appear as a national figure and take the place in public consciousness that he was to hold for seventy years. In this week of June, Rick was preparing to race 300 miles in a blunt-snouted car around a South Dakota cornfield, across the river from Sioux City, Iowa.

The sporting businessmen who built this track had seized on the fascination of speed and were early in the field, because, until recently, moving above one mile a minute had been the prerogative of railroads alone. In 1905, a Pennsylvania train had set the record at 127.1 miles an hour. But the gasoline-powered horseless carriage made its appearance, and those who were familiar with the thundering of fast locomotives heard another sound, what John Dos Passos called "the new noise of the automobile." In 1911, the new noise sounded in a long-distance event when the first 500-mile race drew 37,000 spectators to Indianapolis on Decoration Day. And only three years later, here were these promoters in Iowa, staging 300 miles of racing on Independence Day, with substantial prize money to attract many first-class drivers, who obtained cars from manufacturers and headed for Sioux City.

Rick was captain of the Duesenberg team. There were two other drivers — Tom Alley and Tom O'Donnell — and four mechanics to work on three cars. The splendid racing machines were forerunners of the classic Duesenbergs of the 1920s, but the company had little money, and Rick came to Sioux City almost broke. Unable to pay garage rent, he arranged to keep his cars under the grandstand, the crew sleeping on cots. Next day, the hamburger stand opened, and Rick persuaded the cooks to feed his Duesenberg party on a delayed-payment plan. Rick told friends he was down to $6.75. In Rick's recollection, this sum became seven silver dollars. There was something miraculous in seven silver coins providing food for seven nomadic men. It wasn't a lucky number: out of seven, three were to die in racing wrecks.

As the Duesenberg team settled to preparation, heat came from a sky that was empty and pale at noon. Rick would walk out to his car — white-painted, with its black number, 32 — wearing his fresh white driving suit, and fit his long body under the wheel. When he pulled on the driving helmet, the thought of a knight surrounded by squires would come to an observer's mind. This gave point to an article, "Heroism in the Racing Game," that Rick contributed to the Sioux City *Journal* for June 21. He cited examples of chivalrous conduct, like the time "Smiling Ralph" Mulford shot his car into a cornfield to avoid a spectator who had stepped on the course in a Long Island road race, and the time Billy Chandler, known as the comedian of the pits, had saved Mulford ten minutes by pulling out a gasket that had fallen into the fuel tank, burning his arm from fingertips to shoulder against hot metal while he fished for the gasket with his other hand. And Joe Dawson had almost killed himself when he went through the barrier at Indianapolis to avoid a mechanic who had fallen out of another car. One could understand why newsmen were grateful to Rick for copy of this sort. It helped to satisfy the public appetite for material about cars and drivers, and harmonized with sporting opinion, which held that professional athletes should observe the rules of fair play and scrupulous honesty that amateurs supposedly subscribed to.

Among gentlemen drivers of national rank was the Italian Dario Resta, noted for boldness on the track and also for social charm. Resta had announced his engagement to the sister of Spencer Wishart, the Millionaire Speed King. Handsome "Spence" Wishart was a cotillion leader and had just married a beautiful Indianapolis society girl. He had entered a Mercer Special at Sioux City, and bookmakers rated him the favorite. Wishart's professional rivals, in addition to Rick, included Barney Oldfield; Billy Chandler, driving a Braender Bulldog; Howdy Wilcox, driving a Gray Fox; Billy Knipper, driving a Delage; Mel Stringer, driving his Stringer Special; Jesse Callahan, driving a Stafford; and Harry Wetmore, driving a Chalmers Six. Wetmore had many friends, but the *Journal* said, "The dopesters can't see him with a high-powered telescope." Ralph Mulford came to town with his Peugeot teammate, "Wild Bob" Burman, who tested the course and reported, "This track is very fast." The experts said that if his car stood up under him, Wild Bob had a chance to win "because of his absolute fearlessness."*

* Wild Bob Burman died in a racing accident two years later.

The same sports-page authority noted that Burman wasn't the only driver who competed to the point of recklessness. He turned his attention to Rick and wrote, "This boy has a savage style of driving, and is one of the hardest chaps in the world to overhaul." Rick would break for the front and go around turns at top speed in the four-wheel drift, and devil take the hindmost. Sooner or later somebody would die as a result, and it might or might not be Rick.

This ruthless approach combined with an air of boyish good fellowship to make a strong appeal for newsmen, always in need of copy. And at this early point of his career, Rick had begun to show that he knew by instinct how to play on the press as if it were a musical instrument. Maintaining that whatever brought luck should be cherished in his hazardous trade, he had exhibited a number of charms and amulets, displaying this year a lucky kitten named Duesenbacher, which rode in a box at his side. In addition, Rick had the dried heart of a bat tied to his middle finger. He said his mother had told him a bat's heart warded off evil. Rick also said, when reporters asked why he was not yet married, "My best girl is still my mother. And if I were married, I wouldn't be in the racing game. No, sirree! When I get the matrimony bug, it's quits for the gasoline course. Still, they say, once a driver, always a driver, so I had better not make any rash boasts."

As the Sioux City hotels and boardinghouses filled up, the *Journal* reported a tent city around the track, where hundreds of fans, known as "speed bugs," were camping out. A party of fifty Chicagoans who planned to live on private railroad cars arrived under the leadership of a lawyer named Charles Erbstein.* He brought along a Marmon Six, a man named Cyrus Patschke to drive it, and a bankroll of yellow-backed gold cer-

---

* Erbstein was a well-known sporting lawyer. He had represented the mother-in-law of Jack Johnson, the Negro heavyweight champion, in litigation against Johnson.

tificates. Erbstein started asking about odds, intending to bet his roll on the Marmon, and complained, "I don't like the looks of this town at all." But the next day he sounded happier, and said to Allen Rankin, of the Chicago *Herald,* "I've become enthusiastic about Sioux City. The entire police force couldn't drive me out." The Chicago reporter wrote that the streets were crowded and there was "a feeling that anything could happen."

Such a gathering of worldly persons had an attraction for those who disapproved of gambling, drink, and sporting life. Rick and his colleagues were responsible for a flying squadron of men and women from the Anti-Saloon League, who put up handbills, circulated petitions, and carried a banner that read, TREMBLE KING ALCOHOL. A team of evangelists set up under canvas at the outskirts of town, where they preached against card playing, tango teas, and free love. Intending to break up the service, a gang of rowdies pushed in, but left when the minister drew a pistol. And far from Sioux City, on June 28, a political assassin killed the Archduke of Austria as he rode in his motor car through a Bosnian city called Sarajevo. No one in Sioux City could be criticized for paying little attention to this event in a foreign country when they had such engrossing matters close at hand. It was one of those hinges of history that move without notice when people feel no immediate concern. Later on, they recognize the irrevocable placemark.

While interesting events were taking place nightly in the week preceding the race, Rick was going early to bed. He considered this his most important training rule, and said to reporters, "Boys, the Queen of Sheba herself couldn't keep me up until after that race is run." All through the night before the race, bookies were posting odds that changed in a startling manner. Big money came in on Charley Erbstein's Marmon. Some said that Erbstein's connections were such that his entry could not lose. The bookies took 5 to 1 on Burman and Mulford as an entry in their Peugeots. There were strange bets offered and taken, such as 10 to 1 that Mel Stringer would not finish, and even money that no foreign car would finish first, second, or third. Excepting Wishart from the betting field, a bookie offered 200 to 5 that no one could pick a winner. The longest shot — 100 to 1 that it wouldn't finish first — was the Moon, driven by a local sport, Ely Caillouette. At three in the morning, the *Journal* man telephoned his office that "Spencer Wishart, the favorite, has been hammered from five to one to the lowest price in the book, four to one." Rick remained 8 to 1, sleeping peacefully while the reporter finished his dictation with "this crowd thirsts for blood."

Early on race-day morning, a crowd jammed the bridge over the Missouri. Others crossed in launches, and then took buses down hilly Big Sioux Road into the speedway grounds. About 30,000 spectators filled the stands and set out picnics around the infield, taking their places before noon, when the race was to start. They sustained themselves with 100,000 bottles of pop, two tons of peanuts, and a large quantity of grilled pork sausages between freshly baked rolls. The heat grew intense, acute indigestion felled some of the speed bugs, and the South Dakota National Guard Medical Corps carried them to the hospital tent. Two companies of guardsmen stood by to help the sheriff's deputies keep order.

At the gun, twenty contestants shot away from the starting line, and the roar of the crowd became one with the roar of motors, which deepened to an overpowering, continuous growl; the spectacle of cars endlessly chasing each other added to the hypnotic effect. Barney Oldfield drove a strong race for the first hundred miles and dropped out with a broken radiator. Wishart then took the lead, with Rick in pursuit. Reporters in the press box noted that Rick would "make a reckless dash for the turn" whenever he saw a chance to come into the stretch ahead of Wishart. Wild Bob Burman was not the man to back off when these two crowded him, and held his own until the Peugeot's gas line failed and he had to quit. Those bets against foreign cars began to look good when Ralph Mulford, Burman's partner in the Peugeot entry, had to withdraw because of similar trouble.

A flare-up of gasoline at the pits burned the hands of Rick's teammate Tom Alley, and he had to drop out. Mulford was not under exclusive contract to Peugeot, and he took Alley's place in the second Duesenberg. Then, for the last 150 miles, Wishart and Rick raced hub to hub and hurtled from dust clouds side by side. But Rick gained a lap at the 186th mile and held it until he saw the winner's flag. Wishart closed forty-eight seconds behind. Rick then circled the track three times, to make the victory certain, as he later explained. When Rick steered toward the pits, one of his tires exploded.

Third place went to Mulford, in the other Duesenberg, and Cyrus Patschke in the Marmon ran sixth. Charley Erbstein cried out in protest; he wasn't the only questioner of the official results. Spencer Wishart lodged a protest, saying that when he pulled in at the pits, halfway through, the recording device had taken away a lap for which he should have received credit. Wishart claimed that this lost lap made the difference between his performance and Rick's and that he should be declared winner. The newsmen thought that Wishart would get no satisfaction but that Charley Erbstein would be able to alter the results. In spite of these complaints, all wire services sent out Rick's name as winner of the race.

Starting at seven-thirty that night, officials went over the timing and scoring of laps, as a typewriting device similar to a stock ticker had recorded them on tape. They finished checking at eleven o'clock Sunday night, and on Monday morning the papers reported a change in standings. Rick was still winner, Wishart second, but the officials had moved Patschke and Erbstein's Marmon from sixth to third. Rick had agreed to this, and Wishart telegraphed that he was satisfied. It was strange that the scoring should be muddled, and it did not sit well with Rick.

On Tuesday, July 7, promoters and newspapermen gave Rick a banquet. When he rose to answer a toast, he showed a lifelong characteristic: if something displeased him, he did not hesitate to say so. His afterdinner remarks resulted in the headline RICK MAKES UGLY CHARGE. He said about the scoring, "I know for a fact that officials sent here from other cities were responsible for the trouble, and I also know that some of the officials placed bets on the final outcome of the race, and on a certain car to finish in first place." But even at that early date in his career, Rick had a reliable feeling for audiences, so he used the bad-news, good-news formula to cheer his listeners. The good news which now came out was that Duesenberg Motors planned to move from Des Moines to Sioux City, bringing jobs and prosperity while making its new home town the automobile-manufacturing capital of the world. This brought the banqueters to their feet, applauding, waving napkins, and upsetting glasses. Since no one knew how sorely Duesenberg needed Rick's prize money, the evening ended with cordiality on all sides. Next morning, Rick posed for a photograph at the railroad station, as he accepted a $10,000 check. Smiling in his straw hat and blue summer suit, Rick was handsome as a movie star. America had found a new and engaging hero who perfectly expressed the aspirations of his time.

Rick now went on to another national sporting event, the road race on a course that wound in and out of woods at Elgin, Illinois, which he entered on August 21. The distance was 301 miles, and the presence of Spencer Wishart added a personal note, for the disputed finish at Sioux City was still a subject of discussion among speed bugs. Wishart was there with the blunt-nosed Mercer, and Rick was ready with the Duesenberg, a car of equally uncompromising outline, which had defeated

Wishart and his mount in the South Dakota cornfield. For 180 miles the lead shifted between Rick and Wishart. What happened next Rick recalled as follows: "Spencer Wishart was driving the big Mercer. I was coming up behind him on the straightaway when his car started wobbling, left the road and crashed into a tree. The rear end rose up and smacked into the tree so hard it wrapped around it. Spence was killed instantly. His head left a mark on the tree ten feet from the ground. Regardless of my emotions, I had to keep going . . ."

On the third lap after Wishart's death, the fast driver Bill Endicott hit a bump in the road, swerved broadside in front of the Duesenberg, and Rick went into the ditch as Wishart had done a few minutes before. Rick hit the fence, bounced back and up the other side, heading for a telephone pole. He cut to the left, swung down through the ditch, again bounced off the fence, and came back, only to see another telephone pole looming ahead. Then he skidded into the ditch a third time, and once more the fence slammed him back on the road. He nearly hit a third telephone pole, but returned to the course. All this bouncing in and out of the ditch had taken place in a few seconds. The strain of it bent the rear axle, which fell apart. Rick managed to get off the road, bucking and dragging, out of the race at 202 miles.

While Rick was taking his chances under the sky of an American summer, the armies of Europe were producing death beyond anything that newspaper readers could accept as real. Today it is evident that the First Battle of the Marne, from September 6 to 9, 1914, was the battle that solidified the war into four years of trench fighting, instead of bringing about the quick decision everybody expected. General opinion had held that no nation could stand for more than half a year the financial strain and loss of life demanded by modern war. Plain Americans in Rick's part of the country felt the power of the Marne battle in a personal way. Willa Cather put the feeling into *One of Ours:* a young Iowa farmer has heard that there is a battle going on which may decide the war, and he can't get to sleep. "He knew he was not the only farmer boy who wished himself tonight beside the Marne . . . its name had come to have the purity of an abstract idea. In great sleepy continents, in land-locked small towns, in little islands of the sea, for four days men watched that name as they might stand out at night to watch a comet, to see a star fall . . ."

Early in 1915, a nightmare invaded Rick's mind and stayed with him after he woke up. In the dream, he had been on the track, heading for a crash with no way around it. He couldn't get back to sleep, so he pulled a blanket around his shoulders, sat in a chair, and looked back over his life. He could recall fourteen narrow escapes from death. After the time of the horse car there had been five more escapes in his youth, plus eight on the racetrack. When he came to write about this vigil, Rick stated, "It seemed to me that the Lord above had shown a special interest in protecting me through so many hazardous experiences. It was about time, I realized, that I began to show some appreciation of this Divine consideration. The least I could do, in addition to keeping my faith steadfast, was to improve the condition of the body and mind that the Lord was obviously saving for some purpose."

In February 1915 Rick left the Duesenberg camp to become racing manager of the Maxwell crew. He displayed another lifelong characteristic shortly after he took charge. This was his habit of drawing up rules and regulations: "Always conduct yourself as a gentleman. If you do not, you not only inflict discredit upon yourself, but also upon automobile racing, the means by which you earn a livelihood." The closing paragraph was impressive:

If you don't like the way we do business, if you don't like your teammates, don't grouse and don't go around with a long face.

Quit this job and get another one somewhere else. The trouble
with a lot of people is that they are not willing to begin anywhere
in order to get a fighting chance. My advice is: Throw away that
false pride. No honest work is beneath you. Jump in and demonstrate your superiority. Once you get on the payroll, make up
your mind to master everything about your own job, and get
ready for the job at the top. Your particular task is merely one
end of a trail that leads to the driver's seat. That is my philosophy
of success. It works, I have tried it and proved it.

There was more to Rick's instruction than a rigmarole about
getting ready for the top job, which he must have picked up
from some traveling evangelist of boosterism. Where common
sense began was in painstaking rehearsal of how to handle a
racing car in the pits. Rick showed leadership here, and it benefited those whom he led, for they shared prize money. He tried
to figure out every man's assigned activity in advance, beginning with trips to the latrine before the race began so that nobody would feel nervous or uncomfortable while cars were on
the track.

Rick wanted nothing on the men's minds but the pit operations, which they practiced at the rhythmic direction of a mega-
phone. They drilled until they could remove a wheel with one
blow on the wing nut. "We practiced it until we could do it,"
said Rick. "Every man had a specific job in the pit. Mine, for
example, was to stop the car in the exact spot, then check the
right rear tire, which is the most important tire on the car. To
change it, I pushed the jack under the car and the handle
down in one motion. I hit the wing nut once, removed it, removed wheel, replaced it, replaced nut, hit it once — and
jumped in the car, confident that all tires were changed if necessary and gas and oil added. Our four-man crew could perform the entire operation in 39 seconds." They worked like a
champion naval gun crew.

Rick spent the spring of 1915 competing in California road

races. He continued to cause excitement by his insistence on taking the lead no matter what driving tactics the course might indicate. He would whirl off the road, and somehow no tree or telephone pole stopped him. If he turned over, they would find him on his feet, grinning, when the ambulance arrived. It was a question of luck holding out, and luck of another kind came in profusion when Rick discovered the delightful city of Los Angeles.

People had started complaining that Los Angeles covered too much ground long before Rick came to town, went up the inclined railway on the Third Street hill, looked out over the city, and liked what he saw. As an automobile enthusiast, he drove his friends far and wide under the eucalyptuses, pepper trees, tropic palms, yuccas, and jacarandas. His artist's eye observed the heliotropes, the jasmines and geraniums, and roses that looked as though scene painters had painted them. Like Edith Wharton, Henry James, and Rudyard Kipling in the same period, who liked nothing better than to bowl along in the country and stop for a picnic lunch, he developed a taste for motoring as a pleasant pastime. Rick drove his young ladies from one seaside resort to another, from Santa Monica to Ocean Park, Venice, Playa del Ray, Hermosa, Redondo, and Corona del Mar. It is a strange fact that Rick was introducing to the town he liked so much the machine that would probably, in the end, destroy it. But in 1915 the automobile seemed to bring a final touch of convenience and happiness to Los Angeles County, which covered 4115 square miles.

Among Rick's friends in the recently formed movie colony were the director Mack Sennett and the prince of comedy Roscoe "Fatty" Arbuckle. Rick would visit the Sennett lot to watch the filming by such artists as Mack Swain, Snub Pollard, Charley Murray, and Al St. John, along with Marie Dressler and Mabel Normand. It impressed him to learn that the comic business which produced paralyzing laughter in theaters resulted from painstaking labor before the camera. Rick admired the actors for working all day to perfect one bit of slapstick, for he respected wholehearted effort in any line.

When Rick returned to Sioux City for the 1915 running of the 300-mile Independence Day race, he was the subject of stories in every large newspaper in the country. With the experience of 1914 to draw on, the promoters now talked of 35,000 speed bugs in attendance. The presence of such a crowd would show the country that the race in Sioux City had become an institution, and would unquestionably be repeated for years to come. The boosters had to admit that the Duesenberg Company had not yet built a Sioux City plant. But there was no denying the publicity value of Eddie Rickenbacher and the other drivers who began to arrive at the end of June, just as they had one year before.

When Rick came into town, the Sioux City *Journal* had given him an eight-column top line on the front page, or "outside" as the make-up men called it: EDDIE RICKENBACHER ARRIVES IN CITY READY FOR BIG AUTO RACE.

A reporter wrote, "Rick wears the same old smile." Another asked, "Are you going to win, Eddie?"

The answer was, "I have no doubt I'll win."

"Who will you have to beat?"

"Resta."

The newsmen noted that Rick was driving for Maxwell this season, and asked about the lucky cat named Duesenbacher. Rick said, "She had kittens and I left her with the Duesenbergs." He did not need an appealing little mascot this year; his mastery of the press was now a perfect thing, and the newsmen put his name outside every day until the race was run.

The estimate of speed bugs to be expected at the track held at a possible 35,000 on Thursday, July 1, but steamy heat, combined with intermittent showers, caused gloom at the Commercial Club. Maybe there would be only 25,000 bugs present when the starting bomb was dropped from an airplane. The traditional celebration was unsuitable for Sunday, July 4, and the business interests did not like Monday holidays. So the drivers were ready on Saturday morning.

One of the experts had written that Rick might "overestimate his mount's durability." It was the old question of betting on the jockey or the horse: prospects looked best when both were trustworthy. Since taking on the Maxwell colors, Rick had not driven to win except for a twenty-five-mile sprint on May 15 in Columbus. On that day, Rick tried for a second win at the same distance, but went through the fence when a tire exploded on the seventeenth mile. The car had broken down in California road races in February, March, and May, and on July 26 he ran third in 500 miles at Maywood, near Chicago. About this showing, the expert concluded: "If his machine will hold up, Eddie will stay in the race." What the writer had in mind was Rick's driving strategy of going to the front and hanging there. The crowds loved a driver who raced according to that plan. But in Sioux City the money went in on Rick's old teammate Tom O'Donnell as individual favorite, and on his Duesenberg team to finish one, two, three.

Rain had come across the prairies, and the test run on Friday showed soft spots on the track. On Saturday the track was what horse racing men would call slow. Over this surface, automobile tires had a tendency to form clods of mud that shot back like projectiles, making the course extremely dangerous for drivers closing from the rear. The sky was cloudy when the participants held a brief memorial ceremony for Spencer Wishart. Wishart's name was still painted on the pit he had used the year before; now a crew of workmen covered the letters with fresh white paint while starter Fred Wagner and seventeen drivers stood with bowed heads. Wishart's sister, Mrs. Dario Resta, laid a band of black crepe along the rail. They stood for a moment, then turned to final preparations. The ab-

sence of ceremony and oratory gave the brief gesture of re-
membrance a penetrating emotional quality. There would be
more work for the painters before the day was done.

At half past noon, a canvas-winged biplane came rattling
overhead and dropped a bomb that exploded above the starting line with a crack and thud, and left a globe of whitish tan
smoke dissolving in mist. Seventeen cars lunged off on the wet
track. Rear wheels shot back streams of water and lumps of
mud for those behind to deal with as they saw fit. It was a bru-
tal race on a dangerous track.

At the end of the fifth lap, the crowd jumped up yelling —
Rick had moved into the lead. There was no question that he
was the popular favorite, no matter how the gamblers believed
the race would go. Charley Cox in the Ogren Special followed
close. Then the nose of O'Donnell's Duesenberg came out of
the pack. Rick and O'Donnell went into the north turn on the
fifty-fifth lap side by side; O'Donnell in the outer groove could
have touched the Maxwell without stretching his arm full
length. He gripped his own wheel as eight tires sent up a foun-
tain of mud while the crowd gasped like a huge monster inflat-
ing its lungs. The racers drifted around the turn together and
squared away for the straight. O'Donnell pulled ahead. The
speed bugs were howling as they went past the stands.

On the next lap, Rick and O'Donnell dueled again in the
pocket of the track, and this time Rick came out ahead. Now he
had to cut down the Ogren Special. At 140 miles, the seventieth
lap, Rick drew alongside on the straight and dashed into the
turn ahead of Cox at the Ogren's wheel. The track was starting
to dry, but mud was still churned up in the corners, and the
Maxwell sent back a volley of it. A reporter penciled, "Rick
kicks gumbo — Cox blinded —" and then leaped to his feet
along with everybody as Cox skidded into the ditch and turned
over.

The ambulance started across the infield. Part of the crowd

stampeded over the track to the wrecked car, and guardsmen ran to herd them away. Meanwhile, the stretcher crew had picked up Cox and mechanician Victor McGraw — nobody could say how badly they were hurt — and backed the ambulance onto the track just as O'Donnell loomed up from the turn. He almost hit them head on. The ambulance went up the homestretch in the face of half a dozen drivers rounding the turn after O'Donnell, their engines bellowing. But the roar of the Ogren Special was no longer heard.

As Rick approached the judges' stand on the other side, they gave him the pull-in flag. Next day the papers reported that this stop had been called to warn Rick about "foul driving." They said he had cut too close in front of two cars.

Back in the running on the 142nd mile, Rick lapped the field amid a hail of gumbo. At the end of 200 miles, he was holding steady. The Duesenbergs under O'Donnell and Tom Alley would come alongside, push their noses ahead, and drop back in the merciless cornering. At 275 miles, the experts in the press box said, "Rick looks the winner for sure," and they called his last twenty-five miles "a joy ride." The winner's flag went up for Rick at the finish; O'Donnell and Alley ran second and third in the Duesenbergs. When Rick pulled up the first thing he said was, "How is Cox?" The reply was "Charley's had it. Vic may live." When the reporters asked Rick about the race, he said, "Conditions were very rough out there. I won because the car stood up." Rick had no banter for the newsmen, and this time they didn't expect it.

Rain began to fall, and the fans were soaking by the time they got back to town. The promoters gave Rick $10,000 without ceremony, he saw to the loading of his cars on the train, and started for Omaha, 200 miles downriver. Charley Cox died early Sunday morning. The men in the Commercial Club talked about another race next year, but Sioux City never again held a big one. Their important race meeting in the cornfield was a casualty of the war. The *Lusitania* had gone down on May 7, when a German submarine fired a torpedo that tore the liner open below the waterline. Almost 1200 people had drowned; of these, 128 were Americans. Many other Americans then decided that sooner or later we'd be in the fight.

Rick went to Sheepshead Bay near Coney Island on May 13, 1916. There had been grand weather in the area, with those clean, washed evenings that bring a gentle close to the most feverish New York day. The Metropolitan Speedway Championship Race had drawn a crowd of well-dressed people, the women wearing long skirts and fantastic hats, flowered cartwheels on the slant, or frivolous constructions of silk and velvet, all of entrancing effect when worn by girls of spirit. Men walked happily beside these delightful women, and stylish escorts they were, in their lightweight suits and hats with club or college ribbons around them. Or any ribbon — it didn't matter — for O. Henry's gentlemanly safecracker Jimmy Valentine, or mounted policeman O'Roon on a day off looked no different from Richard Harding Davis or Ted Coy, the Yale football hero. Any of the four could have modeled for the popular artist J. C. Leyendecker, who drew the type of handsome, assured young athlete called "the Arrow Collar man."

Rick was noticeably taller than the average man of that day, his face had strength, and he was unquestionably the popular heroic type in looks, although the late Spencer Wishart, Smiling Ralph Mulford, and Dario Resta had something to teach him in the way of smoothing rough social edges. Rick profited by their example, and during the years he was associated with them he acquired his agreeable style of dealing with other people. Basic to his personality were the underlying decencies of what he called his plain midwestern rearing, which he credited to his mother; a commendable desire to please; the charm of a master salesman; and a simple delight in being alive.

But Rick was thinking of war that spring at Sheepshead Bay.

He had been talking about the need to get ready, and he spoke of the contributions racing men could give as a group. Who, he asked, would make better military fliers? He got no official response, and it didn't seem to disturb him. He would have lunch at Lundy's, Villepigue's, or the Beau Rivage, with their breeze-swept dance floors, and tables on decks over the water. Shaded lamps were put on the tables after dark. Observers noted that Rick's girls were always as pretty as any in the crowd, and when he strolled from Villepigue's on Metropolitan Race day, with a girl clinging to his arm, the men called, "Hello, Eddie!" whether they knew him or not, and said to their own lunching companions, "There goes the winner of the race we're on our way to see."

The speedway officials set this big race at 150 miles, which was a good distance for Rick, whose luck had not held up at 100 and 350 on this track the year before. Now it might turn out to be one of his most profitable afternoons, but Rick was in fast company, which included Resta and Tommy Aitken, in Peugeots; Ralph De Palma, in his Mercedes; Barney Oldfield, in a new machine called the Golden Egg; and Carl Limberg, in a Delage.

Away they went, on "the fastest track in the country." The field broke ahead of Rick, who was trailing the Delage ten miles out when Limberg skidded into the wall. The shock threw Limberg and his mechanic fifty feet; both were killed instantly when they hit the ground. One half of the Delage landed in front of Rick, the other bouncing over his head. He recalled, "A complete picture was stamped on my brain . . ." There was a cloud of dense black smoke, and the other drivers had no idea what was in it. They therefore slowed to feel their way through, whereas when Rick came around again, he sailed in fast and drove blind, depending on his memory of where the wreckage lay. This put him ahead, and the Maxwell team won $25,000 that afternoon.

Seconds spent in the pit could mean winning or losing, as Rick and his men showed at Tacoma, Washington, on August 5, 1916. They went all out for 300 miles, with Ralph De Palma the man to beat. On the rough, tire-chewing track, De Palma's Mercedes was the fastest car. "Just on speed," Rick said to reporters before the race, "we don't stand a chance." He pushed the Maxwell, but at 225 miles De Palma was ahead. Both drivers went to the pits. They worked on the Mercedes for sixty-two seconds, but Rick and his crew took only thirty-two seconds to change rubber all round. From then on, the Mercedes failed to pass, and Rick won by thirty seconds.

Rick turned out at Indianapolis for a special 100-mile race on September 9, 1916. Favored to win was Tommy Aitken, in the same Peugeot Rick had ridden off the track at Chicago three months before. Rick knew the car was ten miles faster on the straight than the Maxwell Special. He later wrote that the Peugeot "would squat down on the curves and stick like glue. I had to take the curves even faster."

At ninety-five miles, Rick held a slight lead; both drivers were going above the track record. Then Rick heard over his right shoulder "a sound like a rifle shot." A wooden spoke in his right rear wheel had broken, which meant additional strain for the remaining spokes. Two or three more of them cracked, and the wheel began to wobble. Track officials, pitmen, and drivers began pointing at the wheel and waving Rick down. He made for the homestretch with four wheels still under him. Then the right rear tire exploded, Rick skidded to the right, the wheel collapsed, and the car began to spin. The left rear wheel broke down, tires and wheels spun off in all directions, and Rick was whirling around, metal screeching and sparks flying, like a pinwheel on the Fourth of July. He came to a stop off the track, unhurt. It is easy to imagine that somewhere above Rick's head an angel of the guardian kind was hovering.

Rick by now had put into full operation careful plans for

self-improvement. Like Jay Gatsby, formerly James Gatz, he marked periods of the day for exercise and reading, and also improved his name. He wrote his name over and over, adding a different middle initial each time, and finally decided that "Edward V. Rickenbacher" was most pleasing to his eye. Then he selected "Vernon" as the name for which the new initial should stand. The full name, Edward Vernon Rickenbacher, had cadence — four trochees, with a tendency to lengthen into spondees; most impressive. And the additional *n* sound set up a pleasing consonant rhyme in the last name.

At the time of his autobaptism as Edward Vernon, Rick came to a conclusion with which many will agree. He made it a practice never to settle on an important decision before noon. His reasoning was that during the night, when people lie horizontal in their beds, more blood flows to the brain than in daylight hours. Therefore, Rick said, night is the time for imaginative and creative thinking. One would suppose by the same token that nighttime would be best for coming to decisions, but Rick said no. He had the common experience of waking with what he took to be a tremendous conception in mind, scrawling it on a tablet, and finding by the light of day that it made no sense. His researches in practical psychology were much to the point. They showed how little formal education matters, in respect to worldly success, when inborn intelligence is accompanied by the quality defined as drive.

In the late fall of 1916, Rick went back to California for the Vanderbilt Cup and Grand Prize events, which were to be held at Santa Monica. He had taken a leave of absence from the Maxwell team to drive these races on piecework terms for Duesenberg, and put in two weeks of preparation for the start on November 16.

A few days before the race, an important thing happened. Rick had gone for a drive in a dealer's car, and was enjoying the fresh air at Riverside, when he came to a grass-covered field and saw an airplane parked near a small hangar. He drove onto the field. A young man came out, recognizing Rick, whose picture had been in the papers during the past week, and said, "Hello, Eddie. It's good to see you. My name is Glenn Martin." What Martin had on the field was a two-seater biplane of the sort that barnstorming aviators were flying at county fairs. When Martin offered him a ride, Rick climbed aboard and took the rear seat with considerable anxiety, because he was afraid of heights. Martin swung the propeller, the engine caught, Martin jumped in front, they rolled in a half-circle, straightened for the takeoff, bumped along the ground, and for the first time Rick felt the cessation of contact with the earth that marks the beginning of flight. Martin took him over the tan California terrain and pointed out the landmarks. Rick felt no anxiety when he looked down, and decided that his dislike of heights did not extend to aviation. Back on the ground, Rick thanked Martin and then "hurried to the track in order to do a little bragging to the other drivers. I had flown in an airplane!"

The feeling of gratification at conquering his fear of heights in Martin's airplane did not hold up at the racetrack on the 16th, when the Duesenberg failed 49 miles into a 294-mile race. On November 18, another race was set for 403 miles, and Rick bowled along for 209 miles before the car broke down and he was off and out. He then decided to stay in California for a 200-mile race at Ascot Park, in Los Angeles, at the end of the month.

Sometimes Rick found it restful to go for a drive in the country, as on the day he had met Glenn Martin. He was taking such a drive when he saw another airplane. This was a single-seater that had come down in a field not intended for landing. The pilot had not been hurt, but his dejected attitude indicated that he was confronting a mechanical failure beyond his ability to repair. Rick asked if he could help. The pilot said help would be welcome; he introduced himself as Major T. F. Dodd, of the Signal Corps, the service branch then in charge of aviation. He said the engine kept losing power, a more serious trouble in the air than on the road.

Rick suggested that Major Dodd start the motor so that he could listen to it. This was part of the lifelong conversation between Rick and internal combustion engines. He thought that he could hear what they were trying to tell him, and there is no reason to say this was not so. Rick listened to the engine of Dodd's airplane and almost at once heard that the trouble lay in its ignition system. He found that the coupling had slipped off the magneto, which he put right. Rick's notes of this affair read: " 'Try it now,' I said. He spun the prop again, climbed in and revved up the engine. It sounded fine. 'Thanks a lot,' he shouted. 'Glad to help you,' I hollered back. He took off, and I went back to my car."

At the moment Rick's mind concentrated on the 200-mile race at Ascot Park, in which he proposed to give the Duesenberg another trial. Some businessmen had built a speedway to promote the Ascot Park development in what was then a no man's land south of the old ball park where the Hollywood Stars of the Coast League were to play through the 1950s. The promoters had paved the track with a composition surface that had failed to provide good footing for drivers in other locations, and both Resta and Aitken refused to enter the race. But Rick agreed to compete on this track. Earl Cooper, Eddie Pullen, and Cliff Durant also came in, with a number of local drivers and lesser-known performers from other parts of the country making up the field. Rick won that afternoon in his perfected style, firing the Duesenberg like a projectile on the last ten laps.

In five years Rick had conquered the press and captured the public. Since he never won the 500-mile race at Indianapolis, the question rises as to how good he really was, compared with the best in the game. We can give a precise answer. By 1913, the American Automobile Association had set up a system of rating drivers by points. Like boxing judges, they gave credits for aggressiveness, so that a driver who always fought for the lead would gain merit even if he didn't win. In that first year of national ratings, Rick's first places were few, but he finished twenty-seventh from the top, with 115 points. For 1914, Rick came up to fifth, with 754 points accumulated in his career. At the end of 1915, after wins at Sioux City and Omaha, Rick still held fifth place, with his score increased to 1785 points. And at the close of his final year of racing, 1916, Rick was the third-ranked driver in the country, with a lifetime total of 2910 points.

The racing at Santa Monica had a curious by-product because of an affair that showed how lightly Rick bore the demands of publicity and how well he got along with press agents and newsmen around the circuit. The publicity man for the Santa Monica track brought a reporter from the Los Angeles *Times* to Rick with the suggestion that they get together on a hoax which would supply some laughs and help gate receipts. The newsman wrote a story about Rick's not being an American at all but a European nobleman, the Baron von Rickenbacher, a Heidelberg duelist who had also been such a daring road racer that he had gone into racing as a professional and come to the United States.

The story drew a few smiles and was forgotten. At least, Rick thought of it as forgotten, though he himself apparently did not realize that Germans were becoming unpopular in the United States. After all, Rick was a good American. What matter that both his parents were of north European origin? They, too, were good Americans. What possible harm could there be in a bit of lighthearted nonsense on a Los Angeles sports page? In normal times, none whatever, but these were strange times.

Curious events impressed the strangeness on Rick when he visited England, early in the winter of 1917. Louis Coatalen, of the British Sunbeam Motor Works, invited Rick to become his consultant, inspect the plant, and take charge of a racing team in the United States.

Rick accepted the offer and booked passage on the *St. Louis*. He found himself in a cabin with two Englishmen, who ate breakfast, lunch, and dinner at his table, shared drinks in the smoking room, and seemed to like him so much that they could not bear to leave his side. In the customs shed at Liverpool, Rick was called out of line by a nasty, long-nosed sergeant, who began to grill him about his purposes in England, and delivered a lecture about the use of steel in racing cars, to which Rick answered that he was not an official of the Sunbeam company, only a consultant.

The sergeant returned Rick to his cabin, where the two companions were still hanging around. Revealing themselves as British government agents, they began to cross-examine Rick about his ancestry and his purpose in coming to England. These men were basing their suspicions on the name Rickenbacher and the news clippings about his being a German baron. Somehow, they had picked up the newspaper story, although they had never heard of Columbus, Ohio, or the American Automobile Association, which might as well have been on Mars for all the good they could do Rick when he cited references. The agents went through every seam in Rick's clothing and even pried the heels from his shoes. Rick's baggage got the same treatment. Then they told Rick he could not enter England but would have to stay on the ship until it returned to the United States. And they wouldn't let him telephone his employer, Louis Coatalen.

Rick suffered confinement for three days, until December 24, when the authorities announced he could go ashore under guard of the two agents. They got drunk at Rick's expense, decided he wasn't such a bad bloke after all, and allowed him to telephone Louis Coatalen at Wolverhampton, who had no notion of what had become of his consultant. After he heard Rick's story, Coatalen put a call through to London, where his contacts told him this was just another example of foolishness in the British Secret Service. By tea time Rick was told he could proceed to London alone.

At the hotel in London they made him go to a police station to be fingerprinted before he could have his room. Rick got to bed at 3:00 A.M. His baggage was not released until the next day. Then Coatalen got Rick down to Wolverhampton, where he had to report to the local authorities. Rick would be allowed to work at the Sunbeam plant but must report to the police night and morning. He maintained his good humor. On weekends he went up to town and stayed at the Savoy, although he had to report to London police night and morning.

Things looked good at the Sunbeam plant, and then, on February 3, 1917, the United States broke off relations with Germany. Rick recorded that date as the end of the Sunbeam racing team, and joined the Americans trying to book passage home. He got a berth on the *St. Louis,* and as he boarded the ship, there again was the churlish, long-nosed sergeant making himself disagreeable. And there were the two secret agents. They interrogated Rick for two hours before granting him clearance to sail. Rick went into the smoking room for a restorative Scotch and soda. Here he met one of his pals, the Broadway songwriter and showman Gene Buck, who had the latest news. "You know why the ship's delayed, Eddie? We've got a big German spy on board!" "Pull up a chair, Gene, and I'll tell you all about that German spy. It happens that I've known him for years."

Although Rick had always managed to finish a day's racing with no worse injuries than bruises or aching ribs, his luck in the matter of physical harm sometimes ran bad away from the track. For example, he had nearly lost the sight of one eye in Omaha on a day when he was crossing the viaduct over railroad tracks and a hot cinder blew under his left eyelid. For the rest of his life, Rick had a blind spot because of the scar. Returning from England, he felt soreness in his throat, and the doctors said his tonsils must come out. They gave Rick general anesthesia, and when he regained consciousness in his hospital bed, blood was running from his mouth. Rick felt himself drifting away as though floating on a tide. He had heard that this was the sensation of dying, and he tried to compel himself to hang on. At this point the surgeon appeared, forced Rick's mouth open, and saw that he had cut too deeply; and prompt measures were used to staunch the bleeding, but several weeks passed before Rick recovered his strength. What he remembered was the delicious sensation of drifting, an almost overpowering urge to drift out of life.

Rick was still preaching the necessity of a racing man's air unit when he turned his attention to business and decided to see if it would be possible to take a purse before going to war. Although he had no way of knowing it, he had run his last race, at Santa Monica, in the previous fall. Now he agreed to drive a Mercedes in the Decoration Day race at Cincinnati. A German car entered on an American track emphasized the emotional question about Germany to which no answer was available. Cincinnati had one of the largest groups of German-American citizens in the country, and Rick was aware of it as he settled in his room at the mansard-roofed Sinton Hotel, on Fourth Street, and started daily visits to the track, where his German automobile was waiting for its test. The track was built of boards, a good surface for the heavy power of his machine, and Rick told the *Enquirer* man, "I think you'll see us up there at the finish."

Coming back from an afternoon of time trials, Rick heard the telephone ringing when he approached his door. It was one of his friends, Major Burgess Lewis, calling from New York City: "Rick, we're getting up a secret expedition to France. We need staff drivers. How about it?" Rick asked for a night to think it over. Major Lewis was on the line again at eight the next morning, and Rick said he'd join him right after the race. Lewis said, "If you aren't in New York by tomorrow, there's no use your coming at all." Rick said, "I'll be there." So it was farewell to Cincinnati. Late that afternoon, Columbus slid back from the club car window under the hazy sunset of central Ohio. New York in the morning was full of uniforms and flags.

Rick was sworn in as a sergeant on the following day, and on the day after that he sailed with the first detachment of the American Expeditionary Force. It was the personal staff of General John J. Pershing, who was to command the armies of the United States as soon as they could take to the field. Staff executive officer was Captain George S. Patton, Jr., about to emerge from the obscurity of peacetime soldiering. Rick was the best-known man in the detachment, one of the first celebrities to go into uniform. Among others in the party was Major Dodd, the man whose engine Rick had repaired less than a year before. Also on board was Rick's friend Major Lewis, who had recruited him. There was a great happiness over all the men, for excitement of war combined in a powerful way with satisfaction of getting in at the start. Eastward lay France and the Marne.

# CHAPTER II

# To Make the World Safe

THEY SAILED out of New York Harbor in the rain. Gulls cried, and settled on pieces of floating wood in that self-possessed way which had fascinated generations of travelers. In addition to "Black Jack" Pershing, who wore the two stars of a major general, the party consisted of 59 officers, 108 enlisted men, and 2 news correspondents. They had all checked in at Governor's Island, and marched onto a ferryboat, which took them through the Narrows to Gravesend Bay, where they boarded the White Star liner *Baltic*.

Rick saw land moving slowly in the rain as he felt vibration in the fabric of the ship. When the land pulled back into a line that represented Coney Island and Sheepshead Bay, where Rick had won prize money, he went below to inspect his quarters, and found himself confronting the matter of rank. The accommodations for Rick and the other sergeants were like those of a jail, for the transport officers had crowded these men into an airless hold, where they shared triple-deck bunks with rats and roaches. But Rick had lived hard and was a born forager. He found two sergeants of the Medical Corps sharing a comfortable cabin. They explained that they were *first* sergeants. As soon as possible, Rick spoke to Major Dodd, who, by a stroke of luck, was the personnel officer. Rick said he needed a promotion to first sergeant then and there. Major Dodd told Rick that promotions followed meritorious service, but it could be assumed that Rick would qualify on that count. So a first sergeant he was from that time on, and got a decent berth and mess out of it.

Ten days later they landed at Liverpool. There was the quality of a recurring bad dream for Rick in the sight of his old enemy the long-nosed sergeant, now a captain and still inspecting travelers at the pier. Rick thought this Dogberry and his superiors would not be able to cause more trouble, but he was wrong, because a country at war is a forcing ground for organized stupidity and, at all times, a threat to the individuality of a man like Eddie Rickenbacker. What it amounted to was that in a war, a man had enemies on his own side as well as in the opposing forces. Rick had yet to learn that outside of people in your own outfit you couldn't trust anybody while a war was on.

A legend was established that Rick served as Pershing's chauffeur and that he frightened the general with breakneck driving on French roads. Rick later denied the report many times but let it pass during the war as a favor to newsmen. Although Rick had sustained harm as a result of the Baron von Rickenbacher hoax, this tale of driving Pershing at high speeds seemed harmless enough.*

Early on June 13, 1917, the Pershing detachment took a channel boat to France. They came ashore at Boulogne-sur-Mer, an agreeable resort known to British trippers in time of peace. The members of the French military reception committee at Boulogne were not of startlingly high rank. Big brass waited 175 miles away in Paris. There was one Frenchman, Brigadier General Jacques Pelletier, whose appearance told more than rank when Rick observed the scars on his face and

* A large advertisement appeared in the Columbus papers for July 17, 1917, proclaiming that "A Powerful Hudson Super-Six Is Used by General Pershing and Is Driven by 'Our Own' Eddie."

the empty right sleeve folded under his belt. In Paris, the leaders of the nation received Pershing and his party. There were Paul Painlevé, Minister of War; rotund Marshal Joseph Jacques Joffre, who had met Pershing in the United States; and Premier Georges Clemenceau, old and tough. As for the people, they came from offices and shops to crowd the streets between the railroad station and the Hôtel Crillon. "Paris had long since lost its gaiety," Laurence Stallings wrote in his account of American doughboys at war.* "Everywhere one saw women in black, and most of the men were old. Yet the people gathered to see the long-awaited Yanks." They threw flowers into the cars, and many wept. They gathered in the street before the Crillon, calling for Pershing, who returned to his balcony again and again to salute the crowd.

Shortly after the headquarters detachment settled to work, articles about Rick appeared in two periodicals, *L'Auto* and *Sporting.* The magazine *L'Auto* began an adulatory piece by stating that Rick's technical knowledge had immense value, which made him more important than an ordinary soldier. The writer proceeded, "Tall, blond, broad-shouldered, with two large expressive eyes brightening his beardless face, 'Eddie' is the perfect type of American sportsman." The article in the other magazine was an interview, in which Rick praised the French as steadfast people who had endured three years of war. Rick's words were tactful: There was no hint of boasting about American power, which would soon make itself felt. He stuck to his point, the appreciation of French sacrifices, and concluded, "France is a great nation." Rick was proving that at the age of twenty-seven he knew what to say and how to say it.

Instead of settling to an agreeable routine, Rick started to hunt for some way out of his headquarters job. All he asked was the privilege of risking his life in an apprentice air force against Germans who had become deadly fighters during three

* Laurence Stallings, *The Doughboys* (New York, 1967).

years of war. Eddie awoke before first light by lifelong habit, and when he looked into that darkness he must have been tempted to leave well enough alone so far as combat flying was concerned. But day would dawn, and Rick held to his purpose of challenging the formidable enemy in the air.

By September 5, the Pershing party had grown to several hundred officers, plus complements of enlisted men acting as clerks. On that day Pershing and his followers moved 163 miles from Paris to the small ancient city of Chaumont-en-Bassigny, capital of the department of Haute-Marne. Rick went along in the chauffeurs' pool, driving for Dodd, who had received a promotion to colonel and carried out important administrative duties.

Twice before, Rick had acted out an element of the Horatio Alger saga, in which the poor but alert and skilled young hero helps an influential man, to his own benefit. In repairing Firestone's machine, Rick had fulfilled all the Alger casting directions, for he was young and poor. When Rick listened to Major Dodd's airplane engine, he was not quite so young, and no longer poor. Now, in the fall of 1917 on a road in France, for the third time Rick performed the Alger drama. Out driving with Colonel Dodd, Rick came on a stalled American car. He concluded that the strainer in the carburetor wasn't letting the gas through. "I took it out, and, sure enough, it was clogged with dirt. After I cleaned it, the engine ran perfectly. The officer to whom the car was assigned was impressed. That was the first time I ever saw William 'Billy' Mitchell, America's great air pioneer."

And that was the end of Rick's association with Colonel Dodd. Mitchell, who also had recently risen in rank through wartime promotion, had influence in places where Dodd was merely another rear-echelon desk officer. Colonel Mitchell had a smart touring car, and, as Rick put it in his clear-eyed way, "He wanted a well-known racing driver to go with it."

Seated in front as they whirled along the roads, Mitchell often talked about aviation. He said the United States' contribution to war in the air would have to be pilots rather than machines. This surprised Rick, who had believed that the old American know-how could solve any problem on short notice. Rick gave Mitchell a demonstration of the know-how one afternoon when a bearing in the connecting rod burned out. The car had to limp into the nearest village, where Rick found a small garage. He recalled, "I heated some Babbitt metal* with a blowtorch, made a mold from sand and water and poured the Babbitt into it. Then I filed it down and made it fit. We had a bearing. When we were on the road again, Mitchell could hardly believe it."

They went on to the town of Issoudun, where Mitchell believed a school of aviation could be set up in the nearby wheat fields. Like Chaumont, Issoudun was very old. It had been there before the Romans, and soldiers of Richard the Lion-Hearted had successfully defended it in 1195 against King Philip of France. This summer, the wheat grew as it had always grown, while two Americans from the Middle West studied the lay of the land.

Billy Mitchell was the grandson of a Scotchman who had been such a formidable acquisitor that he put to rout the merchants and brewers of Milwaukee, where Billy grew up. Commissioned on the field in the Spanish-American War, Billy became an officer of the sort who goes on unusual missions, often in civilian clothes, and frequently writes his own orders. At the time of the First World War, he was an apostle of military aviation and had ruffled higher authority with public statements on the subject.

Rick admired him without reservation, but Mitchell strained the friendship by losing his temper one afternoon, when the car broke down while he was giving a French officer a ride, and

* Babbitt metal is a low-friction alloy of copper, antimony, and tin.

upbraiding Rick in a way he would hardly have permitted himself without the protection of rank. A resolve to have this out at some future date formed in Rick's mind. But Mitchell soon did Rick a favor by approving his transfer to the air force. A few days after that, Rick got orders to report for the pilots' medical examination. At twenty-seven, he was two years over the age limit. But medical science solved the problem when the doctor wrote down his age as twenty-five. Rick then got his commission as first lieutenant, but it appeared that his desire to fight in the air would be frustrated, for orders came through making him engineering officer at the Issoudun airbase, which was now taking shape according to Mitchell's plan.

Rick was a busy ground officer, but he managed to get flying lessons along with the cadets, mostly college men in their early twenties, who were training at Issoudun before they went on to gunnery school. He admitted to himself that he felt uncomfortable around these youths, whose manners spoke of prosperous families and superior education. And he took what he later recognized as petty satisfaction in ordering the collegians to pick up stones from the flying field. The cadets, in turn, complained about the "Prussian officers" at Issoudun — Spaatz, Wiedenbach, Tittel, Spiegel, and Rickenbacher.* This was forgotten in March, when the graduating class went on to gunnery school at Cazeau, and Rick went with them. After Cazeau, Rick joined a new unit, the 94th Aero Pursuit Squadron. He wrote, "It had taken me almost a year to reach the front as a combat pilot, but I was there."

Second in command at the 94th Squadron in its airdrome near Villeneuve was Major Raoul Lufbery, an American born in France who had become famous in the Lafayette Escadrille. Lufbery gave Rick some coaching and escorted him on patrols,

---

*Eddie began to sign himself "Rickenbacker." Newsmen discovered the change, put it on the press association wires, and the entire country learned that "Eddie Rickenbacher has taken the Hun out of his name."

during which no enemy aircraft appeared. This did not mean that Rick escaped hostile fire. On his first patrol, with Lufbery and another new pilot, Lieutenant Douglas Campbell, he flew over an antiaircraft battery between Rheims and Verdun. Rick had been frightened from the time he left the ground, and after half an hour he felt that the fear was going to make him vomit. That was when the first "Archie" shell burst nearby. There was a crack and thud, like that of the starting bomb at Sioux City, and a flash of light. The plane bounced and yawed. Again the explosion, again the plane shuddered — and then Rick was flying, unhurt, the engine talking to him sweet and high, the wings in place with no hole or tear in the fabric. The shock cured Rick's nausea, and after that he was able to bury his fear of being hit when he flew on combat missions. He never succeeded in destroying the fear, but held it under such control that he could do his work.

At this time Rick started his war diary, and its entries show that bad weather kept the 94th Squadron idle for most of March 1918. On April 4, he learned that the outfit was to move in the morning to a field thirty-five miles in the rear. They got there fairly close to schedule, considering the weather, and landed twenty planes out of the twenty-two that started. Next day, Rick went to Epernay and took delivery of a new coat with lapels, on the English model, worn with a soft shirt and tie. The sight of such a garment would have caused Black Jack Pershing to call the military police, but he might as well have been in command of the Russian army, as far as Rick was concerned.

By now, Rick had concluded that the 94th was never going to do anything but fly aircraft from one field to another, and he began to work on a transfer to the Lafayette Escadrille. This was for the practical reason that the Escadrille had just been equipped with new Spad* planes, which were said to be equal if not superior to Fokkers. John Gilbert "Gil" Winant, of New

* Spad was an acronym derived from Société pour Aviation et ses Dérivés, the makers.

Hampshire and Princeton, had come visiting in a Spad and had loaned it to Rick for a test flight. Rick knew at once that it was the best fighting machine he had yet flown; hence his desire to join a squadron in which every pilot flew a Spad.

On Sunday, April 7, came news that caused the pilots to dance, hammer each other's backs, and throw their caps in the air. The 94th was ordered to immediate active duty at the front; it would cannibalize the 95th to make up the requisite number of planes. The squadron was to receive "guns for everybody." And for home base it would take over a French airdrome at Toul, ten miles from the front. Weather closed in before the squadron could get away, and two days later, Rick went to Neufchâtel for a talk with Colonel Mitchell. Rick asked about the prospects for action, and Mitchell told him there would be plenty for all.

The 94th settled in at Toul, and Rick found quarters with room for his bed and a table for correspondence. He noted that things were so convenient and comfortable, it was hard to believe they were at war. On Saturday, April 13, orders read that the squadron would start combat duty the following day, and Rick's Flight Number 1 would lead off at six o'clock in the morning.

Up they went, through mist and low-hanging clouds. The town of Nancy was fifteen miles east, with Lunéville twelve miles beyond. The road from Nancy to Lunéville paralleled the front, and the enemy shelled it every day. But from Lunéville to Switzerland the action had slowed like a puzzling dream. Sentries stood watch on both sides but their commanders said that the terrain, running into the Vosges Mountains as it did, was too rough for ground combat. North and east lay a city whose name sounded like taps on a drum — Verdun. In 1916, the Germans had attacked this fortress of the French, and nearly a million men died where the rallying cry had been "They shall not pass."

After their failure to reduce Verdun, the Germans had had

to keep pressure on the place, for if they went around the city, they would release an army in their rear. Therefore, the Verdun sector always afforded action. And the 94th Squadron would be making its entrance at a place the world would be watching to see how it met the test.* Censorship could be invoked to hide disaster, but the men of the 94th gave no thought to the possibility that more experienced pilots might shoot them out of the air. Rick's flight encountered antiaircraft fire but did not meet any Fokkers, and when fuel ran low they turned for home. The haze had thickened into fog, and the field lay hidden. With only a few minutes left, Rick had to guess where the airdrome was and dive into the fog. Then he saw a landmark and flew into Toul "on the deck," 100 feet aboveground.

Rick's first day in battle added nothing to his record except the good luck he experienced in landing on the airfield instead of against a hill. But for the squadron as a whole, April 14 was a day of triumph. Lieutenants Douglas Campbell and Alan Winslow took off when the alarm signaled that German aircraft were in the neighborhood. These two had been standby pilots, waiting like wallflowers at a dance. They had just taken off when Rick heard an explosion and saw flames beyond the hangar. He thought Campbell or Winslow had crashed, but a mechanic shouted that a German plane had fallen on the field. As Rick ran to see, another German plane fell, about 500 yards away. Campbell had shot down the first, less than three minutes after takeoff. A minute later, Winslow chased the other enemy aircraft into the ground. Both German pilots survived and were taken prisoner. Rick wrote in his diary, "This was indeed a wonderful opening for our Squadron and had the stage been set and the scene arranged for it, could not have worked more perfectly."

* This tactical situation suggested the 94th Squadron's insigne of Uncle Sam's hat in the ring.

For the next few days, according to Rick, the squadron lived on its reputation. Destroying two enemy aircraft on the same day was good work for one squadron at any time; but the betting among French and British allies had been that if planes fell in the territory of the 94th on April 14, they would be American. The veterans had read the situation correctly as far as form would have predicted it, and the results turned out almost that way — defeat for the 94th and death for Rick. This he learned from the captive Germans, who said they had been following his flight, and had been about to destroy it with a thundering assault from above, when the Americans disappeared in fog. The enemy fighters were looking for landmarks and mistook the field at Toul for their home base at Metz. It was then that Campbell and Winslow caught them 500 feet from the ground.

After five days of bad wather, the commander sent Rick up to perform aerobatics for a visiting general. Rick put on the exhibition wing to wing with Lieutenant Hobey Baker, of the 103rd Squadron. Competing as a gentleman driver, Hobey had raced against Rick the professional a few years before in a motor steeplechase on Long Island. Between them, Rick and Hobey, a Princeton football and hockey star, personified the ideal of young America. Now they stunted for the brass in good style, but after the flight Rick discovered a broken distributor. Men were working on it when the alert sounded for a strafing run on German trenches. Rick couldn't go because the mechanics had taken apart his engine. He was already competing for victories and air time in combat territory, which was the spirit of his automobile racing, with its points for finishing and for going off, if go he must, ahead of the pack until fences gave way. A few days later, Rick answered an alert for the sighting of an enemy plane and had almost closed to shooting range when he recognized it as an English Spad. Somebody shot down a German plane that day and failed to claim it, a mystery that was never solved. It is possible that another German destroyed this plane, in an error like the one Rick had almost made.

On his next combat mission, Rick found a German photographic biplane at work near St.-Mihiel. As he approached this prey, one of the fast Albatross monoplanes pounced from a cloud, and Rick corkscrewed up and over, planning to pull straight and dive on the enemy with hammering guns. As he turned to attack, the German flashed past him and joined two other Albatross planes. The three reversed direction by upward rush and backward loop, and formed in echelon above and to the rear of Rick's Nieuport. If the first man didn't get him, two more were ready to try. Rick dove 2000 feet, leveled at top speed, and headed for his airfield. The Germans weren't interested in coming close to Toul; they made a token gesture of further pursuit, like cats concealing embarrassment at failing to catch a pigeon, and turned for home.

After a day of rain, Rick went over the lines with Major Lufbery. They met no enemies and returned to base through clear skies. While they were having tea, they talked about what to do if a plane caught fire. Lufbery had given this much thought. The brass denied parachutes to pilots flying combat missions, and Lufbery agreed with Rick that this was criminal. It showed the black stupidity of the professional military mind. But Lufbery had thought it out. If ever his plane caught fire, he would stay with it. He said, "Ride her down, Rick. Ride her all the way." They also discussed techniques of falling sideways so that wind would blow out the flames. Wind was hardly the treatment of choice for burning gasoline, but at least it would be doing something, and to jump without a parachute meant no chance at all.

A few days later Rick went out with Captain James Norman Hall,* and they caught a Pfalz fighter flying alone. Hall and

* Coauthor with Charles Nordhoff of *Mutiny on the Bounty.*

Rick maneuvered their enemy into position for the kill, with Rick above and behind as the German headed for his home lines. Rick pressed the triggers, and tracers showed two streams of fire going into the tail of the fleeing plane. He lifted the Nieuport a touch, which was like raising a garden hose. The tracers moved up the Pfalz fuselage into the back of the pilot's seat. Rick had destroyed his first plane and killed his first pilot. A second victory, based on similar tactics, ensued within the week.

When Rick started fighting in the air, he also started a diary, and on one of its earliest pages had written that he would never take unsportsmanlike advantage of an enemy. Hobey Baker and Rick would have agreed that shooting a man in the back did not appear to come within any definition of fair play. But this was about the only way to do it when you were fighting with guns fixed to the frames of aircraft. You had to play for position, and when you got it, move in for the kill. The enemy would do the same to you. Rick recorded this first victory and wrote no more about sportsmanship in the air.

On Sunday, May 19, Rick went fifteen miles into German territory, where he exchanged fire with an Albatross that "showed good fight" before it broke off and headed for Metz. Fuel ran low, and Rick went back to Toul. As he came in, Rick saw a crowd in front of the 94th's hangar. He jogged across the field to find the reason for this gathering, and learned that Major Lufbery had been killed a short time before. The major had taken off to attack a photographer's plane high above the airdrome, and word had just come back from witnesses who had seen the end, a few miles away. Since the observation plane was armored, Lufbery's opening bursts had done no damage. His guns jammed, he circled while clearing them, took a burst in the engine, and flames broke out. The witnesses saw him crawl toward the tail of the plane. The fire reached him — and he jumped at a height of 200 feet.

There was a rivulet running through gardens on the outskirts of a village near Nancy. It appeared that Lufbery was aiming at this water when the plane, flying at 120 miles an hour, gave such impetus to his jump that he hurtled along parallel to the ground and crashed through a fence into a garden. An old woman who lived in the house ran out and saw Lufbery's body demolish the fence. Then the body stood up and appeared to bow.

On the following day they buried Lufbery, and Rick led a flight that dropped flowers on the grave. Four planes flew in a V, with a space where the fifth plane should have been, the "missing leader" formation. Two days later, Rick went on patrol with Lieutenant Reed Chambers, who had been his closest friend at Issoudun. With them flew a Lieutenant Kurtz, a gunnery instructor sent to Toul for combat experience. Rick suggested that Kurtz maintain position above and behind, and not move in and fire on German planes, if they should meet any, unless the odds looked good. He repeated the maxim "Avoid a fight unless you can maneuver to best advantage."

At around 15,000 feet, three Albatrosses swooped down and flew through the 94th's formation, blazing away and missing. Rick went after the last one and saw him falling within German lines. What he took to be the other two Germans now got above Rick, and he decided to pull for home. One of the planes started to overhaul him, and Rick was about to fire on it when he recognized the red, blue, and white rings of the U.S. Air Service. It was Chambers, who saw just in time that Rick was preparing to attack, and, like a puppy rolling on its back in a mock fight, banked to expose the insigne. Rick and Chambers landed and stood watching Kurtz, who was circling the field. Suddenly, the Nieuport crashed and exploded. When they reached it, they found that Kurtz had burned to death. They thought a stray bullet might have wounded Kurtz and that he had fainted just before getting home. It turned out that Kurtz was subject to spells and shouldn't have been flying at all.

The death of Kurtz caused Rick to think about something he had begun to notice. This was the evident fact that first sorties into combat ended fatally more often than statistics of probability would have indicated. Yet the chances that any *one* flight would prove fatal were small. In the mathematical view, it was repeatedly going out that made the fatal sortie more probable. There was no answer to it. As Mr. John Oakhurst of Poker Flat observed, "Luck is a mighty queer thing. All you know about it for certain is that it's bound to change." Next day, French observers at the front sent confirmation of the downed Albatross, which was Rick's third victory.

This third kill earned Rick high standing in the masculine, sporting world of Squadron 94. His mates gave him the approval a halfback would have gained by good running and a touchdown in an important game. Those who had been at Issoudun in the time of the gathering of stones forgot their resentment. Rick in turn had been able to reveal his natural amiability, and the other men felt it. For all their air of assurance and competence, most of the men of the 94th had been college boys a short time before, whereas Rick was a man of the world. And his edges were undergoing a smoothing process. He did not really wish to be the stage sergeant major type of man; he wanted to be someone not startlingly different, so far as exteriors were concerned, from well-mannered youths who had been given what old-fashioned people called "advantages." Meanwhile, the officials of Counterintelligence at last gave in on Rick, and some odd-looking agents masquerading as airmen packed up and disappeared. If Rick was a German spy, they must have reasoned, the way he maintained his cover by destroying German airplanes justified their leaving him alone from then on.

On the weekend, a troupe of entertainers from the States gave a show. Rick met a girl from Indianapolis, a Miss Best, and had a grand time. The following Tuesday fell on May 28, and the page heading in Rick's British-made diary read, TRINITY SITTINGS BEGIN. This might have seemed an auspicious day, but Rick missed the dawn patrol. He went out later with Douglas Campbell, and, using the Nieuports' speed to stay on top, the two sparred with six Albatross biplanes. The fight drew antiaircraft fire, which added to the hazard. The American pilots could not tell whether friend or foe was firing from the ground, but Rick shot down an Albatross for his fourth victory, confirmed next day. After he and Campbell got back to Toul, Rick had a funeral to attend. Lieutenant John Mitchell, Billy's younger brother, received military honors. His had been another of those early combat deaths. He had chased a German back toward enemy territory and had turned over and crashed in the *pique*, or attack dive.

The end of May saw Rick win his fifth victory, over another Albatross. Rick had plunged into a confused battle against a flight of Germans harrying twelve British bombers on their way home. One of the enemy planes fell out of the sky because of Rick's marksmanship in a rescue of Lieutenant James "Jimmy" Meissner of Brooklyn. The wind had torn canvas from Meissner's wings, and Rick shot up the enemy that tried to bag the cripple. Meissner limped home and later got credit for destroying a Fokker before his Nieuport started coming apart.*

The competitive aspect of millitary aviation among men on the same side took public form in scorekeeping like that of prize rings and playing fields. Newspaper readers in England and the United States were well prepared for personal records in the air because of the statistics from cricket and baseball. For these games, painstaking scorers noted every play and pub-

---

* Victories were not official unless confirmed by ground observers, and the aces destroyed more aircraft than they got credit for. An examination of Rick's record shows fifteen occasions when it was probable that he had put a German plane out of business, but he made no claim, because the enemy, presumably hurt, had retreated beyond Allied observation.

lished the results in annual volumes that carried the authority
of Scripture for the fans. American war correspondents decided that any pilot who got official credit for destroying five
enemy planes should receive the designation of "ace." The survival of the ace through his five confirmed victories meant that
he had probably gone into ten or fifteen fire fights. According
to the *Oxford English Dictionary,* the Royal Air Force gave the
title of ace to any pilot who shot down three of the enemy. The
RAF expected a pilot to survive no more than four weeks of
combat. The designation of ace was a source of pride at home,
for the censors made no objection to dispatches announcing
that a pilot had achieved the ranking.*

On Friday, May 31, Lieutenant Campbell got credit for a
biplane, probably an Albatross. The make of the plane didn't
matter, because French Eighth Army observers affirmed that
they had seen the enemy go down. Rick recorded that this
made Campbell the 94th's first ace. It was true that the French
had confirmed Rick's fifth victory the previous day, but he did
not yet feel entitled to claim the title. He had shared the plane
brought down on April 29 with Captain Hall, now listed missing and presumed dead. To Rick's sense of fair play this made
his record only four and a half victories, so he congratulated
Douglas Campbell and told him he was "going some." Stepping
aside in this manner was not easy for Rick, but he felt that he
had to do it. It was the cry of "Good shot!" when the opponent
put the ball beyond your reach on the tennis courts, which was
expected in those days.

Rick had become acclimated to fear, and no one denied that
there was plenty of fear. Flying a fragile machine two miles up
in the sky and hunting for opponents who could send bullets
through your body, or explode a tank of gasoline in your face,

* The papers proclaimed Hobey Baker an American ace when he had not in
fact listed the required number of victories. The squadron he led got into action late, on a quiet sector, and he recorded three kills before November 11,
1918. A few days later, Hobey died in a crackup.

was an act that began with anxiety and continued with terror. Yet they kept at it whenever the weather was flyable. Rick, Reed Chambers, and many others put in voluntary hours of additional patrol duty to add to the time in which they sought danger.

This kind of war made an emotional burden that each pilot carried in his own way. Rick said he was able to keep his wits about him in "close calls" by postponing fear until he was back on the ground. He had achieved self-control on the racetrack by a similar method of running ahead of the nervous breaking point just as he tried to run ahead of the other cars. The surroundings at airdromes were similar to racing pits and set familiar nervous reactions going. There were the same crews of mechanics, the roaring of engines, the note of chivalry, the feeling of squires preparing a knight errant for the quest when the ground crews helped Rick to his place at the controls before wheeling out car or aircraft. Flying clothes were the same as racing clothes. In each case he was setting out, gloved and helmeted, to face dangers from which he might not return. Dramatic as the racing pits had been, they did not have the excitement of a lineup for dawn patrol, when Rick would *"coupez le spark"* so that the mechanics could swing the prop and jump clear as the engine caught and the blue green exhaust flame streaked the darkness while Rick taxied upfield for the takeoff.

On June 1, 1918, Rick woke up feeling seedy. His head ached and he was sure his temperature would be high if he allowed anyone to measure it. Instead of doing that, Rick avoided the medical tent and flew his usual patrol over the lines. The 94th patrol met a Rumpler biplane, went after it with crackling guns, received return fire, and the Rumpler got out unharmed. Back at base there were rumors that a big push was about to start. Rick wrote that he hoped this would happen so that he could say he had fought in a real war.

On top of the war as he was, Rick could not form a clear idea of which way the scales were tipping. No one knew for certain. Although some said that American industrial power would crush the German armies, our greatest contribution to the Allied cause was not material things, but men. German intelligence had already reported high quality in the ground troops, and enemy air intelligence warned all flights about the aggressive spirit of the Americans, who would attack formations and would fly with such boldness that care had to be taken against their tactics of hitting from below as well as from above.

A day of bad weather afforded Rick time to work on his mail. He received a cable announcing that the American Automobile Association had made him a life member. That might not be a membership of long duration. Next day Rick got on the tail of a Fokker, but his guns jammed. This happened often, and probably saved enemy lives while endangering his own.

On the following day Rick was appointed deputy commander, which meant that he no longer had to get permission for his voluntary flights but could go looking for action whenever he felt like it. On his first time out under these rules, Rick found an enemy against whom his guns had jammed the day before. And again the guns failed to work. Then Rick's engine "froze" and he glided back to base. Something would have to be done about equipment. Here were guns that wouldn't shoot, engines that quit, and airplanes that tore apart on the dive.

Rick's frustration made him feel generally low, and his bones ached. The medical officer prescribed forty-eight hours' leave in Paris. Rick got up there on Saturday, June 8, had a quiet dinner, and turned in early. Sunday was a beautiful morning, and he went to a nearby airfield with a friend, Lieutenant Cedric Fauntleroy of the 94th, to look at some Spad fighter planes. The sight of the sturdy aircraft excited Rick, and he told Fauntleroy that their squadron must have that plane if they were to accomplish what they had been sent to do. But the weather was so pleasant, Rick couldn't worry about it anymore. He continued to soothe his nerves when they returned to Paris and Fauntleroy introduced him to a young French lady who was a wonderful piano player. Fauntleroy's own young lady was equally good company. Rick closed the diary entry: "Had dinner in the Café Bois de Boulogne, went riding later taking the girls home. It was a most Perfect day."

In the following week, a rumor circulated that Spads would soon arrive for all in the squadron. On the same day, a cable from the Columbus Automobile Club informed Rick of his election as its first and only life member. Again he allowed himself to chuckle at the probabilities: "Ha. Ha." was the entry in Rick's firm handwriting. And the mail continued to pile up, "from real Old and Dear friends all over America."

There was excitement on the morning of June 19, when Rick went out at three o'clock to strafe German trenches at 400 feet, in reprisal for the Germans' use of gas in that sector. When the sun came up, Rick saw that the wind had shifted, as it often will at dawn, and had blown gas back toward the Germans. Later that morning Rick went to Lunéville with a United Press correspondent for lunch. On the way back they saw a family of wild boar. Rick got out of the car, intending to capture a young one for a mascot, or possibly to make the centerpiece at a banquet, but he abandoned the idea when the mother charged from a thicket and headed for him.

At the base, Rick set his alarm for 2:30 A.M., hoping to get an early start on a balloon raid. The observation balloons, which the Germans called *Drachen* (dragons), were useful for bringing fire on infantry, and pursuit squadrons tried to hold them to the ground as much as possible. The *Drachen* had friends who fired explosive bullets known as "flaming onions." Balloon fighting could be suicidal because when a pilot committed himself to his run, gunners on the ground could "lead" him, with a fair chance that his line of flight would intersect their line of fire. This would have given Rick plenty to think about on his way to the *Drachens'* den, but the weather on that day — June 20 — was not for flying, so he stayed on the ground at Toul. Next morning the alarm clock woke him at two-thirty, for the longest day of the year. Again there was no flying weather, and Rick passed his time helping make arrangements for a dance to be held on the following night.

The party was a success, for Rick's social gifts were flowering, and he was "detailed to get the British and French all feeling good as soon as possible, so that they may not become bored." This was like an election to a college prom committee, the sort of social chore given to young men who were sure of themselves and amiable in manner. What had become of that hard-boiled engineering taskmaster? He had taken his place behind an agreeable front as pilots shared dances with nurses and Red Cross girls. Over the ladies' dressing room the hosts had hung a sign reading "No Man's Land." Next morning Rick recorded that everyone had a hangover and no one was "mad at the Boche," their expression for being eager to fly. On the day after they recovered from the party, balloon attackers got off at 4:00 A.M., and Rick found his *Drache* in the air. Flaming onions began to buzz around him as he made his run. He got off twenty rounds, and the guns jammed. There was nothing for it but run for home and leave the *Drache* tugging gently on its cable.

In the morning Rick felt pretty bad. They said he had something called "three-day fever," and obviously he was in poor shape, though he cheered up when word came that a big show might start at any time and the Spads for Squadron 94 would be delivered to take part in it. Rick longed for that plane the way a young sport at college would pine for a Stutz Bulldog or a Mercer Raceabout.

Next day, Rick went to the hospital. All the medics could tell him was that he had a fever. He felt better by the following Monday, and on Tuesday, July 2, went to a nearby château where convalescent officers were resting. Rick passed a quiet day, noting that two pilots of Squadron 27 had been killed, one from Columbus. He must call on the parents when he got home. On July 4, Rick and some other convalescents went to Paris, and he visited an airfield where the French had collected new Spads for the front. The French let him choose one just as though he were in an automobile showroom. In the morning of July 6 — OXFORD TRINITY TERM ENDS — Rick flew the new Spad back to base and landed without incident. First thing he heard was how two members of Squadron 95 "went west" the day before. He wrote, "Hard Luck."

Although the doctors released him from the hospital, Rick was not in good health. He began to suffer pain in his right ear; at times it became excruciating. He gained temporary relief at night from a bag of hot salt on his ear, but when he was found lying semiconscious, the squadron doctor sent him to Paris for a mastoid operation. Rick underwent a second operation before his release, in the last week of August. Tired and weak, he managed to summon strength to sit up and enjoy a concert by the band that Lieutenant James Europe had organized with the pick of army musicians. Jim Europe had been conductor for the dancers Vernon and Irene Castle.* Rick heard the music from a balcony, where he got a visit from a pretty nurse whom he had been longing to meet. She said it was too bad Rick couldn't go down into the courtyard where the band was playing and have a dance with her. Rick's private thought was that he would have given ten years of life for that dance. So they sat there on the balcony for a little while. After dinner she brought Rick some ice cream. This nurse had stirred his emotions more than any woman he met in France.

There was a gunshot case in the next bed, and on Friday, August 23, the surgeons took off one of the man's legs. The

---

* British-born Vernon Castle was another hero of the time. Known for his style and taste as a dancer, Castle had joined the Canadians and later transferred to the American air force. He died in a crackup while training cadets in Texas.

wounded man was none too sure of keeping the other leg, which had a gangrenous hole in the knee. Rick noted that doctors must do their work, but he would rather face fifty Huns than be an army surgeon.

In the last week of August, a publisher's agent came to ask Rick how he felt about writing a book on his experiences in the war. Rick said he would think it over. Then a friend brought in ice cream cones, which made the day a success. On the following morning, he lay in bed deciding about the publisher's suggestion. Rick knew from experience on the racing circuits that yesterday's newspaper was gone like the day itself, and last week's newspaper might as well be last year's. But books went into libraries. Readers walked past shelves and took the books down. They lived longer than the people they told about. At the age of twenty-eight, Rick had decided he was worthy of standing among the people in the books, who kept on living because of what they had done while they were alive. A hero cannot be a man of the shy, modest, and reticent kind — a saint maybe, but no hero. The hero's story must be told.

Next day, Rick felt good for the first time in quite a while. He was able to get up, dress, and go to lunch with Lieutenant Fauntleroy. In the afternoon, Rick watched surgeons taking a piece of shrapnel from a wounded man's lung. By September 1, 1918, the doctors had classified Rick as ambulatory. He was recovering health and spirits by going out to dinner, inspecting airplane engines, reading and answering mail. He had lunch with the nurse who had inspired romantic feelings on the day Jim Europe played, and dinner with Miss Wilson, a librarian.

One is aware, in reading the diary account of these days, of Rick's ability to enjoy being alive. He could stand up to terror and pain. Turn these ailments off, and Rick was happy living from day to day. Boredom was never a problem for Rick. September 4 was his last day at the hospital. He had dinner with Miss Wilson at her apartment on the Avenue Henri Martin. To those who would serve in the next war, Rick's informal ways in the First World War might seem incredible. But the air force had only a few hundred officers and men, compared to millions of enlisted men and thousands of officers in the ground armies. And though it was minute in size, this air arm was doing what higher authority called on it to do, in an admirable manner. Therefore the brass at Chaumont allowed the airmen to administer their affairs pretty much as they saw fit. Commanders did not begrudge a few hours in Paris to young men whose remaining hours of life might be so few. And so Rick had two more days of sunshine on the boulevards, and a country run in a Mercedes that threw its rear wheel at high speed in American speedway style. By Monday, September 9, Rick was with the squadron again.

Bad weather set in, as it always seemed to when Rick returned with hopes of action. This gave him a day off in which he showed a man from the Los Angeles *Times* around the airdrome. The reporter was accredited by press officers who had advance knowledge that at last the big show was about to begin. Rick went out at five o'clock on Thursday morning and saw the opening American attacks at Thiaucourt and St.-Mihiel. That day the Germans killed America's leading ace, Lieutenant David Putnam. On Friday, a day of traditional bad luck because it fell on the 13th, Rick went over the lines on three sorties, once with Reed Chambers and twice alone. Flying under low clouds, Rick took a bullet through the deck of the Spad a few inches from his seat.

Less than a week after his return to duty, Rick scored the sixth victory on his record. Out early and alone, he met four Fokkers with the red wing and white fuselage that identified von Richthofen's Jagdstaffel 91. As usual, Rick was scouting high, and he made a dive at them, getting about 200 rounds into the last plane in line, which went down out of control. One day later, Rick again went hunting early, spied a formation of Fokkers, and finished off the last man with 150 rounds. This seventh victory gave Rick the newspaper title that Putnam had held — America's Ace of Aces. At the time of his death, David Putnam had twelve victories to his credit, mostly from service with the French before the American squadrons came into action. The leading aces did not last long. Lieutenant Frank Bayliss of Massachusetts had destroyed thirteen enemy planes before June 12, when he met death in combat. Lieutenant Paul Frank Baer of Indiana had succeeded Lufbery as champion ace, with nine victories, but two days later the Germans caught him over their territory and shot him down. Baer was wounded, and survived as a prisoner. These events showed that as far as Rick was concerned the immediate future would almost certainly produce injury, capture, or death.

Whatever was to be Rick went out to meet on September 16, in two voluntary patrols without companions. A few hours later he returned, having survived a sparring match with three Fokkers. Rick now learned that his time as champion of all the aces had been brief. For word had come that Lieutenant Frank Luke of Squadron 27 had blown up two enemy balloons within fifteen minutes, which brought his score of victories to eight. Rick saluted Frank Luke of Arizona as an incredibly daring man. Luke had pounced on the *Drachen* as the sun went down, the French mistakenly fired on him all the way home, and he found his way in by the light of gasoline torches. Rick gave a party for Frank Luke the following night.

On Sunday Rick arranged for a troupe of American entertainers to give their show in the 94th Squadron hangar. He thought a young actress named Lois Meredith especially attractive, and it appears that Miss Meredith took the place Rick had reserved for that unnamed nurse who listened to Jim Europe's ragtime and comforted him with ice cream when he was feeling rotten. But Rick couldn't keep the entertainers with the squadron, and after their show, which was a great success, he had to send them on.

The best day yet in Rick's career came on September 24

when orders went out promoting Captain Marr to major and appointing Rick commander of the 94th Squadron. His promotion to captain was coming through. But what cheered his heart was taking charge of the 94th with its traditions of Hall, Lufbery, and Campbell. Only three who had started with the squadron in its early days were still in action — Thorne Taylor, Reed Chambers, and Rick. They and other founders of the 94th had been first to fight as an American flying organization. It had to be conceded that the 27th Squadron, with Frank Luke on its roster, was ahead of all in German planes and balloons shot down. But on his first day in command, Rick set an example of aggressive tactics that Luke himself couldn't have improved on. The date was September 25, and Rick was flying high in an early morning voluntary patrol, when he saw five Fokkers escorting two Halberstadt photographic biplanes. Down he came and shot the rear man to pieces in marauding style. Then he flashed through the formation and broke it up, which gave him a chance for fast return and bursts of fire into the belly of a Halberstadt. The biplane went down burning, and Rick didn't see anybody get out. These kills received prompt confirmation from observers on the ground. That evening Rick helped get a party going, and who should be there but Lois Meredith. Rick had now decided that Miss Meredith was his favorite acquaintance among nurses, entertainers, and ladies of the YMCA and Red Cross.

After the party and before dawn on September 26, Rick heard the thunder of a barrage, which meant the doughboys were moving. Orders came to hold the *Drachen* in their dens that day at all costs, or to burn them in the air if they got out on their cables. Attack before daylight was the word. The mission took off between lines of flares and went to the front under morning mist about 800 feet off the ground. Rick said there were millions of cannon firing, from Rheims to Lunéville. The *Drachen* lay on the ground until Rick and his friends had to withdraw for refueling. North of Verdun, a Fokker appeared out of the rising sun and made for Rick with guns blazing. Almost colliding, the German shot away Rick's propeller, then pulled up for height to dive and finish him off. As it started upward Rick poured fire into the Fokker's exposed belly. In those seconds the fight ended, and Rick watched the burning airplane fall to earth. Lacking a propeller, he still managed to get down at Verdun. Without hyperbole one might call this two days' combat material for Homer or Shakespeare, were they available to write about it. Rick logged the facts and headed his page, "10th Victory."

On September 27 there was too much rain for flying, and Rick drove to Fleury, where he saw Miss Meredith. He came back by way of Verdun, hoping to get news of two fliers missing from the squadron. One of them had gone down on fire in no man's land. Lieutenant Sherry had landed to bury what was left of him. A squad of doughboys, digging the grave, came under fire from a sniper. They caught the sniper and shattered his skull with rifle butts. The day this news arrived saw Rick go out on one of his solo patrols over enemy ground, where he spied a truck hauling a *Drache* to its observation post. Rick aimed the Spad and fired 150 rounds before he corkscrewed off to the right and upward, while the *Drache* shriveled in fire that burst from its vitals when the bullets went in. The *Drache* had defenders, who put a hole through Rick's main tail strut as he got away. This was Rick's eleventh kill.

Sunday, September 29. The Day of St. Michael and All Angels, as Rick's gilt-edged diary leaf reminded him, a Michaelmas well fitted to such of Rick's associates as Lieutenant Weir Cook, who exploded his second German balloon that day, and Frank Luke. Luke marked the day by disappearing forever. His disregard of accepted military procedures had been noticeable even in the air force of that time. The last anyone had heard from Luke was at six o'clock in the evening of September 28, when he dropped a streamer with a note directing observers to watch two nearby locations on the balloon map. As darkness fell, they saw the flare of light that meant the death of a *Drache*, and then almost immediately another burst of flame for the second victim. Rick and the others began to worry about Luke on the following day, September 29, when he did not appear at the 27th Squadron base, and no word came from any French or British airdrome. No word was ever to come until postwar investigation revealed that the Germans had shot Luke down and killed him when he continued fighting on the ground and hit a couple of the enemy with shots from his pistol before he died.

Billy Mitchell came up next day and asked for volunteers to fly thirty miles into enemy territory and locate troop trains moving out of Metz. Rick went on this errand with Weir Cook and Hamilton Coolidge. They came back after dark, searchlights picked them out, and they ran a gauntlet of antiaircraft fire until they saw gasoline lanterns at the landing field.

In 1918, on the western front in France, October was to be the most important month so far in Rick's life, the month in which his achievements would rise to such a level that he would never afterward be able to live as an ordinary man. Luck and his own ability, the scheme of things and his own control of it, were now about to establish him among the personages of the world, who were larger than life size. He was to become one of those people whom you knew, whether or not you had ever met them.

Rick was now flying at least two missions a day, for he felt it his duty as commander to put in more hours of flight than anyone else in the squadron. Hamilton Coolidge and Reed Chambers had almost as many hours in the air as he. Rick had abolished saluting around hangars and tents. The pilots were commissioned officers and the mechanics noncommissioned, socially in the ranks of enlisted men, and Rick did not want them wasting time with parade-ground etiquette when mechanical problems needed solving in a hurry. Everybody thought this was fine, including Colonel Billy Mitchell, who dispensed with salutes when he came to consult with Rick and the others. Rick had assembled what he called "a caucus" of mechanics, and talked to them as he had talked to the pit crews at home. Ground-training doctrine had held that everything was in manuals, such as the *Infantry Drill Regulations.* But no one had prepared manuals for fighting in the air or keeping combat aircraft ready, so the pioneers like Billy Mitchell, Rick, and others set down the principles of what they were doing, as fast as they found out from experience what those principles were. To his brother pilots Rick said that he would not order them to do anything he would not do. By instinct, Rick knew that it was the only way to lead combat troops where actual fighting takes place.

On Tuesday, October 1, Rick was leading patrol formations in the morning and afternoon. Coming back from the last mission, they caught a balloon on the ground and set it afire. Once again, searchlights pinned them while antiaircraft barked all the way home. Oddly enough, Rick did not log this balloon as his twelfth victory, although official records give him the credit and he noted that he had made the kill. Perhaps Rick had some idea of averaging out the victory shared with Captain Hall. He wrote "12th Victory" at the top of the next page, when he crippled a Halberstadt photographic biplane and saw it crawling wounded on the ground near Montfaucon. Rick said this victory, too, was to be divided: Reed Chambers had had a hand in bringing the biplane down. But full credit and the undeniable twelfth victory went to Rick for action that immediately followed on the same day. As usual, the observation plane had escorts, in this instance a formation of Fokkers. They stormed at Rick and he flew up the middle, feeding one of them 200 rounds, which shot it out of action. The others turned on Rick and chased him down, breaking off to avoid plunging into the earth. Rick had escaped so near the ground that he wrote, "Thought my days were ended." Lieutenant Cook got another balloon that morning, west of Grandpré.

The morning patrol next day saw no action, but the afternoon produced two air battles. "Ham" Coolidge blew up a balloon and shared Rick's victory over an enemy biplane, which they turned into a torch. Still over enemy territory, Rick closed with a Rumpler and shot it down. He headed his page, "13th and 14th Victories," noting Coolidge's share of the biplane. The record of shared victories was a matter of bookkeeping, and Rick's log would agree with his official confirmation in General Orders of the Air Force. On October 5 Rick caught a Fokker out of position and sent it down, somewhere north of Montfaucon, logging his fifteenth win. His tremendous month continued on the following day, when he led a balloon-hunting mission and had the satisfaction of watching Ham Coolidge shoot down the *Drache*. Autumnal storms blew up on the following day, so Rick went over to Bar-le-Duc and "had a very pleasant talk" with Lois Meredith. When he got back to base, Rick found that the French had delivered the wrecked Fokker he had killed the previous Saturday. It wasn't merely a souvenir, although Rick and others posed for pictures in front of it. The mechanics took it apart and studied the enemy's motor and weapons.

Rick got to Bar-le-Duc again on October 9 and saw Miss Meredith, who promised to meet him in Paris when possible. He came back and, around six o'clock in the evening, caught a balloon on the ground near Dun-sur-Meuse. Rick put bullets through the distended hide and blew the thing to bits. Next day, he achieved a double victory. He and others, out on balloon patrol, found nothing in that line and were proceeding in the usual formation, when off to the west they saw a patrol from Squadron 147 encounter an echelon of Fokkers. All hands plunged into the melee. Lieutenant Wilbur White of 147 rammed one of the Germans, and they both died instantly. It was White's last scheduled mission before returning to the United States for a visit with his wife and two little daughters. He was one of the few married men flying in combat. Lieutenant Brotherton of the 147th Squadron also went down burning. Germans were out in force that day, and a file of them swooped in among Rick's people. He engaged a Fokker and shot it down. Then another one came at him. He rounded on it and put a couple of bursts into the engine and fuel tank, which sent it to earth, trailing smoke and fire.

The records listed these two victories as occurring at 3:52 P.M., on Thursday, October 10. They were only a few seconds apart, and the two defeated Fokkers hit the ground outside the village of Cléry-le-Petit at almost the same time. Rick's talks with mechanics and armorers had done a great deal of good. From now to the end we do not read in the diary about any more jamming guns or mechanical failures. The great joy the Spad afforded Rick and other pilots, in addition to speed, was its sturdy construction, which held together when the plane was pulled out of dives, for air is solid when you hit it fast.

The weather was bad on October 11 and Rick decided to go to Paris for a few days. He got up to town at midnight and had trouble finding a room. It was still blowing rain next day, but dinner at Maxime's with Miss Meredith made Rick feel fine. On Sunday word came that Germany was making peace on President Wilson's terms. Rick thought he had no more fighting in the air to do, which was satisfactory because he would be glad to live through the war. And he had now been proclaimed American Ace of Aces, which meant that he had combined luck with skill and courage to an extraordinary degree. The official scorekeepers called the double victory seventeen and eighteen, and Rick's accounting totaled one more, which put him ahead of Lufbery's seventeen and the vanished Frank Luke's eighteen. Now one might say that if the Germans were ready to quit, it was all right with Eddie Rickenbacker. On Monday Rick posed for pictures with some motor executives. He was already thinking of postwar employment. Then to lunch at Maxime's and an afternoon of shopping with Miss Meredith.

By October 15, it had become evident that the war wasn't over yet, and Rick rejoined Squadron 94 bringing bad weather with him, as he almost always seemed to do. Billy Mitchell's promotion to general had come through, and he decorated Rick with the Distinguished Service Cross. Rick heard the French were coming with additional decorations for many members of the squadron. The organization did well on the 22nd, when Lieutenant Cook, already an ace, exploded a balloon, and Lieutenant Jeffers killed a Fokker over the village of Romagne. At 3:55 P.M. over Cléry-le-Petit, Rick shot a Fokker to the ground, where it crashed in flames. Rick then damaged a second Fokker, possibly sending it to a crash out of sight behind enemy lines. He claimed only the first one, receiving confirmation five days later.

News came again that Germany had agreed to President Wilson's terms, but Squadron 94 continued to fly patrols. Rick went hunting and saw a German destroy an American balloon, roared down on the enemy as he left the kill, and put him out of action with 100 rounds. Concentrating closely on this pursuit and firing, Rick almost ended his career when he failed to notice five of the enemy who came blazing and chased him home. Officially recognized as his twentieth, this victory over the balloon-killer put Rick into the ranks of those on whom the odds against survival were growing longer by the day. But all flying stopped for seventy-two hours because of bad weather. Rick went to Paris, lunched with some newspapermen, invited them for a meal at the base next day, returned, and tried out a new Spad, which didn't feel quite right and would need some work in the hangar. The day ended with news that Rick's promotion to captain had become official.

October 27 began with no flying weather. The newspapermen came out for lunch, the weather improved, Rick went to look around, and shot down two Fokkers, one at Grandpré, the other fifteen minutes later, near a neighboring village. At about the same time, a few miles east of Grandpré the enemy antiaircraft proved that it could be more dangerous than American pilots cared to admit. Hamilton Coolidge flew into one of the shells at the moment of explosion. Early next morning Rick saw all that remained of Coolidge and his plane. It was about sixty yards from the line, on our side. Doughboys shoveled earth on the coffin while a chaplain read the funeral service. Rick took a photograph for the family and left a wreath on the grave.

On the way home, Rick came near destruction on the ground when shells exploded near enough to shower his car with dirt. Back at base Rick received clippings from newspapers with stories that he was engaged to a young movie actress, Priscilla Dean. He hadn't seen Priscilla for nearly two years, which made the story of their being engaged completely absurd, and he knew through his instinct for press relations that it would die if left alone. All Rick did was write in his diary, "This is not true." Miss Dean ranked far down on the list of ladies who had aroused Rick's interest, which included Lois Meredith; Mrs. Chandler, who was an American society woman living in Paris; Miss Wilson, the librarian; and the unnamed nurse. No woman ever thought it necessary to complain about Rick's conduct, and he never said or wrote a word about the women in his life that could not have been published in a parish bulletin describing a church supper.

On the next to the last day of October Rick pursued a biplane into enemy territory until he calculated he would not be able to get back if he followed it farther. Two hours and ten minutes was the limit with Spads before fuel ran out. One could glide for a long time from heights of 15,000 to 20,000 feet, but meeting an enemy who had fuel in his tanks could be fatal. Rick would spend from four to six hours in the air every day when flying was possible. On this day, he went home for gasoline while it was still light, refueled, and went back at the head of a patrol. Two Fokkers bearing the red paint of the von Richthofen squadron flashed into view. Rick met one, fed him three bursts at close range, and saw him whirl to the ground, on fire.

Over Remonville, five minutes after killing the Fokker, he saw a target directly under his right wing, where "a German observation balloon lay in its bed at the edge of the village." Rick slammed over the rudder, pointed the Spad's nose, and pulled both triggers. He described the action: "I continued my sloping dive to within a hundred feet of the sleeping Drachen [*sic*] firing up and down its whole length by slightly shifting the course of my airplane." Rick zoomed up a few hundred feet for another pass, but it wasn't needed. A pillar of fire shot into the sky, and Rick started home.

Darkness came before he cleared enemy territory. He realized that in a short time he would have burned all the fuel in his tank, and he was too close to the ground. Rick recorded that "real terror" seized him: "Even as I banked over and turned southward I wondered whether my motor would gasp and expire in the turning." He started drawing antiaircraft fire and passed the lines somewhere west of Verdun. When he estimated his position to be about ten miles from home, he fired a red Very rocket, then another, and heard his motor begin its final sputtering. Then he saw the outline of the field as mechanics ran down each side with torches, lighting flares. He struck the ground "with a quiet thud," less than 100 feet from the hangar. Rick had no way of knowing it, but he had flown his last victorious flight.

Making October 30 a double victory day had brought the tally up to twenty-four in General Orders, and eventually the official audits were to show that Rick had won twenty-six victories. The important aspect of the matter was not the keeping of books on Rick's fighting, but the closer approach, every day, of every fighting flier's inevitable end if he kept at it long enough. The records were to show that Rick had closed fifty times with enemies and exchanged fire. Any one of these fights could have been Rick's last. These exposures to fire do not include the numerous missions Rick flew in ground support, reconnaissance, and strafing convoys, where he encountered defensive fire. And bombardment by antiaircraft guns was routine warfare, like the firing of coast defense artillery in the direction of a hostile fleet.

But civilians and soldiers alike felt the fascination of the battles with German pilots, recognizing them as ancient, pure fighting to the death, like the combat of heroes in the Trojan war, who fought and maneuvered in swift chariots. By now, Squadron 94 listed eight aces, counting Major Lufbery, who had come to them with that designation. The outfit had killed sixty-eight enemy planes and balloons. Rick had scored more than one third of the squadron's victories; leaving aside good luck, the performance that Rick displayed, especially during his six weeks as commander, was beyond praise. The army did its best, and Rick received a total of nine Oak Leaf clusters for his Distinguished Service Cross, each one representing an additional citation of the award.

The good angels who had protected Rick on the racetrack had apparently followed him to the skies over France. Every day now meant another mission for those angels, but, for all anyone knew, they might be summoned elsewhere, and there would be national mourning for the young man who had come to represent his nation and carry the nation's luck.

The first day of November greeted Rick with typical Meuse

River fog when he turned out at 4:20 A.M. When the fog lifted at four in the afternoon, Rick flew for an hour and encountered no enemy. News came to the base that evening that Turkey had sued for peace and Austria would do so tomorrow. The newsmen told Rick it was no rumor; they had it from their offices. On Saturday, November 2, Rick flew over the lines and saw American troops advancing. He came back and left for Paris with his pal Fauntleroy, now a captain. They got to town at 2:00 A.M. on Sunday and had trouble finding a room. Paris was coming to life. There were many lights in the streets, and captured cannon on the Champs Elysée and the Place de la Concorde. On November 4, Rick bought a "wonderful" officer's overcoat for 1450 francs, although he thought it might seem foolish. Miss Meredith went along on the shopping tour and bought a hat. They had lunch and "quite some ride" around Paris. This would be a bad time to get killed, but Rick started back to the front at 9:20 in the evening.

Next day he was out on patrol in the afternoon as soon as the weather cleared. On Wednesday, November 6, the weather again closed in. It continued bad on Thursday, when the United Press man told Rick the German peace delegation had crossed no man's land at 3:00 P.M. under a white flag. Rick flew in the lead of a patrol on November 8, although the weather was bad. That day Major Kirby, who was slated to command another squadron, joined Rick's outfit to get combat experience. Rick and the others shook their heads at the thought of it. They had seen men killed on first missions, and felt it would be foolhardy, not to say suicidal, to fly such a mission now, with peace delegates across the table from the Allied command. But Kirby wanted membership in the club of blooded pilots, and, of course, if he insisted, they would accommodate him. Kirby flew with them on November 8 and 9, landing at Chaumont out of gasoline on the latter date, reported missing. Then word came that the major had won his spurs. He had shot down a Fokker, confirmed near Mauecourt, just north of Verdun, at ten minutes of eleven that morning. This raised the squadron's total of victories to sixty-nine, in its last combat of the war.

That evening Rick got word by way of the neighboring 95th Squadron that the Kaiser had fled to Holland, and the war would end on the following day. "Come on over to Ninety-five mess for the celebration!" said the caller. They had a piano over there, a souvenir from the officers' lounge at an abandoned German camp. There was a grand spontaneous uproar. They mixed punch in kettles out of anything alcoholic, paraded regardless of mud after an impromptu band, fired Very rockets, pistols, and machine guns into the air, and danced around a bonfire primed with aviation gasoline. Rick understood what was happening. He wrote later that the pilots had been living for months under tension at the peak of nervous energy, and now tension was exploding like the guns they were firing at the sky. Serious negotiations had begun on November 9, and Laurence Stallings wrote, "While the haggling continued, the doughboys had two more days to fight their savage war."

Rick's diary entry for November 11 tells a plain tale. It records that he went up at five minutes of eleven in the morning, "trying to get to front, was unable." The main thing was that the war was over, with Rick and the rest still breathing. It is useless to try to describe how grand, how welcoming, how infinitely promising the future looked to those who thought themselves winners on November 11, 1918. For his part of it, Eddie Rickenbacker had managed to keep a series of terrifying events under control in wartime. There could hardly be a limit to what he might achieve in civilian life.

# CHAPTER III

# The Personality Market

NOVEMBER 12, 1918, found Rick and his mates planning a victory dinner at the mess. Rick felt especially good because he had ended the war as America's Ace of Aces, and his writing of the title in his private book showed the importance he attached to it. Next day the pilots of Squadron 94 returned 95's hospitality with a dinner and show. Hilarity continued late, but it takes a while for the fact that a war has ended to sink in. The military bureaucracies continue to function, pouring out orders and plans. Both men in the ranks and junior officers almost unanimously want to go home and take off the uniform. They face the question of whether one should go back to the old job or strike out on some new line.

But Rick did not hurry his decision as to future work, and made no move for immediate separation from the air force when news came that Squadron 94 would go into Germany with the armies of occupation. Rick said he had always wanted to see Germany, and it was an honor for the squadron. On November 17, Rick signed a contract with a man named Laurence La Tourelle Driggs for a book to be published by the Frederick A. Stokes Company of New York. The diary notation says that Rick signed "with Mr. Driggs to write or rather assist

me in writing my book."* On the 18th, orders came that the
94th would move to Germany no later than November 20.
Later it was heard that the 95th Squadron would go to Germany instead. Rick immediately sent off an advance party and
tried to reach General Mitchell. They stalled him at Mitchell's
office, but an adjutant whispered in Rick's ear that he was not
to worry. At 2:00 P.M. the next day Rick left for Moers, in Germany, in the old Number 1 Spad. It was grand to fly over Verdun without worry about enemies and to stop on a German
field a short time later.

Lieutenant Douglas Campbell turned up with news that Captain James Norman Hall, now in Paris, had confirmed that Rick
"brought down a Hun in the fight which he was lost in." Rick
now wrote this in his personal scorekeeping as "26th Victory."
But it appears to historians who try to audit Rick's score that
this "Hun" would be the twenty-seventh win on record. On the
following day, Rick gave a little talk to members of the squadron. His subject was the organization's achievement in the war.

Rick decided it would be best for him to stay with Squadron
94 as commander and to come back with the outfit when it returned to the States. Therefore, he found it disturbing to hear
on November 27 that orders were being prepared to send him
back alone to the United States. Rick started at once to
straighten this out. He hurried to First Pursuit Group Headquarters and talked with two colonels who had reliable connections higher up. Rick also managed to get a telephone call
through to a trustworthy major at Chaumont, who said the
orders had come in from Washington. For the moment, the
major reported, the papers were just sitting there, and no one
had taken action on them. With Jimmy Meissner and Douglas
Campbell at his side, Rick made a fast trip to Mitchell's office.

Underlings blocked the way, but Rick pushed them aside and

* The result was *Fighting the Flying Circus* (New York, 1919). Stallings recommended it: "This little book is careless, candid, and charming."

told his troubles to Billy Mitchell. The general sent a telegram to Chaumont, requesting cancellation of any orders concerning Rick's return to the United States, other than such as might originate with First Pursuit Group. Then Rick and his pals took Mitchell and the staff to Thanksgiving dinner at Squadron 94's mess. There were holiday decorations, a fine meal, plenty to drink, and numerous speeches. When Billy Mitchell left, he vowed that he would go all the way up to Pershing if anyone interfered with the squadron's plans.

Major Kirby left on the 29th to take command of the Fifth Pursuit Group, Second Army. The squadron would always remember him as the eager apprentice, mad at the Boche, who had risked his life in their final victory. Most officers who wanted to serve in Germany hoped for commands like the one that had come to Kirby, and they wanted to be based in Hamburg or Berlin, if possible. There could be profitable arbitrage in German, French, and American currency, and the conquerors observed that cigarettes and chocolate were mediums of exchange. The inflation that ate up the value of German money and destroyed the government was getting under way. Rick and his comrades in Squadron 94 were not aware of the condition to which the German people had come. The Allied blockade had subjected the enemy to shortages of food that brought him to the point of starvation. Many German children developed the chicken faces and protruding bellies that were signs of acute undernourishment. They died soon after these symptoms appeared. Rick had blockaded no grain and destroyed no crops. Combat pilots had fought a clean war. Burning gasoline, clothes set afire by flaming onions, bodies ripped by exploding bullets — all this the pilots inflicted on each other, but not on civilians, women, and children.

Early in December, Rick and Douglas Campbell dined with General Mitchell in Luxembourg. The general said that they would soon leave for a trip home and then come back. But they were to say nothing about this around the squadron, as things were not yet clear. A ghost of Baron von Rickenbacher drifted in Rick's direction when he heard from a friend, who had just made an informal survey, that the Germans hated Rick more than any American because he had been born in Germany, had served in the German army, and turned against the Fatherland when the Great War came. Rick could only shake his head at this. It showed how easily fiction could assume the guise of truth and walk along like a zombie beside the living facts of a man's career.

About this time, Rick began pulling wires to get a group of Red Cross girls attached to the squadron on co-ed status. His contacts reported that this business was going forward, when in came a rumor, on December 7, that the entire First Pursuit Group would pack up and move out for America. Rick telephoned a pal at group headquarters, who advised him to send a truck for the girls right away. It would still be possible to get them under the 94th's wing, as the move was not scheduled until Monday. The girls got in on Sunday with all their baggage. Then on December 11, when Rick and a bevy of the girls went sightseeing, he got a private message from Billy Mitchell to stay where he was until orders firmed up. Nothing more was said about the United States.

All this confusion was understandable. Political forces originating at a distance were pressing on group and squadron headquarters, where staff officers could only move in the direction toward which they felt themselves impelled by the most powerful influence at any given moment. Meanwhile, civilians brewed more politics in Paris, London, and Washington; and the military politicians, who also would have something to say about what ultimately happened to Rick, had their heads together at the office of the Chief of Staff. Here were Pershing's enemies, Generals Peyton C. March and Tasker H. Bliss. This side of the war went on with inconceivable pettiness. Gen-

eral March, for example, forbade officers returning from overseas to wear the Sam Browne belt, which had an extra strap
that ran over the shoulder of the tunic and was attached to the
waist strap. March had military police at dockside to confiscate
the belts. And his office sent out so many directives about great
and small matters that countermanding orders sometimes arrived in France ahead of the orders they superseded.

There were two sources of confusion. One arose from an
honest effort to deploy forces in such a way that the defeated
enemy would meet the terms of peace without question, once
these terms were decided. That was sensible enough in conception, although it was to breed bad results because of the Allies'
differing postwar aims. The second source of confusion came
from a disease of human organization, the hatred of one bureaucrat for another, in or out of uniform. This kept everybody off balance, all the way down to the 94th Squadron, so
Rick did not know from one day to the next what he was supposed to do or where he was expected to do it.

On December 13, the squadron finally reached Coblenz,
where Driggs and Rick took rooms at the best hotel and had
dinner beside a window overlooking the Rhine. Then they met
some American newspapermen and moved on to a café whose
proprietor claimed to have been a spy for the Germans in the
United States prior to the war. Nobody held it against the man,
and they passed a convivial evening. Then Rick spent several
days of work with Driggs, together with sightseeing and shopping around Coblenz. He saw Americans fraternizing with the
enemy and noted his opinion that doughboys took to Germans
"like ducks to water." The shopkeepers admired Rick's DSC
ribbon and caused him to wonder if they realized what it had
been given him for.

Next day Rick went to Trier (the former French city of
Trèves), and strolled out for a look around town. He saw two
French officers on horseback order a group of German civil-

ians to take off their hats. When the civilians refused, the officers knocked off the hats with riding crops. Rick reflected that no good could be gained that way. Then he went to lunch with Billy Mitchell, who was full of care and business. The latest word that Chaumont had sent Rick appeared to give him the choice of leaving for the States either in one week or in a little less than three weeks, on January 1, 1919. Rick was ready to be accommodating and was able to understand the tensions of those who did not lunch with generals, pal around with war correspondents, and carry literary coadjutors with them while on duty in the armed forces. Mitchell said that the president of France would confer the Legion of Honor on Rick, who then recorded that the "boys in the Squadron" were afraid he was going home. That made for unhappiness, or at least a feeling of regret. Just as Rick wanted to return to New York with the old outfit, its members wished to come home with Rick at their head.

While the tentative orders whirled around the solar system of military bureaucracy, Rick and Laurence Driggs buried themselves in their book, with Rick talking and Driggs taking it down, sometimes verbatim and sometimes in general notes under various topics. This method of working was congenial to Rick, a natural talker. Driggs gave conventional spelling to the material — Rick sometimes wrote "their" for "there," and he didn't bother too much about French place names — but what Driggs may have contributed in the way of structure is hard to assess. There is no question that it is Rick's speech we hear in *Fighting the Flying Circus;* the style of the diary and the manual for racing mechanics comes through with the authenticity of a familiar voice. By December 17, Rick felt that he had covered his flying career adequately in the little book, and he relaxed at a show given by the 94th Squadron with amateur talent. Rick noted that some of the boys told good stories.

On December 19, Rick went to Chaumont, where he received

orders for America, with a stop in London on the way. He also got an additional Oak Leaf for his Distinguished Service Cross, in effect presenting him with still another decoration of that rank. When he got back to Coblenz, Rick observed that the boys were depressed when word got out that he was to leave them. And he, too, felt unhappy. It was like leaving home. The day before Christmas was cold and rainy in Coblenz, and at lunch General Mitchell gave Rick secret letters for delivery in the States.

Christmas Day in the country of the *Tannenbaum,* the festive tree, was a success. The squadron put on a fine German dinner, and the men gave Rick a silver cup. There was plenty to drink: beer, wine, and schnapps. Rick proved his mettle by getting out of bed at six o'clock next morning. He drank punch, motored to Bar-le-Duc, caught a train for Paris at 10:17, stood up all the way, got in at four in the afternoon, dined at Ciro's, and went on to the Folies Bergère.

On the following day, Rick toured the shops. When he got back, he found a letter, brought by courier, from Billy Mitchell, with more instructions about whom to see and what to say in America. A cable from the New York *World* started negotiations for the newspaper rights in Rick's forthcoming book. This was on December 30, and on the last day of the month Rick noted that there was one thing certain about the coming year: it would not hold the thrills that he had experienced in 1918. But he did not buy another diary in Paris. From now on, whether or not he cared to keep a private record, there would always be a public record of Rick's career.

Rick got to New York on February 1, 1919, before the city had become used to returning servicemen, and he received attention like that which comes to a successful politician. Army press officers collaborated with ship news reporters to stage a scene that was aimed at the metaphorical heart of America. As Rick walked down the gangplank, a lieutenant of military po-

called on the Secretary of War, Newton D. Baker, Rick went
mentally blank, like everyone else, so that the sound of Baker's
voice resembled the murmur of distant surf or the wind in a
forest several miles away. Among other things, Baker said that
Rick was "one of the real crusaders of America — one of the
truest knights our country has ever known." Baker added that
Rick would "find his greatest delight, when the evening of his
life comes, in looking back on his experiences." Unable to get
rid of "about," like Br'er Rabbit struggling to shake Tar Baby,
Baker also emphasized that Rick's life would "always be glad-
dened as he looks about him and sees men and women and
children walking about free and unafraid and when he thinks
that he has given his best and ventured his own life to bring
this about." Then Secretary Baker turned to what was on his
mind. American industry had failed to provide aircraft for our
pilots in the war. The men had made a fine record, but in
French or English planes, practically never in an American-
built ship. Baker tried to talk this fact out of existence, but he
might have done better to leave it alone. Rick started from his
doze when he heard applause at the end of Baker's speech.

Congressman Ireland now made haste to put on the star of
the evening, the clergyman, author, and diplomat Henry Van
Dyke. At the time of this banquet, in February 1919, Dr. Van
Dyke was a leading literary figure. He had been a great catch
for the Contest Board. The only personage of comparable rank
at the dinner was Bud Fisher, the artist who drew a syndicated
comic strip called "Mutt and Jeff." Henry Van Dyke also
pleased a large audience and was Fisher's superior as a speaker,
for he had been pastor at the Fifth Avenue Presbyterian
Church before he became a national celebrity for his writing,
his three years as ambassador to the Netherlands, and his lectures at Princeton as the Murray Professor of English Literature. In addition, Dr. Van Dyke had been a navy chaplain.

He now rose in dress uniform to say a few words. Van Dyke

was sixty-seven years old but held himself straight; his ruddy complexion was set off by silver hair and mustache. Rick gave careful study to this old charmer and noticed that Van Dyke pleased the ear as well as the eye with his agreeable tone and crisp enunciation, which contrasted with Newton D. Baker's monotonous whine. What Van Dyke had to say was brief and simple. His theme was the affection that the country felt for Captain Eddie Rickenbacker. This young man was not only the Ace of Aces; he was the Ace of Hearts. Thereupon Van Dyke called on Rick to stand up, and handed him a jeweler's box containing a pair of diamond, gold, and platinum wings. Rick had not expected to be on his feet at the banquet and had no prepared statement. His inspiration was to hold up the box toward the balcony, and call, "For you, Mother."

Henry Van Dyke knew better than to keep on after that. He pressed Rick's hand, Congressman Ireland gave a formal good night, and the crowd broke for the exits. Many stopped in the bars and supper rooms of the hotel for more drinks, and others headed uptown for some cabaret entertainment or to hear the music of the new Original Dixieland Jazz Band. Rick escorted his mother and sister to their room in the Waldorf-Astoria, then pushed his way through a crowd of well-wishers at the Fifth Avenue entrance, where he hailed a hansom cab and rode to the Plaza for a night's sleep. He needed his rest; plans were afoot.

When Rick looked through his mail at the Plaza on February 18, he found that a letter from an old friend had caught up with him. Addressing him as "My Dear Edward," his third-grade teacher at the East Main Street School in Columbus had written from her home in Milwaukee, Wisconsin. This Mrs. Henry M. Humphreys recalled the school Christmas decorations of twenty years before. She wrote that "you and John Weissinger brought little angels just alike. When we took down the tree, you and John told me you wanted me to have yours.

So I have kept them all these years. Every Christmas they have adorned our tree, and just think how proud I was to show yours with your name signed in your childish handwriting . . ." Rick answered at once: "It seems wonderful to think you have kept the little ornaments that I brought as a child to school to decorate our class Christmas tree, for the past twenty years . . ." What warmed Rick's heart was the way this teacher, Miss Sue Alexander at the time he knew her, had preserved the souvenir before he became well known. Relics always have a part in the hero's life story, and here was a genuine relic. The letter had a singularly encouraging quality and appeared to be a harbinger of good luck.

By a great and continuous struggle of will, Rick had postponed his nervous reaction to the strain of war until after the event. He was now trying to relax, but found it hard to sleep eight hours a night at a comfortable and restful level of unconsciousness. He would often wake with a pounding heart, breathing in gasps and not knowing where he was. He would try to deepen his shallow breathing while he identified his surroundings. In the daytime, relaxation sometimes came in the bustle of going around town interviewing this person and that about future possibilities, giving talks at lunches, and being recognized on Fifth Avenue. Rick's orders specified that he was not in active service after February 28, and he no longer wore uniform unless an arrangement committee requested it on a public occasion. Out of uniform, he liked to turn up the collar of the polo coat and pull the brim of his new fedora down in front.

On the surface, all was well. Rick benefited from his catlike satisfaction in physical existence, especially when there were men to pal around with and women to admire. He had always been like this, and the trade magazine *Motor Age* reported, "Eddie is the same Eddie." The writer observed what the war correspondent Frazier "Spike" Hunt had noticed in 1918: "a warm, friendly sporting smile." But a year later Spike Hunt saw that Rick's face in repose "had become hard and set." And Rick's notes reveal an approach to his renown as Ace of Aces that differs from the way he presented his battle honors to the public in early 1919.

Rick's private written thought had been that the emotional sustenance of living on military glory after a war was like living on cream. When the cream gives out, one must start to live on skimmed milk. Rick had not exhausted the cream in February 1919. Its richness attracted the B. P. Pond Lyceum bureau, whose principals suggested that Rick tour New England and the Middle West, giving a talk on his experiences in the war, illustrated by moving pictures, presumably an improvement on the traditional magic lantern and slides. They recommended that Rick tell his audiences what it was like to be under fire and how it felt to kill an enemy. The Pond office would attend to bookings, supply advance publicity, and provide movie operators along the route. Rick signed a contract to troupe the country under Pond management.

The lecture bureau got in touch with Dr. Van Dyke, who was staging a rally on April 1 at the Metropolitan Opera House for the benefit of French wounded. Van Dyke was delighted to have Rick as the star of his show. Now the managers began working to get Rick on the road at least a week ahead of the Metropolitan engagement so that he could acquire confidence before appearing on a New York stage. Rick wanted all the training he could get, for his character was such that he disliked going into any situation unprepared. Henry Van Dyke had impressed Rick. Modest but effective stage presence, naturalness of manner, simplicity and directness in speaking, with clear enunciation — Henry Van Dyke combined all in a performance that showed what a trained man could do with an audience. With such an example before him, Rick concluded that when he appeared on the platform he must be absolutely sure of his material.

He turned for advice to the Hearst star reporter, Damon

Runyon, whom he had met at Squadron 94 with other correspondents. Runyon was to write the short stories about Broadway citizens that laid the foundation for *Guys and Dolls,* and
Rick could not have found a more knowing helper; Damon
Runyon knew the world and surveyed it with a penetrating eye.
He wrote a speech for Rick that started with a tribute to
ground troops. This was a good suggestion, and Rick kept it in
the speech that he later worked up using the Runyon text as
foundation. Rick memorized it all, but neither he nor Runyon
was satisfied with the effect when he delivered the talk in rehearsal. Runyon said, "The trouble is, you *sound* memorized."
His suggestion was "Memorize by all means, Rick, so you won't
get scared up there. But don't speak from memory." Runyon
then revealed a secret of platform artists, the use of topic cards.
He told Rick to enter each topic with a key word on a card
small enough to hold in the palm of his hand. The speaker
holds the cards out of sight under the lectern, and puts each
one aside as he develops the topic.*

Rick knew that preparing his material was only a preliminary
to delivering the words in a public hall. At Runyon's suggestion
he went to a voice coach, the well-known elocutionist Madame
Amanda. The most beneficial tutoring took place in the empty
Metropolitan Opera House, where Madame Amanda put Rick
on the stage, then climbed to the top balcony, and ordered him
to give his speech so clearly that she could hear every word.
She also equipped Rick with a few stock gestures, entreating
him to make them naturally and not use his arms like wooden
semaphores. Rick told his friends the coach would call down,
"Throw out your left arm. Throw out your right arm. Throw
out your voice." Rick added, "And maybe she said, 'Throw out
your chest,' I just can't recall." Madame Amanda also tried to
clear up Rick's accent, for he still spoke the thickened "th" of
Livingstone Avenue in Columbus.

---

* Rick carried one of these cards, with the word "PARACHUTE," through all his
travels and disasters, and still had it when he showed it to his friends in 1965.

At this time he bought a book called *Modern Eloquence* and subscribed to the Roth Memory School, whose advertisement showed a man burbling, "Of course I remember you! You're Addison Sims of Seattle!" Later on, Rick bought a copy of Emily Price Post's book on etiquette, to serve as a guide in situations where he had no experience. He later said of this period in his life, "I knew that with the title of American Ace of Aces would come an awesome responsibility. I knew it would be easy to fall from hero to zero." The fall would have been instantaneous had any sort of scandal touched the hero's personal life. This was an important consideration, because a large number of girls and women stated that their only aim in life was to meet him. They sent letters, tried to reach him on the telephone, and waited outside the Plaza, hoping to catch a glimpse of him. Some were insane and capable of inflicting harm. Any moron could retain counsel and charge Rick with bastardy or breach of promise when he didn't even know the complainant was a fellow inhabitant of the earth. Pugilists, jockeys, ballplayers, actors, fashionable clergymen — all were vulnerable to such attacks, although some gave grounds for them. Rick managed to avoid the harpies, and the gods decreed that his luck should hold in the matter of undeserved accusations of the kind that would have appeared in big black headlines, with his denials printed later in considerably smaller type and a less conspicuous location in the paper. Bearing all this in mind, Rick returned to Ohio on February 17, 1919, for a second homecoming, in some ways more strenuous than what he had experienced in New York.

Columbus newsmen accompanied Rick and his mother on the train, and one of them wrote an editorial in the *Dispatch* for February 17:

### A MOTHER AND HER SON

. . . That frail little woman was the "Boss," without being "Bossy." At least she wielded the mother-rule; she agreed with the big fellow in most instances; he had his way as he supposed. But back of it all, there was the mother's authority — the most beautiful authority there is.

To her it was not a rugged man who sat beside her. It was only her boy. Had she not nursed him at her breast, a tiny thing? Had she not watched over him in his weakness? Why, then, should she be afraid of the great strength he possessed? Why should she tremble at his words, or fear the decision he might render? He could have his way with others. He could lord it over his opponents. But here, in this frail mother, was more than his master — and he felt it without knowing it. And those of us who watched the two throughout the day upon the train; those of us who heard their little arguments, and noted the splendid devotion between the two — we knew that it was mother and son who did not have to be informed by either.

An official of the Loyal Order of Moose echoed this editorial in a speech of welcome that also was printed in a souvenir booklet sold in downtown Columbus for twenty-five cents a copy. Addressing Rick as "Brother Moose," Grand Master "Doc" Waddell used typographical embellishment to show how he had sounded on the platform: "In and through all this Massive Sway of Honor bestowed, I know your Heart and Love and Thought and Greatest Thanks go out, first to *God,* and then to your best earthly friend — *She Who Bore You. God* could have paid no Higher, Sweeter Tribute to her than Gift of you, for *Such a Mother.* To both, the *Loyal Moose* extend *Choicest Wishes,* and the Prayer for Long Life and Perfect Happiness." Some such tribute certainly seemed appropriate for Rick, as the Doc added that the returning hero had "Soared the Air, and Led Forth the Ever-Coming Morning of the Ever-Better Day."

The souvenir book was published by Walter A. Pfeiffer, president of Columbus Automobile Club, and contained testimonials to Rick from Newton D. Baker; Governor James M. Cox, of Ohio; and William Howard Taft. Pfeiffer got nowhere when he tried to get an encomium from President Woodrow Wilson.

The best he could do was a paragraph asserting that Wilson was a great admirer of Rickenbacker's and had "often expressed himself in the highest terms concerning this daring 'man of the clouds.' "

The story of Rick's appearance at the Waldorf-Astoria had made the New York front pages, one column wide, and continuing inside. This was good, for the front page of a New York paper was a field of competition by stories from all over the world, pushing for place with intensity at the moment, mostly forgotten on the following day. In Columbus, each newspaper gave its entire outside to Rick and recorded his homecoming in detail. An eight-column headline topped the *Citizen:* WINGED KNIGHT RETURNS HOME IN TRIUMPH

It was now six years since Rick had first appeared in the local papers as a celebrity of the racetrack, but during those years the nobles of Columbus had not been knocking each other down in competition to receive him socially or hand him valuable awards. Things were different now: the Automobile Club gave Rick a banquet. And the mayor handed him a pair of platium wings encrusted with 156 diamonds and 66 sapphires. A committee was formed to give Rick a house and lot. The idea was that by accepting this gift, Rick would make Columbus his official home town and voting residence. But Rick's instincts had told him, as he looked around at familiar scenes, that this town would not serve him as headquarters. Like other Americans on the rise in that period, he felt the pull of New York, Los Angeles, Chicago, and, because of his alliance with gasoline engines, Detroit.

Back in New York, Rick consulted his managers, who said he would make his first lecture appearance in Boston. That sophisticated city was accustomed to New York tryouts; Rick therefore worked hard to get ready for the opening early in March. Runyon advised him to make a noticeable stop after each humorous remark and wait for laughs, and to do the same thing when he had made an impressive serious statement. Rick wrote the word "Pause" on his script, for example, after a story he put in to give the proceedings a little spice. A farmer dough-boy, billeted with a complaisant French girl, says, "I suttinly wisht somebody would have told me this was going on before." (Pause.) Another bit of humorous relief told of the doughboy who failed to salute an officer. On being rebuked, he said, "I'm sorry, sir. I didn't know you were an officer. I thought you were in the Air Corps." (Pause.) Rick also indicated timing for the dramatic effects as Runyon recommended. "My God, you've been shooting at another human being." (Pause.) He then would pick it up with "At that moment, I hated and abo-minated war, and all that it meant, more than ever."

Legendary driving for General Pershing also fitted into the lecture. Rick said, "But I didn't hold my job with General Pershing long, because he gave me the opportunity of trans-ferring to the aviation service soon after we got to France." Then Rick got to the first victory, and told the audience it was not so dangerous or spectacular as some that came later, "but it produced in me a sensation I'll never enjoy again. Life holds just one of those sensations." When Rick came to remembered air duels, he spoke in the style of *Fighting the Flying Circus,* and told how he pressed the trigger and could see "tracer bullets sending a stream of living fire into the rear of the Pfalz plane . . . Gradually it settled into the pilot's seat. And now I could tell by the swerving of the Pfalz's course that its rudder was no longer held by a directing hand."

It is possible that Rick looked on the lecture tour as an im-portant passage in his life, a venture that might show him what direction to follow right through to the end. A piece of evi-dence lies in his having started another diary. Rick signed the flyleaf in a bold hand, "Captain Edward V. Rickenbacker 1334 East Livingstone Ave Columbus Ohio," and put his opening entry on the page for March 23, 1919. Here, he recorded his first appearance as a lecturer, which took place later than plans had called for. He noted his arrival in Boston, interviews by reporters from six local papers, and the first presentation of his lecture and moving-picture program, which "sure is a Rickenbacker circus." He was "scared stiff," but drew a fairly good house, and his share of the take came to $461.50. He headed the first page of his lecture log, "A New Start in Life."

On the following day, in Hartford, Rick played to only $65.00, "the smallest first prize I have ever won." Afterward, Rick found two men from Columbus waiting backstage. They were emissaries of the Ohio Gas Company, who had come to discuss a publicity tie-in. They mentioned $5000. Rick said he would think it over and let them know.

Back in New York he had little to do except continue sharpening lines and delivery for the appearance at the Metropolitan Opera House. Rick had his nerves under control and headed the diary page for Tuesday, April 1, "My Metropolitan Opening." He logged it a success and said he was pleased. His cut of the money was $800; Henry Van Dyke worked without charge for the French wounded, who benefited by $1800 on the evening. Rick had faced disaster when the movie projector broke down as he called for his first scene. There he stood, with five floors of the Met looming before him, in a position that would have tried a veteran entertainer. He showed poise by calling for house lights so that the audience would have something to look at while operators struggled to make the machine work. The object of the audience's gaze was a large, embarrassed-looking young man with a disarming grin, which he turned on them in supplication for charity and patience.

Because of Van Dyke and the French relief angle, this was a gathering of rich society people. The thought of it, which might have congealed Rick's naturalness of manner, on the contrary gave him courage; after all, he had survived at the Waldorf-Astoria when Van Dyke left him "on" with no prepared lines. Providential help arrived when someone called out, "Why don't you go fishing, Eddie?" Rick answered, with a helpless shrug, "Don't I wish I could!" The audience loved it, and their laugh was with Rick rather than at him. In a few minutes, house lights dimmed and flickering biplanes took off on the screen to the right of Rick's lectern. His show ended on what *Variety* called "heavy mitting," prolonged applause.

After the performance Rick and some friends went for supper at a cabaret, and he felt as relaxed as he could remember for quite a while, perhaps clear back to the good times in Los Angeles and Sheepshead Bay. Rick was comfortably at home in a metropolitan atmosphere, with his table centering a scurry of waiters. The other patrons stood up, white shirtfronts and bare shoulders theatrically lit by rose-shaded lamps, and peered through the haze of smoke — Melacrinos, Murads, and Egyptian Deities — to see who it was. The bandleader nodded and smiled when Rick and his partner danced by. This was considerably better than having people make fun of your clothes in a schoolyard.

Next day Rick didn't feel like any strenuous effort, and was pleased to do nothing but read good things the papers had to say about his show. The *Herald* man had especially appreciated the way Rick handled the projector's breakdown, and wrote that "Eddie was as good as a vaudeville act when the magic lantern gums up." It was even more encouraging to read in the *World* that "Captain Rickenbacker is quite an adept talker, speaks distinctly and holds the attention of his audience."

On the evening of April 2, Rick turned out among celebrities assembled to show the importance of the midtown neighborhood at the grand international opening and dedication of the Commodore Hotel. The management entertained with a concert in the Palm Court by four of the finest musical artists in the world — Mary Garden, Arthur Rubinstein, Mischa Elman, and Enrico Caruso. The audience thrilled to the performers' talents, and drank health to the new hotel in champagne wine. Men in dress suits were bowing to ladies who looked like Mrs. Vernon Castle, and everyone held hands when the evening ended with "Auld Lang Syne."

Rick was on the road by April 6, when he lectured to a good house in Washington, D.C. After that, the tour became an ordeal, with money seldom coming up to Rick's expectations. He played big towns and small, and often slept in Pullman cars for two and three nights at a stretch. A nightmare caught him outside Louisville, and he tumbled in the aisle, fighting an imaginary opponent. The highest financial point came early in the tour, when he took $900 at the Academy of Music in Philadelphia. Rick went from this to the discouragingly low return of $149 the following night, in Utica. He was young enough to enjoy a consolation prize in the form of a supper party and dance at the country club, but next day he worried over the problem of small and unresponsive audiences. His log reported that he "had been trying to find out why people will not come, it is heartbreaking to stand up on stage & talk to empty seats, however I never received anything in my life I did not work overtime for and this is simply another case of it as I have hope."

It is easy to understand Rick's anxiety and frustration. He had received as much publicity as any man in the country, and everyone knew that there were ways to transmute publicity into gold. But Rick was playing to small crowds in tank towns and second-rate cities. At one place he collected only $8.00. When did the alchemy start? It had better start soon, for Rick had learned on racetracks that yesterday's journalism goes the way of yesterday's wind. He felt like a man in a poker game with a tall stack of chips in front of him, and the house cutting his stack every hand and making it less tall, while the cards continued to follow a losing line. What would he do when all the chips were swept away? It is not mere conjecture to say that

Rick felt moments of panic when he awoke before dawn in hotel rooms.

On May 2, Rick gave his lecture in the university town of Ann Arbor, Michigan. Although the audience was small, its response was so direct and appreciative that Rick felt encouraged about his ability to reach people by speaking before them. He had always been successful with small groups — racing crews, mechanics and pilots in the 94th Squadron — and from time to time, as he trouped his one-night stands in 1919, Rick felt something come back from the people he talked to, a kind of harmonic response. There was something powerful here, and he would learn to understand and control it, as all persons who influence the emotions of others must learn to do. Rick trudged on through April, punishing his digestive and nervous systems with the hardships of hotel living and much sleeping on trains. A few days after the middle of May he reached Kansas City, where the schedule permitted a Sunday of rest and meditation. It was an important day in Rick's life, for as he finished the entry in his log, he wrote, "Today I am thru worrying about Hero's and making money easy in big chunks. It's now I must get down to work harder than ever."

That night Rick left for Omaha, the scene of his entrance into the ranks of well-paid sales employees eleven years before. Omaha was pleased to list itself as one of Rick's home towns, and the citizens gave him a memorable day. There was breakfast at the Athletic Club, with prominent men attending as the waiters rushed in with sausages, ham and eggs, small tenderloins, and stacks of golden wheat cakes on the side, every stack five cakes high, as God intended. Syrup and melted butter added a thousand calories to each helping. Rick was barely able to waddle to the official car, which took him out to the airfield for news pictures. In the evening he sat at a table with twenty rich men at the Omaha Club, a fortress of conservative wealth. Here, he had to run through the high points of the lecture, and got nothing for it but the free meal.

May 20 was gala in Sioux City, but when Rick arrived, he found that the air of excitement and expectancy was due to the presence of a circus in town. He noted, "Drove out to the Speedway where I made my start." At the lecture, boys outside the hall threw pebbles on the skylight over Rick's head until police chased them away.

And so Rick headed his diary page of May 29, "The Last." He left Detroit for Indianapolis by way of Toledo, arrived at 8:15, and went directly to the lecture hall, where a good audience waited. Indeed, this proved to be "the best crowd since talk started." Rick was not ready to admit it, but his two months on the road had been an experience of permanent value. He had seen the country at close quarters and absorbed the tone of it in a way that had not been possible when he played some of the same towns and cities as a racing driver and team leader, preoccupied to the exclusion of all else with questions whose answers might mean life or death. As a racing man, he had pleased crowds with the speed of machines and with skill and courage in danger. Although he used personal charm on newsmen, his performance was impersonal. But when he appeared on the lecture platform, Rick had to make personal connection with each listening man and woman, in addition to his offstage function in the role of a modest, likeable hero leading parades and respectfully listening to rich men when they summoned him to lunch and dine at their clubs. It had been hard work, it had nearly worn him out; but he had derived education from these recent experiences, not so much in the college of hard knocks as in the university of public relations. Rick was now ready to go on the personality exchange, for he had come to understand how it worked and what one must do to sell at the top of the market.

It is safe to theorize that on May 30 Rick felt that a burden had slipped from his shoulders. There were no more lectures to deliver, and he now found himself at the center of automobile racing and sales promotion on the eve of the annual

500-mile race over the Indianapolis Speedway. He had accepted an invitation from the Contest Board to act as honorary starter, which meant that he would drive around the oval track ahead of the field before the opening flag went down. Rick had excellent quarters at the Claypool Hotel, old-fashioned, comfortable, well run, and giving a sense of shelter the moment one crossed its threshold. The deskmen wore buttonhole carnations, instantly recognized every high-class drummer in an area of thirty states, and did not hold themselves above accepting a martini cocktail from an approved client when they came off watch. With so many racing men and industry promoters in town, Rick had no trouble collecting "several of the Boys" early in the day, and they lunched at a round table in the grill room. In came one of Rick's pals, the showman and press agent Christy Walsh. The sight of this old friend delighted Rick, and that night they sat up late, making plans. Walsh couldn't see any reason why Rick should not become a millionaire.

May 31 was race day, and Rick began it at seven-thirty in the morning. The ride around the track as starter drew much applause, and Rick recorded that he "got the Boys started it was a great race Howard Wilcox won same there were 3 Boys killed and several hurt De Palma was going well then motor trouble stopped him."

When Rick got back to the Claypool, he organized a party with Barney Oldfield. He spent most of the next day in bed, and still felt terrible when he boarded the night train for New York. Rick summoned up strength on June 2 for a talk with agents who were working on a movie deal. But it would never work out, and he decided to make an impossible demand so that it wouldn't get around that he had lost a sale. He recorded that he asked $50,000 cash on the table or "nothing doing." So it stood.

On Tuesday, Rick met the musical comedy star Elsie Janis and took her to the Hotel Astor Roof Garden, where trellises set off the tables and the dance floor, and during good weather the place was open to the sky. This was a surviving bit of O. Henry's New York, swept by winds and lit by Japanese lanterns. Miss Janis and Rick were called to the bandstand to receive an ovation from the supper crowd. Waiters tugged at corks, and champagne fizzed in the glasses. Rick slept until noon on Wednesday, June 4; he noted that this meant he was "beginning to relax and forget the World." He spent the rest of the day writing letters and planning a talk that Henry Van Dyke had arranged for him to make on the following Saturday at Princeton. On June 12, Rick gave an unpaid talk in Greenfield, Massachusetts, as personal promotion. He had driven to this New England town in a National Six, with Reed Chambers spelling him at the wheel. The weather was fine, and he spoke to the people from the town bandstand.

Chambers and Rick drove to New York on Friday, and the next day Rick left for Princeton, driving two ladies in a Simplex touring car. Rick was a guest at the class of '99 reunion tent, delivered his talk to the class of '97, and saw Princeton lose a baseball game to Yale on University Field. After that Rick took tea with Van Dyke at Avalon, the professor's house on Bayard Lane. He got back to New York at two in the morning.

Rick left on the overnight train to Columbus, where he talked to Mr. R. M. Pierce, who was planning to manufacture automobiles. He had in mind to ask Rick in on the promotion end. It sounded good, but neither Pierce nor Rick could go all the way to a deal on this first meeting. They parted, promising to think it over. Rick went on to a reception, where he saw "all of Columbus society," and the mayor gave him a jeweled pin representing Uncle Sam's hat in the ring.

The automobile interests of California and the Los Angeles Chamber of Commerce, claiming Rick as their own in the manner of Indianapolis, Detroit, Columbus, Omaha, and Sioux City, had set the date of Saturday, June 21, for a parade in his honor, which they assured him would be superior to anything he had yet seen. Rick started for the Coast by way of Chicago, and there talked to Christy Walsh, who continued to prophesy great things for the near future.

Beyond Chicago he worked on the Los Angeles speech in his snug compartment, with the Great Plains rolling past the window. At San Bernardino a committee displayed signs reading, WELCOME CAPTAIN EDDIE and WELCOME TO THE ACE OF ACES. This looked good to Rick because he had felt that interest in war heroes had begun to cool off. The committee drove him to Riverside, where they dined at the Mission Inn. He talked to reporters and posed for pictures, and went to bed at the inn after a fine evening. In the morning, he stopped for an early lunch in Pasadena, and the parade committee delivered him at the Los Angeles Union Station by twelve-thirty, where the main body was formed and waiting. They had a car covered with flowers in the form of an airplane, and he rode in it over to downtown Los Angeles and then all around the principal streets. The floral airplane is noteworthy as an early example of the Californian folk art of the parade float, which was to develop year after year, to astonishing heights, in the Rose Bowl Festival at Pasadena.

After the parade, Rick was guest of honor at a reception in the Los Angeles Athletic Club, and then he went out to the Coast League ball park on Vernon Avenue, where he received an ovation from the fans and a silver cup from the management. He next went to the house of Marcus Hellman, who gave a lawn party, with caterer's men offering trays of dainties and liquor flowing freely. This outdoor gathering modulated into a dinner party; then a dance band set up and the merry meeting became an informal ball.

Rick had noticed that he was sleeping more soundly now that the lectures were over, but nothing had happened that would end his underlying anxieties. He was putting in days as strenuous as those of a campaigning politician, without being able to say what he was running for. All over the country people looked forward to the year 1920 as the opening of the most rewarding decade in American history. It promised money, and Rick's objective was to get his share. As a man without a job, and no demonstrated ability other than that of a daredevil on the track and a gunfighter in the air, Rick had reason to worry.

June 23 was the Shriners' day for honoring Rick. They added to his jewelry with "a beautiful diamond ring." The Southern California Automobile Trades Association gave a lunch at the Athletic Club. From Rick's point of view, this was the familiar spectacle of admiring faces, an audience he could take under control, if he wished to, with his worn but sincere smile and his new lower-register voice. Then he made several visits around town for drinks, one at the home of Christy Walsh's father, and then with an old friend, Mrs. Taylor, who had a fine house in the hills looking out over the plain of Los Angeles. On June 25, the Elks gave a party for Rick at their clubhouse. His log recorded the entire evening "another Grand success."

A significant meeting took place on June 26, when Walsh introduced Rick to Douglas Fairbanks. The genuine hero shook hands with the hero of fantasy, and each man could see himself in the other. Rick had a chance to see in Douglas Fairbanks the part that he wished to play in life: the good American, helpful, friendly, and charming in his amiable generosity. After dining with Fairbanks, Rick took the overnight train for San Francisco.

His purpose in going there was to attend a lunch given by the Automobile Club of the Bay Area, which turned out to be the usual gathering of sales franchise holders, parts jobbers, and sporty motorists of the sort that liked to wear linen dustcoats, flat caps, and gauntlets. It was obvious that Rick suggested automobiles to the public mind, and he was fortunate to have public stature. He perceived an organic connection between automobiles and airplanes, but the club lunchers became uneasy when he talked about civil aviation. Most Americans then thought that airplanes were either a military matter or the province of eccentric daredevil inventors and sportsmen with goggles and their caps on backward. Henry Ford was moving toward the sale of more than a million cars a year, and it was evident that nearly everyone would have some sort of self-propelling vehicle and that fortunes would be gained, not only by manufacturing the cars but by selling them.

The idea of selling as a special function, separate from what happened on the assembly line, was beginning to take form. Alfred P. Sloan, Jr., was thinking about it in his office at the Hyatt Quiet Roller Bearing Company. Soon he would start to move. At the moment, Rick took his friend Billy Hughson for his first airplane flight, and then they went to dinner and a show. Afterward they ran into Fatty Arbuckle at the St. Francis Hotel and spent a few hours in his company. Arbuckle was a friendly fellow, and, when traveling, always held open house in his hotel suite. Nothing untoward came of the evening except that Rick mislaid his polo coat. He found it the next day with no trouble and left for Tacoma, Washington.

The trip was similar in purpose to Rick's Indianapolis visit. There was a motor racetrack at Tacoma, with two races scheduled for the Fourth of July. Rick was to act as honorary starter, an opportunity to appear in newspapers throughout the country and to scout among the promoters and manufacturers who would gather for the races. He pulled out Monday morning on the Union Pacific. The train ran through country so beautiful it became almost dull. When he got to Tacoma, a reception committee headed by the mayor with a brass band marched into the shed and drew up in line to greet Rick as he stepped from the train. The mayor advanced with his silk hat at port arms, and the entire marching body wheeled and escorted Eddie to a dock, where he boarded a yacht that had been waiting, with steam up, to take him along Puget Sound to Seattle. The party lunched on board and got to Seattle in time for an open-air banquet. Then there was a dance at the Flyers Club, where the members made Rick an honorary member.

The next day held few surprises for Rick, who was by now well used to the routine. He autographed menus at lunch and dined out with the Commercial Club at a banquet, where the toastmaster handed him a diamond and platinum stickpin in the form of an airplane propeller. Rick left Seattle on July 5, thinking over the only offer of money he had received, a suggestion by local promoters that he fly over Mount Tacoma as a publicity stunt for a fee of $150 and expenses. Rick feared that the meanness of this offer might be an indication of what he was really worth on the market.

As Rick confronted his dwindling bankroll, with no money coming in, he knew moments of panic. Where would he find his level? Would it be noticeably lower than the position of celebrated racer, and less desirable socially than that of officer and gentleman in the elite air combat corps? These were unpleasant questions, and the answers did not print themselves clearly on Rick's consciousness. They could not at the time, even though he had gone so far in self-analysis as to rebuke his desire for "chunks of easy money." This stand in personal ethics was the part of Rick's character that his mother had implanted, and it had the enduring quality of bare landscapes in his mother's childhood.

His mental and spiritual machinery bore the incised maxim that you must work before you enjoy the reward. Fortunately for Rick, he enjoyed work, with the qualification that he could order the conditions of it. This he had been able to do since he took to the track in his youth, appearing as a free-lance performer and living on prize money. Then, as an enlisted celebrity, he had been under light discipline for a short time, and was writing his own orders soon after he became an airman. Rick now realized that few starting jobs carried the privilege of running the show. And so, except for the fundamental decision on hard work as the main ingredient of the career that he sought for himself, Rick felt but little motivating force. He admitted long afterward that, until about halfway through the year 1920, tides of circumstance had carried him along while he made what effort he could to develop lasting relationships among the men and women who came his way. "Floundering and coasting for a year and a half after the war" was Rick's description of what happened.

He decided to go back east by way of Canada, and at Victoria met a friend from Milwaukee who introduced him to the Bill family of Hartford, Connecticut, who were on their way home after a tour of the Northwest. There were two attractive daughters, Dorothy and Ruth, and he was happy to learn that they would all be traveling on the same Canadian Pacific train. They pulled out for Lake Louise, and Rick had a good time with Dorothy and Ruth, the three of them like characters in one of Ring Lardner's less acerbic stories. As they lunched in the dining car, gazed on scenery from the observation car, and took tea in the club car, it became evident that Rick preferred Dorothy. All stopped over at Lake Louise, where Rick and Dorothy strolled on a woodland trail, with lake and mountain as backdrop, "a most wonderful place to fall in love with a Fair maiden." Rick spent the next day with the girls, and they enjoyed a boat ride up the lake after dinner. He recorded that, on their return, "Dorothy and I took a walk in the Woods. Oh how enchanting."

On July 11, Rick went on to Banff, where he had agreed to give a talk at the hotel. He wrote in his log that when he left Lake Louise, "everybody came down to say good-bye as though I was a newly wedded Man at the Depot." Next day photographers and reporters were waiting for Rick at Banff, the summer and winter resort town, and he faced a capacity crowd when he delivered his talk after lunch in the central hall of the principal hotel. This was a lofty room with rough-hewn walls punctuated by stone fireplaces and windows looking out on the Canadian Rockies. Rick gave his prosperous vacationing Canadian and American listeners a session of prophecy, as he gazed into the future and concentrated on air travel. What he saw was breathtaking. He started by asserting that the government should get to work "laying out the air routes and photographing every inch of them, and preparing maps for air travel." Then Rick began to spin ideas.

The question of safety came first to mind then as it does now when commercial aviation is considered. Rick assured his audience that it was

> possible to design planes with a string of kite parachutes which could be released as the machine is landing, making for a much softer impact on the ground. Eventually this will develop into planes being designed with propellers turning vertically, which could be used in maintaining a position over a given spot after the ship had taken the air. It also could use reversible propellers as a transatlantic liner does when docking. They will carry headlights and navigation lights the same as are used on the high seas.

Rick had never flown in a plane larger than the Number 1 Spad, and he had seen no airplane that carried more human beings on board than pilot, gunner, and bombardier, in the heavy aircraft of the RAF. It was therefore natural for him to give some thought to small aircraft in civilian use, and he said he had reached the conclusion that it would be a good thing to design "a single-seater plane for peace time — you would have safety, comfort, and low cost of maintenance. Then there should be a three-seater sociable plane capable of seventy to eighty miles per hour with a very slow landing speed which should be enclosed like a limousine, with non-shattering glass, for passenger-carrying comfort, and safety should be considered first."

Rick saw rivalry between dirigible airships and planes, and predicted that until the middle 1920s the dirigibles would be preferred for long-distance freight and passenger work, "due to their state of perfection and factor of safety." He told his hearers to expect to see something

> having an immense body similar to a fish with a series of wings and instead of several small engines to propel it there will be one large power plant of several thousand horsepower, centrally located in the hull. This power will be transmitted by shafts to the respective propellers. It will have promenades out on all the wings permitting a given number of sightseers to stroll upon them without affecting the stability of the ship . . . It can be made as long as desired up to 2000 feet long, and carry from five to six hundred passengers and their baggage. The airships will have all the comforts of the best ocean liners including elevators to the roof, which will be known as the promenade deck.

Air travel either by dirigible or plane would have control from the ground. Rick said he expected

> wireless-controlled compasses on all planes for land work such as going between New York and Chicago. There will be stations at Buffalo, Cleveland, and Toledo. By special electric wave lengths these compasses will be controlled from these stations, keeping planes on their paths . . . All pilots will be forced to pass a government examination before being registered and examined again every six months by a board of doctors as to their physical fitness. Planes will also be registered by the government and examined at definite periods to determine their condition. Pilots and passengers will be able to get insurance at a nominal rate as on railroads or steamships.

What Rick was saying appealed to the audience as though someone were reading them pages from the romances of Jules Verne and at the same time giving assurance that what they were hearing would actually take place in the near future. Rick went boldly at the most astonishing idea of all, the possibility of overseas flights. There was no question about it: dirigibles and long-range airplanes would have regular schedules, New York to London, and "would be controlled by directional wireless from both sides in a similar manner to land flights." He asked the listeners to take transatlantic flights for granted, and consider instead the sources of power. Air-cooled engines of the radial type would furnish the motivating force for small planes. The huge transports would have "a centralized power plant similar to the present day steam turbine, using crude oil for fuel." Rick then carried his prophecy to "the day when all these types will be discarded for the electric motor which will receive its current from wireless stations on the ground, thereby eliminating the necessity for fuel tanks and increasing the useful carrying capacity of the aircraft, in addition to providing an increased factor of safety, as present day electric motors are practically foolproof."

Those of his listeners who had seen airplanes take off and land had been present at primitive, makeshift airports that were scarcely recognizable as such. "Cow pasture" was the term most frequently applied to them. Rick said, with emphasis:

Every city should have a municipal airdrome. And be sure to select your field as near the heart of town as possible, so that streetcar or automobile transportation is always available. By so doing you will encourage air travel just as the numerous garages all over the world encourage touring. The day is not far distant when every large city will have a landing field on the roofs of buildings in the downtown districts. They eventually will be built of universal height with the streets bridged over for many square blocks — making it possible to land within fifteen or twenty minutes ride of your office or destination. Central Park with all its natural charms will be utilized for this purpose . . . The roof will be one large flat surface on which ships will land from all four corners of the world.* There will be elevators for the passengers and freight of the different lines. The upper ten floors will be reserved for garaging private planes with immense elevators on all sides of the building to take your plane down to its stall on arrival.

Having spoken in a severely practical way, Rick now turned his talk to speculation that reminds one of Kipling's early aviation story, "With the Night Mail." Rick asked the audience to join him in a flight of imagination, and began it with:

Here I am in Seattle. What a beautiful evening it is as I gaze up at the North Star which is shining so brightly. I feel that I am living in a new era ten years hence, and that North Star is the shining headlight of a large passenger plane just arriving from Alaska. Then I see other headlights not so bright, far out over the Pacific — meaning more planes coming from the Orient, possibly Japan. I wait until they land — one, two, three, four, and five of the ordinary size, carrying an average of from two to three hundred passengers. Then the last, the sixth, an immense airship — down it comes slowly, landing like a bird. From the top deck I hear a voice shouting, "Hello, Rick!" — and as I gaze up I wonder if my eyes are not deceiving me, for can it really be my old friend Captain Ransom. Then I reflect. Why, I just had a cable from him in London only a week ago stating that he was sailing for America. Here I wonder if I am not dreaming, when up dashes my friend with a hearty handshake. Looking him in the eye, I said "What do you mean, Cap, by having some friend of yours wire me from London only a week ago that you were sailing for America?" At that he laughs and a hearty laugh too, and takes out his purse with a long strip of paper resembling a ticket with every color of the rainbow in it. I asked him what it was. "Why, do you mean to say you do not understand?" "Certainly not!" "Well,

* Rick was not alone in visualizing airports on stilts or rooftops. Plans of such projects, with pictures of how they would look, may be studied in Sky and Stone, *Unbuilt America* (New York City, 1976), and Conrads and Sperlich, *The Architecture of Fantasy: Utopian Building and Planning in Modern Times* (New York City, 1962).

Rick, you must wake up. You are living back in the old war days. This is my passage on this ship. It is the new *Lusitania* of the air and belongs to the International Air Service Company which has passenger carrying ships to every important city in the world . . . Why don't you cancel your railroad ticket and buy passage on this ship for New York and share my cabin? We'll be there tomorrow noon." Without a second thought I agreed.

Now it is 11 P.M., and the propellers are starting to whirl. I hear a very loud blast, similar to a foghorn, and we are off. Faster and faster we climb until the western horizon gets brighter and brighter and then a beautiful change. The sun is rising again on the horizon of the Pacific — a massive red ball. Could it be possible that the sun was rising in the west or was I again dreaming?

Rick concluded the dream with rapid arrival in New York, where he entered his hotel with all his baggage a few minutes after landing on the roof over Central Park. After the speech, Rick "met the Bill family just coming in." He accounted for the remainder of his time at Banff with the entry "Spent the rest of the day with Dorothy left for St. Paul 7:40 P.M."

Dorothy Bill was not for Rick, and we catch no further glimpses of her. Rick was moving too fast to settle down with a wife. Sometimes during this period he would go for two weeks, passing as many nights in Pullman cars as in hotels.

Arriving by train in St. Paul on July 14, Rick went to a friend's house for dinner. Then he was off to Chicago on the overnight train. When he got to Chicago, he showed how restlessness was digging into him by leaving the same day for Detroit. Like Charley Anderson, aviator hero of *The Big Money*, John Dos Passos' story of postwar America, Rick was "ready to go to Detroit any time." He found a booming city with a herd of new skyscrapers downtown that faced across the river into Canada. Various men showed Rick the sights, and talked in large but indefinite terms of motor making. He called on Henry Leland, a veteran auto man with whom he had already talked on one occasion but hadn't been able to reach a deal. Leland talked big, but he was bluffing on the strength of having been president of Cadillac. Enemies had pushed him out in 1917, and he was now looking for a proposition.* Rick believed Leland had Detroit bankers behind him, and thought it would be a good thing to represent him in New York City, selling whatever Leland planned to make in the motor car line. When Leland found that this caller didn't have a job or money, he backed off, said he'd keep Eddie in mind, and got him to the door, patting his shoulder and urging him outward at the same time. Rick boarded the Wolverine for New York and smoked Mr. Leland's cigar after dinner.

The object of all these interviews was simple. Rick was searching for a man who thought Rick could help his business and had the authority to put him on the payroll. But this simple objective seemed unattainable, and the task of pursuing it endless. A man would be cordial, but Rick wouldn't be able to reach him later on. A man would say, "Rick, we ought to be able to work something out," but then add that he should talk to Joe, Tom, or Lester, down the hall, before they made final arrangements. Then Rick would find himself staring at a frosty stranger, who would say, "Now just what is this all about, Captain Rickenbacker?" — and Rick would reach for his hat.

But you never knew when the right contact might come along. Rick thought he made it on that same train from Detroit to New York City. In those days, important trains sometimes resembled ocean liners in being the means of allowing one to meet important people. And on this trip Rick got acquainted with William C. Durant, head of General Motors, who talked with him about business conditions and the automobile industry. There was also some mention of Durant's son Clifford, the amateur race driver whom Rick had met in his first California racing days, and of Clifford's wife, Adelaide. Rick played it

* Henry Leland developed the Lincoln car, which he sold to Ford.

straight, as though he didn't have a care in the world, and Durant told him to come up to General Motors headquarters in New York and maybe they would talk some more. Rick said he'd be delighted, and left it indefinite, knowing the next move should come from Durant and that if he, Rick, seemed eager and went up to the GM building without invitation, he would be back on the street. Slight and seemingly unimportant matters could make enormous differences in where one started on the corporate ladder, and it was better to bluff through a period of indigence than to start below a certain mark. Therefore, a young man in Rick's position had to use delicacy and tact in handling the possibility of interviewing the president of a company on his own ground.

Not hearing further from W. C. Durant, Rick decided he'd better do the Mount Tacoma flight for the fee plus expenses. The Banff prophecies had made press association wires, and follow-up was needed. But it turned out that the people who had suggested the Tacoma flight had changed their minds. Finding himself unwanted even for a promotion stunt gave a jolt to Rick's self-confidence, but he absorbed it, and instead of Washington State went to Washington, D.C., where he saw "some of the old boys" and had a talk with Billy Mitchell.

A few days later W. C. Durant asked Eddie to stop in at the GM Building, up near Columbus Circle, just south of the developing Central Park West area, where people said the finest apartment houses in the city would be built. Durant put Rick on the defensive by saying, "Well, Eddie, what do you think you can do for us?" Rick said that what he had in mind was to collect a general commission, called an override, on all GM cars sold in New York City. This was a tremendous plum and only for a politician, which Rick was not. Durant needed some overrides himself, if the truth were known. He eased Rick out. But Rick felt that he had gained something simply by being asked to Mr. Durant's office. He kept after the New York override, talked to a GM official named William Portner, who was encouraging, and on July 22 took the night train to Detroit.

Rick lunched next day with two GM officials at the Detroit Athletic Club, usually referred to as the DAC, and then went for dinner in the country with Christy Walsh. This indefatigable promoter said Rick and the motor industry were natural allies, and a conquest of aviation could grow from the relationship. Walsh stirred things up for Rick, and on the following day they met at the DAC with a Mr. Eastman of GM, later had dinner, and took in a show. Back at the hotel, there was a telegram asking Rick to see a Mr. Jackson at Willys-Overland in Toledo as soon as possible. This sounded fine, and next day Walsh said he had "a new proposition up his sleeve." Rick put a note in his log, "Have a Date to meet a young Lady whose name I know not." It appeared that things were developing when an offer came from Curtiss Aircraft suggesting that Rick join for 25 percent of the profits and "a minimal salary." But when Rick considered this, he saw that the principal return might be 25 percent of nothing, and asked for more time to think it over.

Next morning Rick received another call from the Willys-Overland plant. This was on Saturday.* The message said Willys wanted him right away, but once again it was what a later generation referred to as the old runaround. Later in the day he went to the Lincoln plant and talked to a Mr. Williams, who turned out to be another of those who can turn you away but lack the power to admit you.

Rick left Detroit that night, arriving in New York on July 31. At the hotel, he found an urgent call to see Mr. Willys of Willys-Overland at the New York office, yet the magnate was

---

* In those days, all offices were open and running on Saturday morning, and some continued under full steam all day. Employers who dismissed office help at 1:00 P.M. on Saturday considered themselves to be paragons of kindness and indulgence on the order of the Cheeryble brothers in *Nicholas Nickleby*.

unavailable when Rick got there. The highhanded treatment
was almost unbearably vexatious to Rick, who was always courteous and careful about keeping engagements. He decided to
drop these tiresome people, for the time being, and on Saturday went over to Bayside, Long Island. This was one of the
most attractive parts of the metropolitan area. Here he met
W. C. Fields in the bar at the Bayside Yacht Club. Rick wrote in
his log, "Fields has the golf act at the Midnight Follies." Actor
and aviator took to each other, and Fields telephoned two
young ladies from the chorus. The foursome drove out to
Travers Island for a beach picnic. Motoring back to Manhattan,
the party stopped at a "wayside inn" for "many drinks," as Rick
recorded.

Curtiss Aircraft got in touch with Rick again on Monday,
August 4. The business of dealing in government surplus
goods was then just beginning, but far-seeing men sensed the
possibilities in it. There had dawned an elementary idea — to
take booty *at the expense of one's own government* in buying war
goods for less than their worth and then selling for more.
Curtiss had been manufacturing the JN-4 "Jenny" Trainer, and
Rick heard that a friend of his was now buying back about 2700
of the aircraft at a nominal rate. But Curtiss would have to be
taken care of, and big money was expected to accrue for somebody. Rick thought about this as he dressed for dinner and the
theater, Fay Bainter in *East Is West.*

In the morning Curtiss Aircraft made an offer: Rick would
join in their promotion activities for $25,000 a year plus
$10,000 for expenses. This at a time when $5000 a year meant
a comfortable living and $10,000 was a benchmark of achieve-
ment, putting the recipient within the ranks of success. But
Rick didn't jump at it. For all his prophecies about putting a
roof on Central Park and operating aircraft with 600 passengers, Rick was not absolutely sure that now was the time to get
into aviation. He told the Curtiss people he would give them

his answer in two weeks. They had done him one tremendous favor by making a hard offer with money attached. They had given him market value, above the stuntman, headline-hunting category, and had furnished him with a negotiating base. In asking for two weeks to think it over, Rick showed his characteristic prudence and his lifelong habit of scouting important moves in advance and avoiding leaps in the dark. His confidence restored by the Curtiss offer, from that time on Rick played the personality market with the requisite combination of coolness and skill.

August 6 saw Rick calling on Charley Browne, another of the surplus-plane operators, hoping to arrange some way to get a percentage of his business. Browne said he'd let him know. Christy Walsh came to town and suggested that Rick should be in Detroit on Monday, August 11, and Rick was on the Sunday night train, where he met a young lady who told him she knew Eddie Rickenbacker very well, "but not quite so well as she thought when she found I was the original." Walsh had arranged for Rick to see the Chalmers Motor Car people, and Rick did so, but the New York override wasn't available. On Tuesday and Wednesday, Rick went easy, hanging around the DAC and having drinks with pals. On August 14, he went to the baseball game and had dinner with a Mr. Gertsinger of GM, who said there was a possibility of Rick's getting the California override, which would be worth a fortune. This had the effect of making the Curtiss offer seem smaller, although it still appeared to be the bird in hand.

Reed Chambers came to town, for Detroit was a big-time city, at the crossroads for all who looked to the gasoline engine for lucrative careers. Chambers had been talking aviation around the country, and he brought a Spad fighter to Selfridge Field near Detroit. Rick went out there and took the Spad up, his first flight since leaving the front. A first flight after the end of hostilities had killed Hobey Baker, but Rick put on a show of stunting, and astonished the natives with a falling-leaf maneuver that had them yelling to look out, he had lost power and was falling to his death. Luck held, and Eddie took Chambers to the DAC, where they talked about the 94th Squadron and other things until a late hour.

Through these days, the tone of Rick's log had become cheerful and confident, almost as though written by a different person, a stranger to the tired lecturer trouping the boondocks and working small houses in the tank towns. It is probable that spending time in the company of W. C. Fields, matching wits with W. C. Durant, and running into young ladies who claimed that they were intimate friends had acted on Rick in a stimulating way. It was natural that he should kick up his heels, for he now knew he was a $35,000 man, after eight months of adulation and anxiety, encouragement and disappointment, and incessant travel. These had tended to erode Rick's mental and physical equipment, which he kept going with nerve and stamina rather than reserves of strength. During the war he had spent more time in hospital than many who went home as invalids, and throughout his days and nights in France he had eaten poor food and forced himself out of bed in the dark on many a morning, to wait for sunrise like a condemned man.

Instead of what Rick had gone through since the Armistice, a wise physician would have prescribed six months of relaxation in some Adirondack lodge, where nothing at all would be seen except the activities of squirrels, chipmunks, and deer. The diet to be carefully controlled, and, above all, no eating on the run, no cabaret life, and no arguments, no anxieties. But it is obvious that Rick was doing the opposite of what a prudent regime would call for. It may not have been good for his health, but it gave him a feeling of excited anticipation, and now, as the summer of 1919 approached its end, Rick had reason to expect a dramatic adjustment of his affairs.

That two-week option to accept the Curtiss offer would be

up on August 18, and Rick was in Detroit when the day came. Word was out that Curtiss wanted Rick and that good money was involved. But if he did not take up the offer on the due date, its continuation would become doubtful and its negotiating value shrink to the point of disappearance. Rick did not reply, one way or the other, to the Curtiss offer. The reason was that on this Monday Mr. Gertsinger, the high GM official, told Rick things looked favorable in California and he would have definite information in a few days. So Rick kept silent on Monday and passed Tuesday waiting for word, but got none. This was an all-too-familiar situation and caused Rick extreme psychic discomfort, as it does all who must abide the decisions of other people.

News came on Wednesday, and it was shocking. GM had given the California override to somebody named Murphy, in Los Angeles, and Rick was out in the cold. It became known that this Murphy was in Chicago at the moment, and Rick telephoned a New York agent to get out there at once and try to secure a cut of the money. Rick himself couldn't go to Murphy hat in hand. Murphy now left for Detroit, and the agent followed but couldn't get in to see him. And now nobody would come on the phone at GM, and even the indefatigable Christy Walsh looked unhappy. Rick went to Chicago to ask a banker about a line of credit that he could show to Mr. Gertsinger and the other GM officials as proof that he was worthy of commissions on their cars. They liked to deal with people who already had money in the bank. Rick went back to Detroit without a letter of credit, but at least he had been courteously received by the Chicago financier, who authorized him to say that the bank expressed interest in Rick's doings. There was a meeting with Mr. Gertsinger, who now appeared to have lost his enthusiasm for Rick. On his part, Rick noted that he had "lost some confidence in Gertsinger."

Things now began happening with the rapidity of a knockabout sequence by Rick's friends at the Sennett lot. On Thursday, August 28, Mr. Snyder of the Automobile and Abstract Title Company gave Rick 100 shares in that concern, apparently out of disinterested generosity. On Friday, Rick visited the Dodge plant and talked to sales department heads. They had no suggestions to make, and gave Rick reason to feel that he was no longer a $35,000 man. There was nothing for it but the DAC bar, dinner in the grill, and the night train for Chicago.

He was going through Chicago to spend Labor Day with friends in Wichita Falls, Kansas. In the station he saw in newspaper headlines that he was about to marry Elsie Janis. He wrote in the log, "immediately denied same," and went on to St. Louis, arriving Monday, September 1, in Wichita Falls. His friends took him out to their ranch for an old-fashioned buffalo barbecue. Rick's note was, "Met the Village Queen. Enjoyed myself very much."

On September 2, Rick's friends took him to see the sights, which were mostly oil wells. Rick's log read, "The Wild Western Days are not over Yet." A telegram from Mr. Gertsinger on September 3: MURPHY IN TOWN WANTS TO SEE YOU. Rick thought it might signify the end of his troubles if he could go along beside Murphy on his California override. At any rate, sound tactics now required that he answer Curtiss, or they might tell everybody they had hired Rick and fired him almost at the same time. There was no reason to be abused for nothing. Rick sent a telegram from Wichita Falls, saying he could not entertain the proposition at that time, but perhaps they could take it up later. He wrote in the log, "It was hard to turn down $25,000, but I truly don't want the job." It is noticeable that, in recording his refusal of this opportunity, he took off the $10,000 in expenses so as to make himself feel the salary was all he turned down.

General Motors was like an astronomical mass, attracting

Rick by specific gravity. And if they said, "We hear you didn't make it with Curtiss," he wanted to be able to reply, "It was I who closed out the deal." Rick was aware of the delicacy of balancing one prospective employer against another. It was a matter of precise weighing, down to the last scruple, of the two prospects' actual need of one's services together with the vanity of the executives concerned. That the tinhorn and the fathead were not confined to lower corporate reaches, Rick had well learned by now; the business brigadiers were almost as stupid as generals of the military kind. They hated to pay out money, and they hated to see a man better himself, for another at the trough meant less all around. Nevertheless, they admitted young men to the highly paid ranks when it appeared that they must. GM had blown hot and cold with Rick for weeks. Now the time had come to take him in or let him go.

On September 4, while Rick was on his way to Detroit, the railroad managed to send his trunk to Whitesboro, Texas, where it was found some days later. There is nothing more disconcerting to a traveler. Rick was in Detroit on September 6, where Murphy had asked to see him, so he suffered no loss of face in calling on the California overrider. Murphy turned out to be a glad-handing type whose jolly manner concealed a keen brain and far-reaching connections in southern California. Early in the interview Murphy said, "Rick we want you on the team." Then he stated the deal. Rick was to serve Murphy's California GM franchise for $25,000 in salary the first year, plus 10 percent of net profits. That metallic little word "net" was what worried Rick. When they start figuring the net for purposes of dividing shares, terrible shrinkages can set in. And now came a shocker. In the second year of service to Murphy's dealership, Rick was to get only $15,000 in salary, with 20 percent of the net. Of course, 10 or 20 percent of the *gross* sales would make a splendid income, but Murphy — now promoted by Rick to Mr. Murphy — didn't want to talk about that. Rick disliked the idea of being Mr. Murphy's employee, cut off from direct connection with Detroit. He stalled for time and said he needed a day or two to make up his mind.

On Monday, September 8, Rick got word of "a tire proposition in Pittsburgh." There was no question that cars had to have tires, and Rick did some figuring. He telephoned the Pittsburgh man to report in Detroit right away. Meanwhile, Rick interviewed someone from the Refiners Oil Company. Automobiles fed on gasoline; maybe this was where he belonged. But Rickenbacker gas didn't sound right. It was useless to differentiate brands of gasoline, and Rick realized that fact.

The tire man from Pittsburgh proved to be a disappointment. He was a barfly. Nevertheless, Rick talked to Walter Flanders, an experienced operator in the automobile trade, about the possibilities of the tire deal. But Rick feared the tire fellow would crawl into a whiskey bottle. He was convinced that this had happened when he waited all day on Saturday after the man's return to Pittsburgh, but received no call. Rick went to Chicago, where he met an old girl friend, who was accompanied by her mother. He gave the ladies lunch at the Blackstone Grill, with its green-shaded lamps and red checked tablecloths, and saw them on board the train for New York.

Back to Detroit for Rick, where he waited to hear from Mr. Murphy about an improvement in the California terms. Nobody called. The log for Wednesday, September 17, had three words: "Same Old Story." On Thursday he wrote, "As Ever," and on Friday, "The same." For Saturday and Sunday, blank pages appear. The blanks continued through Monday and Tuesday. On Wednesday, Rick played pool with an old flying pal, Dick Richards, at the DAC. Thursday remained blank. On Friday, he went to Cleveland and talked to various men, with no progress in any direction. Rick was still in Cleveland on Sunday and made a visit to a country club, of which he noted, "Played first game of Golf and Oh Boy what a game. Ha. Ha."

By September 30, he was in Jackson, Michigan, having gone there by way of Detroit. There was a motor car manufacturing plant in Jackson, and the people at the plant told Rick they thought he should join them. They would let him know more in two days. But he did not hear from Jackson Motors until eighteen days later, and by that time the deal was dead. Back in Detroit he received word from Joe Fields, of Liberty Motors, that his company was "very much interested" in Rick. And then Rick heard that Willys-Overland wanted to have further talks. He told Christy Walsh, "I guess they know where they can find me."

On Saturday, October 4, Rick came back to New York City. There was nothing like early autumn in the metropolis, and it appears to have done Rick good to walk on Fifth Avenue again. He lunched with a friend, met a lady, and took her to dinner. On Sunday, he drove to Long Island with this lady, unidentified in the log. Rick loved the quiet expensive roadside inns, which he had first seen as a sixteen-year-old riding mechanic from Columbus, helping his employer try for the Vanderbilt Cup. Then he had been too young and poor to command the amenities of such places. Now he could stroll in with attractive ladies and enjoy his money and success. Whether the money would last and the success prove permanent he could not tell. But anxiety grew less in these circumstances, even though it might be waiting at his bedside in the morning like a patient animal.

The page in Rick's log for the next day, Monday, October 6, is the most significant in his record of the efforts he made in 1919 to plan his future course. There are two paragraphs. The first indicates that Curtiss Aircraft made one more effort to get Rick into camp. As he recorded, a Curtiss official called on him and renewed the offer. Rick refused it, and noted that he found it hard to turn down $25,000 in salary and $10,000 for expenses, showing that he now appraised the offer at its real worth. Thus, he closed off the possibilities at Curtiss, and he ended the paragraph with his familiar question, "Is it a mistake?"

The second paragraph noted that Rick had dined with Harry Cunningham, a veteran in motor car manufacturing, who knew the workings of finance, engineering, production, and marketing, all topics of interest to Rick. They had a long, gratifying session of shop talk. Rick then returned to the Plaza, where he wrote in his diary that as he listened to Cunningham, his own thoughts arranged themselves, and a master project took shape in crisp, rational outline. What had happened was that during the conversation "a Great Idea Came to Me of a Rickenbacker Motor Car."

This was a different idea from a proposal of June 9 at Sandusky, which had been to run up a car in someone else's shop, to be identified with Rick only by a label as it rolled out the door. The new idea was for a personal creation, a car built to Rick's own specifications, embodying what he had learned about gasoline engines on the track and in the sky. It was no easy-money dream; Rick would work day and night to express himself as engineer by designing the car, as financier by raising the money, and as salesman by seeing that America bought the Rickenbacker, "The Car Worthy of Its Name."

# CHAPTER IV

# Assembly Line

THE INSPIRATION for the car worthy of its name had come from Rick's nocturnal wrestlings with his desire to establish himself as a leading citizen. This was a hard problem, because the public had more interest in Rick than in the average man, and he was conscious of the scrutiny. He could not escort Elsie Janis in New York, for example, without starting the rumor that they were engaged to marry; and Priscilla Dean was the love of his life, according to Los Angeles tabbies, who were nourishing the infant science of movie gossip for the Hearst press.

It had happened that Miss Dean was in Vancouver at the time Rick got there. Miss Dean was registering at the desk when Rick walked in. One of those ubiquitous pals hastily ushered him out a side door. It wouldn't do for Rick and the movie actress to be seen in proximity to each other in a hotel lobby, for everybody knew what that could mean. Fifty years later, Miss Dean or any other woman could enter the place arm in arm with Rick, travel the world with him, bear him a child, and give interviews on whether or not it would be advisable to marry him. If he had been Priscilla's traveling companion in 1919, they would have stopped at separate hotels and exchanged visits with great prudence and discretion. Rick did not hesitate to follow his helpful friend out the side door.* Coupling his name with that of the actress would have made him unacceptable to the Bill family; but that no longer mattered, and Rick got up, the morning after he had seen the vision of the Rickenbacker car, facing several things that did matter very much indeed.

More cautious than ever about gossip, and firm in the resolve to build an automobile with his personal integrity behind it, Rick again sought out Harry Cunningham and enlisted him as partner. Many business meetings followed with men in Detroit, Chicago, and New York, and the atmosphere was cordial, now that Rick was no longer a job-hunter, but a promoter with an obviously sound idea. Rick was relaxed because he was selling the idea and not himself. After careful discussions, Cunningham found three seasoned men to help make and launch the car. They were Barney Everitt, William Metzger, and Rick's acquaintance Walter E. Flanders. These three had originated the Studebaker, and Flanders had been the leading production man for Henry Ford. Cunningham said the associates would work together in Detroit to develop a Rickenbacker car on advanced engineering principles, but this might take as much as a year at the drawing boards. However, now that Rick had his own car in view, and four such tested and reputable associates, his immediate job problem faded away. It happened that Gen-

---

*The incident had been sufficiently alarming to stay in Rick's mind, and he dictated an account of it many years later for his unpublished notes:

I was standing in line, when Harry Van Hoven gave me a shove and pushed a newspaper before my face and pushed me over into a corner. He said, "Keep still. Keep still. Wait until I get a chance to tell you." So I did. When he had maneuvered me to a place where I could not be seen I said, "Hell, what's happened?" He said, "Priscilla Dean is in the line just ahead of where you were standing, just four or five paces ahead." One chance in a million for that to happen, you know, but had we met the newspapers would have picked it up, the romance would be publicized, and no one would have believed it was merely a coincidence. I would have been unable to explain it. I would have been a goddam liar, and everything else. She didn't know I was there, of couse, and did not know until years later.

eral Motors needed a California sales chief for the Sheridan car, and W. C. Durant gave Rick the job. Although he was able to do Rick this favor, Durant was losing control of General Motors.

Alfred P. Sloan, Jr., had come into General Motors, along with his Hyatt Quiet Roller Bearing concern, in 1916. They made him vice president in charge of accessories, and by 1918 he was on the executive committee, in the confidence of a large GM investor, Pierre du Pont. When money ran low at GM in the wavering business climate of 1920, Sloan sent a report to du Pont, casting doubt on Durant's management of the company. It also came out that brokers were pressing Durant about his personal investments. Soon Dwight W. Morrow and the millionaire politician John J. Raskob got together with du Pont and the Morgan bankers to put needed money into General Motors and get rid of W. C. Durant. Sloan wrote that they "all tried to be just in a difficult situation." Durant resigned on November 30, 1920.

William C. Durant had run to type in having an expensive, charming, scapegrace son, who lived at a fast pace and received the title of "sportsman" in the papers, usually preceded by "millionaire" or "society."* Clifford Durant was a driver who spent money freely on cars and crews, but did not achieve a listing with champions or even among occasional winners. However, Cliff kept up racing connections because it seemed appropriate to his father's position, and he liked the exciting life.

During the days that W. C. Durant was riding high, Clifford had pleased his father by marrying a girl of whom the old man thought highly. The young lady was Adelaide Frost, of Grand Rapids, Michigan, and her background was unusual. Her fa-

* The sporting idler whose father is a self-made millionaire may be studied in many of the O. Henry stories about New York and in the fiction of Richard Harding Davis. Douglas Fairbanks, Sr., played the type on the screen in *The Knickerbocker Buckaroo, American Aristocracy,* and *Say Young Fellow.*

ther was Stoel Meech Frost, a man of English Quaker stock, whose wife died young, leaving two small daughters. One of her sons, William F. Rickenbacker, said of his mother's early life: "Adelaide was raised by her grandmother, whose passion was to take the sick into her home and heal them. The young girl was marvelously beautiful and had a singing voice that demanded, and got, professional attention. Before she was sixteen she was singing in churches all around the state; before she was twenty she was singing in Detroit, and not in churches."

Miss Frost met and married young Durant in Detroit. This match between handsome magnetic young people looked good, and everyone approved. The couple later moved to Los Angeles, where Cliff took a house surrounded by extensive grounds. The kitchen was larger than the entire Detroit apartment. Adelaide directed a staff of servants and acted as hostess at parties, for the gregarious Cliff Durant liked to have a crowd around him. Sometimes Rick was among the guests, along with other members of the racing and movie set, and Adelaide tried some matchmaking for him, continually bringing up attractive girls. The nickname for elegant Adelaide Durant was "Ma," and often, when he ran into Cliff, Rick would say, "How's Ma?" Cliff would reply, "Fine as silk, Eddie old man! How about coming over for a drink?" Durant was an early model of what came to be known as a playboy, and extremely poor husband material. The marriage died the year before old Durant ran into trouble at General Motors. In spite of the difficulties swarming around him, W. C. Durant had taken the time to settle a trust fund on Adelaide. He said he made this gesture in gratitude because she had done her best in a lost cause.

As he approached the rank of manufacturer, Rickenbacker's good fortune sometimes operated by keeping him out of unpleasant publicity that would have risen to haunt him in mature years. The Dick Richards New Year's party in New York at the end of 1919 is a case in point. Rick's account of this affair in his unpublished notes says that his friend Dick Richards, "one of the toughest bastards that ever lived," shared his quarters at the DAC. The cronies decided to spend the New Year's holiday in New York. On the Wolverine they ran into old friends, Mr. and Mrs. Charles Van Sicklen. Nothing would do but to dine with the Van Sicklens in New York at the house of a rich English uncle. Dick and Eddie would have liked to skip this, because they "had come to town for a fling." And just as they feared, liquor did not flow freely. They got one cocktail before dinner and a thimbleful of brandy afterward. Rick "finally sold the old man into giving a second one." The four went on to Justine Johnson's Little Club, downstairs in a theater near Times Square. However, with the Van Sicklens along, Dick and Eddie weren't having much fun.

> Finally a friend of mine by the name of Elgin Brane came over and whispered in my ear, "There's a swell party up on 54th Street. Come on over." This was about two o'clock in the morning. I couldn't figure out how to get away from Mama Van Sicklen. They were out on the floor dancing. I told Dick to tell her when I was out dancing, that I was getting a little too much, and the sure sign was when I started to drink two glasses of whatever it was, at the same time, filling one from the other as I emptied it. I came back and Dick gave me the wink. I picked up two glasses and went to work. She said, "Now, Eddie, you've had plenty." And of course that was my cue. Then she wanted me to go home, which was what I was after, so we left them at the Commodore Hotel and went over to this apartment where the party was going on.

The party was in a town house on East Fifty-fourth Street, the sort that sometimes was later converted to an expensive speakeasy. Apparently, anyone who wished might come in. There were bars all over the place and a small jazz band on the landing of the magnificent staircase that greeted entrants to the lower hall. The first thing that happened after Dick and Eddie checked their coats was that a pretty girl, dancing alone to the jazz, snapping her fingers and shaking her slender shoulders, tripped against the banister, hung there for a moment, and fell fifteen feet to the hallway beneath. The luck came in because this young lady wasn't even severely shaken up. Soon she was dancing again, and nobody gave the mishap further thought. It would have been different had she broken her neck: GIRL DIES AT RICKENBACKER PARTY . . .

After looking over the crowd, Dick and Eddie decided that they liked a vivid, handsome girl, who turned out to be their hostess. The trouble was her close attendance by a best beau, who obviously held office as what would now be called her boy friend. He was "a great big fellow, six feet four and all he-man." They decided on a stratagem. Eddie said, "Women always fall for a man in distress. You get sick and I'll be your nurse." Accordingly, Dick Richards began groaning in the kitchen while Rick applied damp towels to his head. Nurse and patient refreshed themselves with brandy and champagne, waiting for news of Dick's trouble to reach the hostess. But at last, instead of the beautiful girl, the enormous boy friend entered the kitchen. He said, "Come on, Dick, it's time to go home." Richards answered with one of his usual oaths, and the big fellow grabbed him by the neck. Dick Richards was too drunk to fight, and Rick was laughing so hard he almost fell down. In a few seconds, the big man deposited Richards on the sidewalk and put his hat on his head. Rick went, too. The boy friend said, "Good morning gentlemen," and locked the door.

The next scene that came out of the murk was the front entrance of the Commodore. Here they found a policeman talking with the doorman, and invited them to come up to the Richards-Rickenbacker suite on the twenty-second floor for a few nips. There was only one elevator running, and they persuaded the operator and an early morning maid to join the party. At seven-thirty, the assistant manager called up from the lobby, begging the return of his help and his elevator. The manager said, "You're disorganizing the whole place." Dick Richards said to come on up, and the manager said it would kill him to climb twenty-two floors. At last they made terms and went to breakfast in the big Terrace Restaurant at the east end of the main lobby, where the waiters unsuccessfully attempted to seat them at an obscure table in the corner.

Rick and his pal were up that afternoon, and they went to "somebody's country place or country club and had dinner." Rick's unpublished record then reads:

> Neither of us could dance very well, and I said to Dick, "We're going to learn how." He said, "O.K." I said, "We'll start tomorrow. Let's find out where we can go." We asked everybody, and finally someone suggested Chaliff's, on 57th Street, between Fifth and Sixth. The next morning I made arrangements and Dick and I were up there at eight o'clock every morning. We did that for four mornings, but you wouldn't get any of those goodlooking gals they had as instructors to be there at that hour, so we decided that wouldn't work. We didn't learn anything about dancing. We gave it up.

Rick assumed his Sheridan duties at the end of 1920, expecting to work as California sales manager during the time his associates were developing the new car in Detroit. There was no help for it if Sheridan reduced the market for his own car when it was ready. The men in Detroit wanted the automobile industry as a whole to prosper, and planned to price the six-cylinder Rickenbacker a grade above the Sheridan, which had four. Rick had landed on his feet, and much of the wartime nervousness disappeared, never to return. Business conditions were beginning to look bad, but it was almost impossible to worry in California, in those days a place of overpowering promise and charm.

When he decided where to establish headquarters, Rick passed up Los Angeles, though he still loved it, and settled in

San Francisco. The city had not yet become self-conscious, and was indeed a delightful place to be, especially if one was young and lively. Rick understood that introducing an unknown product required all the publicity he could get. For gaining attention, he would have to exploit his career and personality, and since the obvious way to do this was through aviation, he decided to become the first sales manager to cover his territory by plane. He found a single-seat Bellanca in San Francisco and arranged to lease it whenever he opened a new agency. Rick would fly over town, to land in "the nearest cow pasture," as he put it, and be met by the Sheridan dealer in the new car. These methods were successful in drumming up sales, and in his first California year, Rick established twenty-seven dealerships, which sold 700 cars.

Flying up and down California, with frequent trips to Detroit and New York, Rick was happy as he watched his plans mature. He released a painful old psychic tension in the autumn of 1920, and felt much better for it. Easygoing Rick, calm on the surface for the most part, could harbor deep emotions, and he knew some of them to be ugly. He had said to himself during the war that the thing he was fighting was an evil thing, and he had learned to hate. He recorded in his notes, "I had to learn to unhate after I got back. Sometimes I think I haven't gotten over it yet." He did not direct all his hatred at the enemy. Some was reserved for authorities on his own side, if not specifically at the men themselves, certainly at some things they did. Even Billy Mitchell had stepped over the line of decent conduct, and Rick found himself still unable to accept Mitchell's having yelled at him in front of a French officer. Rick confided to his archives years later: "The French general was someone Mitchell wanted to show off before, and he was boiling to think I had hurt the chain guard, when I might have wrecked the goddam thing completely. I made up my mind he'd pay for that, some day, somewhere." Sooner or later, this bad feeling would have to come out in the open. There might be violence. And the ventilating of hard feelings finally came, in October 1920, under circumstances of physical danger to both Billy Mitchell and Rick.

The drama began when Rick took a party of friends to Ebbets Field in Brooklyn to see a game of the World Series between the Dodgers and the Cleveland Indians. Rick and some DAC pals had rented half a floor at the Biltmore, and it occurred to him that Mitchell might like to join them. He wired an invitation, which brought the general from Washington, ready to go on a frolic. Rick's crowd had cocktails before lunch, and he noted that General Mitchell was in full uniform, "with six rows of ribbons and a swagger stick. He was hotter than a firecracker."

When they returned from the game, rounds of highballs appeared, and the general suggested they go out on the town. Rick answered, "Nuts to that. I'm not going out with any billboard like you. Get into civies and I'll go out with you." Rick's notes continued, "Well, out of the lot of us we put him into mufti; we got him a suit, hat, shoes, socks, everything. We took his uniform from him." After some hours, only Rick and Billy Mitchell were still on their feet. "We wandered from one gyp-the-blood to another down in Greenwich Village."

All the while Rick's memory of Mitchell's unkindness kept coming back more strongly. He wrote that he was thinking, "How am I going to make him pay?" At 3:00 A.M. they entered a gin mill in the Village. Two girls came over, and Rick bought drinks. His head seemed to be clear, and he thought, "Now I'll let him have it. I'll tell him how I feel in my own way." At this moment Billy Mitchell said, "Eddie, there's something I've always wanted to tell you. I owe you an apology. You remember when I bawled you out in France? I've been sorry for it ever since." Eddie noted that the telepathy going on was unbelievable. He said, "Bill, goddamn it, now we're friends! I was about to tell you, you owed me an apology. Up to now we have not been friends. You may have thought we were, but I know better so far as I was concerned. But now everything is out the window. We will start over."

They shook hands; then Eddie realized something was wrong. His watch was gone. "It was a beautiful watch which the City of Detroit had given me, with a platinum chain. I had it when I came into the place, so it was probably still there." People had been maimed and killed in such places and dumped in the alley. Rick told Mitchell to prepare for trouble. Then he called the waiter and said, "Get the manager." A shifty-looking man came up. Rick said, "I had a watch. I had it when I came in. It was a keepsake, a gift. The girls were here and they're gone. I would like to have it back. Please get it for me." He added, "You'll find my name on it." The manager looked them over and sensed something about Rick and Mitchell that warned him to have a care. The man murmured he would see what he could do, and went away. In a few minutes, he came back with the watch. Rick's engraved name had been all he needed to make him extremely nervous until the owner and his friend were out the door. In those days the New York police were a fine body of men, and zealous in protecting citizens, especially those who were famous and popular like Captain Rickenbacker.

From then on Rick had no more ill feeling toward Billy Mitchell, who returned to Washington, wearing uniform and decorations, much refreshed by the holiday. He needed relaxation to get him in shape for his battles with army and navy bureaucrats over the modernization of their flying components. Rick wondered what lay ahead for his friend, but now had little time for anything but unveiling the Rickenbacker car. Advance trade notices were so favorable that during the last three months of 1921, the company sold $5 million worth of stock to 13,000 investors. Rick and his partners retained 25 percent of the total, and turned to their advantage the general shakiness of business when they got the chance to buy a factory in Detroit, at advantageous terms, from a firm that was giving up the fight.

The Rickenbacker car, carrying the hat-in-the-ring insigne, went before the public in the first week of September 1922 at the New York Automobile Show in the Grand Central Palace on Lexington Avenue. There wasn't a name in American motoring too fashionable to feel at home in this collection, and people came by thousands to see the new cars displayed against a proper background. Rick's rivals formed an impressive array. Strolling at random, one could inspect the Peerless, Velie, Franklin, Haynes, Case, Kissel, Kline Kar, Sayers, and Dixie Flyer; and there were seventy-one more brands to be examined by the critic of automobiles. Aside from the Rickenbacker, new cars included the Ambassador, Bournonville (with rotary motor), Apperson, Earl, Goodspeed, Handley-Knight, Kelsey, Leach-Bitwell, Wills St. Claire, Itala, and Vauxhall. The Rickenbacker space was on the fourth floor, and, in addition to the $1485 roadster, Rick displayed a sedan for $1995. The cars made a hit with the crowds. Elegant, slim lines and low-slung bodies suggested speed and dependability, and put one in mind of Rick himself. Orders poured in, and the founders of Rickenbacker Motors were as happy as producers of a play with lines forming at the box office. And the old squadron's hat-in-the-ring insigne appeared on the radiator of every car.

A friend who had helped arrange the flowers and decorations for the Rickenbacker exhibit was Adelaide Durant, now divorced from Clifford and living in New York. For some time, Adelaide and Rick had appeared together at parties during his frequent visits to town. Sophisticated, handsome, and popular, they held membership in a set of stylish, prosperous people who would carry the banner of "café society" during the 1940s. Rick proposed marriage, Adelaide accepted, and the wedding took place at a chapel in Greenwich, Connecticut. The Reverend Jacob Pister, of the Rickenbachers' Lutheran church in Columbus, performed the ceremony, which showed Rick's feeling for the roots of home.

He started a new diary on the wedding day, September 16, writing at the head of the first page, "The opening of a New chapter in my Book of Life." His record of the wedding ceremony was "Adelaide looked beautiful and inspiring, *it was a wish that made it so*" (Rick's italics). They went to New York at once, to sail at midnight on the *Majestic* for a trip to Europe that was to be of almost three months' length. Rick was able to do things in style, and he wanted the world to see his handsome Adelaide. They found their stateroom filled with flowers, and the pageboys kept coming in with telegrams. Rick wrote, "It's a real sense of satisfaction and pride to know you have married a girl whom it seems all the World Loves and Admires." He went on to record that Adelaide was "a peach" and a "Wonderful Pal to share and suffer through life alike. May God help me to make her life one of Bliss and Happiness." They learned that the purser of the *Majestic* was an old friend; he had met Eddie on the *Adriatic* when it brought him back from the war. So Rick and Adelaide dined at his table, which was accounted to be more entertaining, with younger people than one encountered at the captain's table. And it was all a tremendous lark for Adelaide and Eddie, for passage to Europe on the *Majestic* was an experience that cannot be duplicated today.

Luxurious travel by ocean liner was still in its glory when Adelaide and Rick chose the *Majestic* of the White Star Line. This ship had started in life as a German, carrying the Hamburg-American flag. And being of Germanic origin, the ship lacked grace but made up for it in grandeur. The American Ace of Aces and his bride came aboard to find themselves in an entrance hall two stories high, with Corinthian pilasters on the bulkheads. All around were oval Empire tables and vast velour armchairs, resembling furnishings in the public rooms of grand hotels. Adelaide and Rick then passed through an arched entrance into the Palm Court, similar in appearance and size to that of the Plaza in New York. Living palm trees rose to the domed ceiling twenty-five feet above their heads. Having arrived at this point, passengers were properly on board, as could be deduced from the many tables of convenient size and location, with call buttons in their tops by which one could summon servitors bearing any kind of refreshment and at any time. This Palm Court was the town square of the voyage, only one of half a dozen meeting places offering equal spaciousness, convenience, and comfort.

In addition to lounges, bars, sheltered sunning places on deck, and the dining rooms, Adelaide and Rick had access to a ballroom, library, gymnasium, Turkish bath, and two swimming pools. Eddie liked to walk with Adelaide, and the two handsome young people drew admiring attention as they strode arm in arm along the tarred lines between planks on the spotless boat deck. This comfort and luxury took some living up to, for several changes of clothes a day were required, and first-class globetrotters might carry as many as twenty trunks. Taking it from Rick's point of view, it is hard to imagine anything more pleasing than to be young, part owner of an automobile factory, just married to a wonderful girl, and sailing to Europe on one of the finest ships afloat.

The stunning effect of Adelaide's looks and style furnished entries in the log from that time on. And the late hours of dancing caused the Rickenbackers to sleep late, with Rick contentedly reflecting that they must be the laziest couple on board. They made some friends, among them a congenial older couple, Mr. and Mrs. R. T. Burge of Los Angeles. "Mr. Burge evidently is retired," Rick noted. The voyage ended on Thursday, and Rick and Adelaide were on their way to Paris by the following day. Somewhere Adelaide lost a fur neckpiece that had cost $325, and Rick recorded, "I as usual made an ass of myself by losing my temper."

But there could be no jettisoning of luggage, and when the Rickenbackers reached Paris, they found their trunks waiting in a long row outside their suite at the Crillon. They danced down the hall on top of the trunks, a routine for the Castles or Fred and Adele Astaire. In that dancing mood, they took a Sunday trip to Fontainebleau, and Rick wrote that at times he wondered if it could be true that life contained the happiness he was feeling. But on September 26 he gave way to irritation at "Adelaide's bad habit of losing things." Rick and Adelaide visited the Argonne battleground, and then at the end of the week Adelaide broke two vanity case mirrors, thus assuring fourteen years of bad luck, as her husband calculated. But he added in the log, "Luck is what we make it."

The visit to the Argonne put Rick in a thoughtful mood. He had not lost sight of the miseries of ground combat, having run his own risks in the kind of fighting where casualties were high, but dust, dirt, and mud not part of the picture. Seeing the burned-over battlefields started Rick on a line of thought he pursued to the end of his life. He noted that he was now beginning to mistrust all statesmen and all governments. Rick wrote that he would like to see the day when, instead of people being the victims of government, the statesmen and government officials would be victims of the mistakes they made. What Rick saw around him showed that there hadn't been much profit for the suffering people of Europe. He looked beyond the luxury of fashionable Paris and realized that peasants and small tradesmen were just barely getting by.

Rick dressed for dinner at Ciro's, which had changed but little since last time. And on October 30 he and Adelaide took a train for Berlin, stopping at the Adlon. Berlin didn't look as a world capital should: Unter den Linden was dirty, the people shabby and discouraged. The inflation of money was frightening. Rick gave some tips to maids and floor waiters, which he thought amounted to $123.50 each. When he figured the exchange rate, he realized he had given each about six cents. He went back and brought the gratuities up to what he had meant to give, which required bundles of banknotes. Rick said that the German people themselves did not seem to believe what was happening.

A visitor came to the Adlon and asked to see Captain Rickenbacker. He was Ernst Udet, who had succeeded Baron von Richthofen as leading German ace, and he carried a dinner invitation from a group of former pilots. Rick accepted, and the party took place in the back room of an obscure restaurant. Rick's German was rusty, and he talked mostly with Udet, Hermann Goering, and Erhardt Milch, a brilliant pilot and technician. These three spoke English and had much to tell their former enemy. Rick later recalled that Goering was definitely the leader of the group. Addressing Rick as "Herr Eddie," Goering delivered a speech in which he said that the German Empire would be recaptured by air power. First he and his fellow airmen would teach gliding as a sport to young men, then build up a commercial airfleet, loaded with planes that could be converted to bombers. After that would come the administrative plan for a military air force. Germany would be on her way to glory, and this time she wouldn't fail. Rick decided he should report this in Washington. He planned to suggest a scheme to alleviate economic troubles in Germany and get these industrious people working along peaceful lines so that they wouldn't start another war.

The Rickenbackers went back to Paris on the night train and had to contend with insolent customs officials at two in the morning. The scene was better next day at Lanvin's, where models displayed gowns for Adelaide's approval. Rick wrote, "I was King of the Harem, only man in the place." He also recorded that he heard an American say he would like to meet a French bootlegger and get a glass of water. On Sunday, Rick and Adelaide went to the races at Longchamps with Mr. and Mrs. Harry Crosby.* Rick achieved Lardnerian diction when he wrote in his log that the fashionable racecourse "was no place to take one's Wife there are too many ideas to be had for beautiful clothes." Bad luck came when Rick bet on Parnassus, left at the post.

That night Adelaide lost a diamond pin, but Rick kept calm. He told her it was probably only mislaid, and put down a bet that she would find it, for he was becoming accustomed to the amount of gear that had to be spread about their rooms to keep a lady of fashion in trim. Then came something good. It must be one of the leading human felicities to celebrate a birthday in autumnal Paris, all the more so if the anniversary is in the early thirties, when life still leaves room for changes and improvements. Rick had this experience on October 8. He lunched with Harry Crosby, and found his friend "so nervous he could get a bumble bee excited by association." They went shopping and strolled in the afternoon.

That evening they toured what Rick called the "Latin quarters." He and Adelaide had a fine time next day, and attended a performance of *Thaïs*. Rick observed with distaste how Frenchmen kept their hats on, stood up, and "quizzed" the audience. The Rickenbackers retired at the end of the third act, "leaving the French opera to the Frenchmen."

In these days Rick grew to resemble still another figure of American literature, the narrator of Ring Lardner's *Gullible's Travels*. Lardner's man was not gullible at all, and neither was Rick. Both travelers had an understanding of the human race and so did not put their expectations unreasonably high. Rick's

* Caresse Crosby had been Polly Peabody of Boston. Interested in avant-garde art and publishing, the Crosbys were among the most celebrated American expatriates of their time, noted for wit, style, and a daring manner of living.

clear-eyed view of others guided his pen when he wrote in the log about Mr. and Mrs. George Robertson, of Paris: "Both real good Americans, she having been here three years hates the French, true of all real Americans from every viewpoint."

There was rejoicing on October 13 when the missing trinket turned up. Rick was proud of himself for not having got excited about it when the loss was noticed a few days before. Now he could write, "Adelaide found her diamond pin as I predicted she would, in some of her pink things. I win a thousand francs."

In the following week the Rickenbackers prepared to start serious globetrotting, and Rick's log entry was concise: "With Adelaide's trunks on top of the Packard, and enough baggage for a trip around the World, we started for Nice." They stayed that night at a plain country inn, and Rick noted "the first cold bain in months, must admit it was not so bad." On October 19 they reached Grasse, in the flower-growing district on the hills above Cannes, a center of the French perfume industry. Rick visited a perfumery and recorded, "After being shown how they make it, I was used as a test stand for all these different concoctions. If only I could have entered the DAC smelling as I did on my exit, it was so strong I near became ill on our way home."

At the Italian border Rick declared the cigarettes in his baggage to customs officials, and maintained that he had no more than the legal amount. He lost that argument, and the agents pocketed five packs for themselves. Rick meditated, "What a fool. Never again will I declare anything less than a house and lot." They arrived in Rome, took a suite at the Excelsior, and Rick proved himself a good sightseer while inspecting the city for two days. Then they were off for Naples and Pompeii. On the way they saw a villa named BROOKLYN NEW YORK. The fascists were out in Sorrento, blocking streets and creating an uproar. Rick's comment was, "The organization is similar to our American Legion only we do not resort to violence as they have." Moving on to Naples, the Rickenbackers visited the National Museum, where Rick liked the exhibits, "especially the nude art." They then went on to Florence by way of Rome, and by October 28 were living in a suite at the Danieli in Venice.

Rick in Europe showed neither the sensitivity of Henry Adams nor the anxiety of Henry James. European travel for him was what you did for enjoyment if you could command the time and money, and the way you did it showed who you were. Rick also demonstrated by taking this extended trip that he was not the obsessed businessman who refused to leave the office for longer than a weekend. He had left good people in Detroit and relied on them to see that no detail went unattended in his absence. And what happened in Europe was of no concern to Rick, although he could see that another war might be brewing, as a cloud presages a thunderstorm. But even that would not concern him directly, as he saw it, which was the usual American opinion. This time, he believed, the United States would stay out of the fight, having learned a lesson in the previous war. On October 29 Benito Mussolini and the fascists had marched into Rome, and it is interesting to note that Rick did not find this worthy of written comment. He shared the American impression of Italy as a place that one did not have to take seriously. No foreigners could be trusted to do anything right; nevertheless, some of them had a pretty touch with machinery, and two days later, in Turin, while Adelaide went shopping, Rick enjoyed a celebrity's tour of the Fiat plant and admired what he saw.

Over the Corniche to Nice the Packard hummed through fine weather on October 31. The sun was setting, and Rick said he had never seen such colors. But the travelers did not linger, and on November 3 were thankful to be "home again," for by now they looked on the Crillon in Paris as their European home. Rick went out for a stroll and ran into a friend from the war, Webb Miller, of the United Press. As they sat in a corner of the Ritz bar, Miller said the Italian fascists would make trouble before they got through. Rick opined that Germans also would behave badly if they saw fascists enjoying success. It was like a mean dog teaching the neighbor's dog bad habits. He remembered Goering and his speech to "Herr Eddie." Those fellows had little to lose.

The Rickenbackers put in a "huge day" on Sunday, for they had decided to move on. After arranging for trunks to follow, they took a plane of the recently organized British Airways to London. There was risk in passenger flights, and the run they were on had seen two London-to-Paris planes collide over Beauvais, killing six people. Only two months before Rick and Adelaide made their flight, John Galsworthy wrote to the *Times* recommending that all aircraft should be banned, owing to their unacceptable dangers. Rick was out early next day to look over the auto show at the Olympia. His own car was not represented; he saw a British car that was smaller and lighter than the lean Rickenbacker. Several advantages became obvious as he looked it over, and he thought there might be merit in passing a law that permitted only a stated amount of horsepower to each 100 pounds of weight. It would save materials and fuel, reduce prices to users, and help preserve roads. This was a surprisingly disinterested idea for a motor car maker to entertain.

After his day at the auto show, Rick took Adelaide to see *Loyalties,* the new play by Galsworthy. This is the story of an ex-officer reduced to cheating a rich Jewish social climber. The ex-officer's pals cover for him; that's how the loyalties go. But at last he commits suicide. There were shattering scenes in the Galsworthy play, and their effect may have remained in Rick's mind on November 11, when he dined at Romano's and then dressed for the Armistice celebration at the Savoy. The Rickenbackers had an American couple as guests at their table in the ballroom. Rick recorded the evening in telegraphic style:

Mr. and Mrs. Keeler were delayed 40 minutes, account of traffic jams for it seemed everybody was going same place. At Savoy every inch of space reserved for guests, all in their best, beautiful women and handsome men soon played as Kids, it was a Gala night for all but the poor and unemployed, ex-soldiers selling shoestrings, matches, how the spirit of Humanity would be benefited, if the millions spent on pleasure could be given to a better cause and the spenders stayed a night at Home.

It was a big night, and so strenuous that Rick used Pepysian honesty in his log for November 12: "Spent most of the day in bed getting over Armistice Night. After tea we dressed for dinner in the Hotel and danced, I getting on my ear and making Addie feel badly." Next day he was well enough to lunch at the American Club, "a nice place with plenty of Americans." That night Rick and Adelaide went to a musical comedy and then danced at the London branch of Ciro's until closing time. They finished a quiet week, taking in the Tower, Harrods department store, and various theatrical performances, including a clutching-hand melodrama, *The Cat and the Canary,* which they enjoyed. While investigating London life, Rick sometimes encountered things that seemed inexplicable and even foolish. But when he thought of these people, who conducted their affairs in such strange ways, he always told himself, "One must remember they are English." And he saw cloth-capped men marching in orderly ranks with a red flag to demonstrate in front of the Prime Minister's house at 10 Downing Street.

Even though he devoted attention to motor cars, Rick always had aviation on his mind. He lunched at the Royal Automobile Club, and, while paying polite attention to the shop talk of his hosts, he subconsciously arrived at a plan to manufacture an airplane. He recorded the inspiration: "I decided to build a three-motor plane, with body hinged at the wings and long enough to transport one of our cars ready to drive away upon landing. This will be one of the greatest advertising stunts ever put over in the auto Industry."

On November 22, the Rickenbackers boarded the *Majestic* at Cherbourg for the voyage home. Rick recorded that he had never been happier, and he hoped that was the way Adelaide felt about things. On the first day his log was pure Lardner: "Awakened with Sun shining and with a boat so steady one feels as though they are on land." Next day, Rick dressed for dinner in a hurry and tied his tie wrong side out, showing the maker's label "like an advertisement." The calm sea of Rick's first entry grew rough, and a lady lost her hat to the stiff deck breeze. "Next time around my cap left me suddenly but landed on a life boat. (Lord always protects his lambs.)"

Financial weather continued favorable throughout 1922 for the owners of Rickenbacker Motors, as they saw the price of plant machinery rising, and were happy that they had acquired theirs at the bottom of the market. The odd, countrified, horse-trading aspect of selling motor cars extended from offices in Detroit and Indianapolis all the way to local banks, where persons of good repute could finance their car buying, if they wished. The conception of the motor car maker himself acting as banker had yet to be born in the brain of Alfred P. Sloan, Jr. When it came, this method of selling had the majesty of a great idea: you sold your customer a car, you sold him money to pay for it, and you held the car as collateral until he retired your loan. If the customer went broke, you took back his car, sold it to someone else as used, and signed up the used-car customer in debt for another installment loan. This wasn't the way they had sold the Mercer and the Stutz.

Lending money to the customers was one thing that Rick failed to prophesy in the 1920s. But he made a number of bold predictions that have since come true. For example, he stated in an interview that the aviation industry would find places for women employees, both on the ground and in the air. Rick said that manual skill and moral courage were the two essential qualities in making a successful pilot, and as women possess these attributes more frequently than men, there was no reason women should not enter the field. And he ran the risk of not being believed, early in the 1920s, when he said he was sorry for those who had their money tied up in railroads. Talking for an automobile trade magazine, Rick went on to say that such investors had only themselves to blame "and must pay for their foolishness." This was in a time when New York Central "Fives" and securities of the Pennsylvania Railroad were valued threads in the fabric of commerce. The editor remarked that if a nationwide election could be held, Captain Rickenbacker would easily win "the post of director-general of aerial transport in the future."

Rick was by no means presumptuous in offering his opinions, for the public already had conferred the position of oracle on him. The principal of a high school in Trenton, for example, asked him for a letter of advice to the pupils. Rick answered with four pages of good sense about work habits and goals in life, along with the assurance that "this government stands for good and good only. It is the fairest and most liberal government in the whole world. And it holds the key to world peace."

The year of 1923 saw Rick's acquisition of an associate who would see that all his utterances, whether to students, other celebrities, or the general public, would be preserved. It was luck that brought Marguerite Shepherd to his service when Rick asked the personnel department to engage a secretary. Returning from a trip, he found Miss Shepherd at the desk she was not to relinquish for more than fifty years. He described Marguerite Shepherd as "an attractive, well-educated and serious young woman from Hamilton, Ontario, Canada." The young lady's integrity and ability were obvious; in fact, Marguerite was such a prize that Barney Everitt tried to get her away after she had worked in Rick's office for a few weeks. Rick said, "If you continue as you are, you'll have no regrets." In time, Miss Shepherd became office manager, with secretaries of her own; more than that, she was Rick's confidential aide, personal accountant for him and Adelaide, and practically a member of the family.

Instead of taking the presidency of Rickenbacker Motors, he had heeded his partners' suggestion that he would be of greatest use as vice president and sales manager. This was a field he dominated by instinct. He showed his command of basic tenets when he addressed the Rickenbacker dealers of Los Angeles in August 1925. On this occasion, Rick talked for more than an hour. He had stenographers taking down his discourse, and, pointing out that repairs could be a profitable sideline, Rick told his dealers to convince the prospect that

> you are rendering him a great service and you are only enabled to keep going in business when you have rendered to him the best and highest possible service available at the minimum cost.
>
> Remember, gentlemen, it is being done by these little garages all over the country. So why shouldn't your service stations do the same? Gentlemen, do not compel the used-car department to absorb your loss in maintaining your service department. I tell you it is rotten business to have to do it. It is not complimentary to you or to me, because, after all, your best business is in your used-car department, when you have the kind of product that we have, a car that will frankly please the eye, a car famed for its comfort and ease of operation. If you do that, then I tell you you will have no trouble in selling the prospect by the time the sample drive has ended and he has appreciated the thrill that goes through that steering gear and motor. And when the time comes for you to pass upon the price that you will pay him for his old car, he is interested . . ."

The horse-trading aspect of automobile selling lay beneath Rick's manual of tactics. While the floorman played his customer, he had to have a croupier's brain balancing all the figures going into the deal. As Rick said, the floorman was buying and selling at the same time — buying the customer's car for resale at a profit, selling him a new car at a markup that would afford something for everyone along the line, including the dealer's landlord, and tribute in the form of taxes and license fees to the civil servants of his town, plus any undisguised graft he may have been compelled to pay. The graduate schools of business couldn't make a tougher theoretical problem, and well did Rick know it, for the *third* man, the man who made the whole thing work, was not present when floorman and customer cried done and done. This third man was the purchaser of the used car. And where was he? Somewhere out in the street, or on a trolley car that he was tired of riding to work, or counting a raise in his pay and planning to give some girls a ride.

Rick had found the root of this matter, too. It had dawned on him that the huge mass of metal torn from mountainsides and folded into boxes with wheels on the corners and engines under the fronts must *keep moving* — not only when the first owners got in and started off, but in a sense that touched both physics and economics, so that the roofed-over showrooms fed the open-air used-car lots, so that the course of profit and pressure, *the factory*, should continue the insectoid procession of new cars that steadily crawled from their doors and out to every corner of the land. "Gentlemen, some day every car in the United States and in the world will be wearing out and some day will have to be replaced, and that means some twenty-odd million . . ."

Rickenbacker Motors prospered throughout 1923, for a superior car such as Rick had to sell was bound to gain acceptance. And in that year Rick called his partners into council on the matter of four-wheel brakes. He told them he had driven racing cars with four-wheel brakes and so had personal proof of their superiority. Rick got to the heart of the discussion: "It is a straightforward matter of arithmetic. Four is greater than

two." So in 1924 the Rickenbacker car came before the public
with a brake functioning on each wheel. Here is Rick's account
of what happened:

> What I did not realize . . . was that the other automobile compa-
> nies could not afford to be taken unaware. The industry had
> hundreds of millions of dollars' worth of automobiles with two-
> wheel brakes in inventory or in production. There were cars in
> showrooms, cars in warehouses, cars en route to the dealers, cars
> on the assembly line and cars in pieces en route to the assembly
> line. To sell those cars the entire automotive industry had to con-
> vince the public that four-wheel brakes were inferior, even un-
> safe.

The Rickenbacker cars with four-wheel brakes went well in
1924, but not so well as the makers had expected. Dealers
began to report that they were hearing rumors about the safety
of the braking system. Some dealers suspected a whispering
campaign; that is, the organized distribution of unfavorable
gossip by professional rumor planters.* Two planters would
ride a crowded elevator and one would loudly ask the other if
he had heard about the Rickenbacker that landed in the ditch
and killed two people because of four-wheel brakes. The other
would answer that the company was being widely sued for
criminal negligence because of the brakes, which interfered
with steering to such an extent that thousands of accidents had
occurred, but it was being kept out of the papers because of
Rickenbacker advertising. That sounded like proof to most
people, who were used to reading of suicides "at a leading
downtown hotel" or shoplifters arrested "at a large department
store" in their local papers. Who paid the rumor planters? The
benefit of stopping Rick's sales went to the rest of the automo-

---

*William C. Esty, in charge of Camel cigarette advertising in the 1930s,
called paid whispering "a diabolical weapon." Competitors put it about that one
cent from the price of every Camel pack went to the Vatican and that inspectors had found a leper at work in the Camel factory in North Carolina. Mr.
Esty said that when he visited a town where the campaign had struck, he could
count Camel packages thrown away in the gutter with cigarettes still in them.

tive industry, and there lay the source of rumor spreaders' fees.

During 1924, Rickenbacker Motors put up a fight by bringing out two new models, including the boat-tailed Super-Sport Coupé, which was a rangy car with some of the cut-down style of the Mercer Raceabout, an immortal thoroughbred of American motor manufacture. The attraction of the product, and Rick's assiduous preaching of his sales gospel, helped to keep the company in good condition. But the tales of snapped necks, cracked spines, and tires that wore out too soon continued to flourish, and the Rickenbacker partners buckled down to trim expenses and make production more efficient. The sport coupé had a soft top, but Flanders and Everitt saw that taste was swinging to hard-topped touring cars called sedans and destined to become the standard family vehicle. Accordingly, they acquired the Trippence Closed Body Corporation of Detroit, thus ensuring a supply of roofed bodies with which to meet future demands. The report by President Barney Everitt, dated on the last day of 1924, showed a net worth of $7,947,248.92, compared with $7,429,250.65 at the close of the previous year. The net gain was $517,998.27, and the company paid $377,870.20 to stockholders.

Rick sent out a poem of his own composition at Christmastime in 1924, and it may have had as stimulating an effect on its readers as Everitt's figures. Every customer, stockholder, and dealer, and all those on a list of friends, received a folded card that opened to twenty by eleven inches and carried the following verses:

When our forefathers drove their oxen across the plains to the sea,
They started a march of progress which never shall ended be,
They ate their Christmas dinner sitting 'round the campfires bright,
And watched for the skulking red man from behind their carts at night.
But they who were timid and lagged behind never reached the promised land,
For we must step with progress ere we grasp success by the hand.

Since the time of the covered wagon we've advanced in science far.
Till today men go from coast to coast in a plane or motor car.
And as I sit at my Christmas board while the flames in the fireplace
    leap,
I thank God for these fearless men and resolve their faith to keep.
They gave their best they had to give and we will do the same,
And progress aid if we build a car that is worthy of its name.

I hope your day will brighter be because you've joined our band,
And that for newer better things throughout the year you'll stand.
May your brightest dreams be realized and naught your vision mar,
And may success ride at your wheel in a Rickenbacker car.

During the time that Rick was developing his genius for salesmanship, Billy Mitchell got into trouble. Mitchell had made high navy commanders look foolish in debate over the effectiveness of military air power. He had gone so far as to sink a hulk target by throwing bombs out of a light plane. The dreadnaught admirals had counterparts in the army, whose influence was strong. They passed over Mitchell's name on the promotion list, and Rick offered him a job at the motor company. Mitchell declined with thanks.

The brass called Mitchell before a court for insubordination. Rick appeared as witness for Mitchell's side of the case, confronting the same sort of officers who had ruled out parachutes for combat pilots. Among other things, Mitchell had demanded a unified air force. But General Hugh A. Drum, one of the judges at the court-martial, said that he could defend the District of Columbia with twelve antiaircraft guns. As the closing witness for Mitchell, Rick clashed with Drum and other judges, including Douglas MacArthur, who had by now achieved two-star rank. Rick said:

Because of the cowardice and stupidity of our own War Department and government authorities, when the Wright brothers went to the government with their new invention, they were refused encouragement and had to turn to France. France saw the possibility. When we entered the war, we had no aircraft industry. Hundreds of lives of our fliers were sacrificed needlessly by defective planes and obsolete equipment in training camps thousands of miles from the front. This nation owes General Mitchell a debt of gratitude for daring to speak the truth. He has learned his lesson from the only real teacher — experience . . . Unified air service is the life insurance of our national integrity.

Rick's appearance at the trial made headlines but failed to exonerate Mitchell. The judges canceled his rank of buck general and broke him down to colonel. Mitchell resigned his commission and became a folk hero in private life. "That was his reward," Rick said, "for the great service he had given his country."

The marriage of Rick and Adelaide was childless. They decided to make a family by adopting two sons, the older born on January 4, 1925, and the younger on March 16, 1928. They named the first boy David Edward Rickenbacker, and the second William Frost Rickenbacker. Neither was "Junior" because Rick detested the name "Eddie," though he answered to it. He said, "To my mind that name depicts a little fellow — and I saw to it that neither of my boys would be so called."

Rick made one of his best speeches in 1925 to the Executives Club of Chicago. He put the audience in good humor by recalling how an Englishman said he had enjoyed reading the dictionary, but "it was rather disconnected, don't you think?" And he nailed them to the chairs with his absolute sincerity when he said, "The only downright fundamental fear I had on the western front was fire in the air." Soon afterward, Rick made his first appearance at Harvard. Public figures seldom refused invitations to speak in Cambridge, and Rick addressed something called the Harvard Aeronautical Society. This was an undergraduate group, of sporting membership, on the order of a sailing, mountaineering, or iceboating club. That didn't bother Rick, who told his listeners that, since they would stand among the country's leaders, they should decide in college where to bring this leadership to bear. Rick said, "Study everything Harvard can give you about aviation. Get yourselves ready, and go into air transport."

Throughout 1925, Rick applied himself to problems of selling. The advertisements in which he announced four-wheel brakes resembled a discharge of cannon on an enemy position. Counterbattery fire was sure to follow, and Studebaker made reply in behalf of the industry. A full page in every big newspaper plus hundreds of smaller publications fired the barrage. According to Studebaker, a car with four-wheel brakes could go out of control at any time, and taking one's family in such a vehicle amounted to criminal negligence.* The cost of each insertion was enormous, far beyond what Rick had to spend. Barney Everitt and the home-office people thought it was Rick's fault for insisting on the brakes. All he could do now was increase his efforts to inspire salesmen. His own brains and energy, his gift for understanding people, had showed him the way. He found the basic tenets: get the prospect's confidence; establish moral superiority over him; but do not expect to close if you give him any cause for offense.

The time required something more, for a business recession came in 1925, and the competitors' whispering campaigns and printed advertising combined with a shortage of cash in customers' pockets to bring down the Rickenbacker Motor Company. Dealers began to fail, though Rick did what he could to keep them going. By 1926 he had signed notes for $250,000, mostly with bankers in Detroit, but had little luck in New York,

---

* The advertisements claimed that Studebaker had tried four-wheel brakes, proved them a failure, and would never put them on cars. Studebaker's copy stated that four-wheel brakes were too complicated, and called for unnecessary parts and maintenance. The advertisements also warned that the brakes had a tendency to lock front wheels and turn cars over.

where he hoped to convince underwriters that they should help the company survive. Miss Shepherd never forgot how Rick went downtown from his New York office in an optimistic mood and came back two hours later with his face white and drawn. He said, "They told me they would find money if we changed management." Miss Shepherd asked what that meant. Rick said, "This is what it means" — and dictated a letter of resignation to company headquarters in Detroit. The men downtown had struck at him as a salesman. What they said convinced him that nothing could save the company, but he was willing to let his associates go on and pull it out with another sales manager, if they could make that work. They could not — this soon became obvious. A year later, in 1927, the Rickenbacker Motor Company went bankrupt.*

Rick appraised his position as that of an unemployed man thirty-five years old and a quarter million dollars in debt. But the very size of the obligation carried a certain advantage. It is hard to grasp the principle that debts can be an asset, but Rick knew the bankers in Detroit, at least, would like to see him make a fortune. Frank Blair, of Union Guardian Trust, was one who would listen to any scheme by which Rick could make money. He would rather see a prosperous Rick than have him represent an uncollectible loan. At this time Rick announced his doctrine that failure was a good thing. It was a privilege to fail: you learned your limitations and applied that knowledge to future plans. Rick was entirely in agreement with Mr. Greatheart, in *The Pilgrim's Progress,* who said, "This Valley of Humiliation is of itself as fruitful a place as any the Crow flies over."

In spite of his financial troubles, Rick was now an insider and so would remain for the rest of his days. If the 1920s gave the

* Forty years later, Rick continued to hear from people who were still driving their Rickenbackers. A man called from California in 1966 and said his Rickenbacker was in perfect shape. He asked, "Don't you want to see it and have a ride?" Rick answered, "Thank you very much, but I wouldn't want to look at it or ride in it. The thought is painful."

United States a feeling of adventure and freedom, together with a false promise of lasting prosperity, ease, and comfort for all, the decade gave Rick something he could cling to — the assurance that he was durable, that his renown had entered the national consciousness as deeply as that of any man in his time.

Rick pondered the tactics of his second foray into the personality market and the world of big deals, and a piece of valuable advice came to him from Detroit, where Frank Blair suggested he might find it interesting to scout the Allison Engineering Company at Indianapolis. James A. Allison was one of the builders of the Indianapolis Speedway, and he had founded his company to make racing cars. Now he had given that up and devoted his small plant to the manufacture of high-precision bearings for airplane engines, superchargers by subcontract to General Electric, and reduction gears for navy dirigibles. Anyone could see that the Allison shop did first-class work, and although it was not a huge concern like the plants that scissored auto bodies in Detroit or cooked metal in Youngstown, Toledo, and Pittsburgh, it was a valuable piece of working property.

Time was when Rick would have asked for a job there. But now that he was broke, now that he had seen the Rickenbacker nameplate obscured in bankruptcy, he made himself no longer a job-hunter. What he sought was the whole thing — he was now a company-hunter. And as far as anyone could tell, lack of money had nothing to do with Rick's estimation of whether or not he was likely to succeed in making a deal. Rick did not hesitate, therefore, to ask Jim Allison to sell him the company. But what it really amounted to was asking that Allison sell to Union Guardian, with Rick as agent.* Allison was getting old and was ready to retire. Rick's recollection of his answer was: "Well, Eddie, I'll tell you. It's true I spend most of my time in Florida these days, but when I do come home for the summer I like to

* Bernard Baruch said the only sure way to make a million dollars was to sell something for $20 million and take a 5 percent commission.

have a desk I can put my feet on. But I have an idea that's tailor-made for you. Why don't you take over the Speedway?"

Asking to hear more about this possibility, Rick added that he was willing to admit it had not occurred to him. Allison explained that the four speedway founders were no longer active. One was dead, another had lost interest, and Arthur C. Newby, like Allison, had come to the point in a successful industrialist's life when he liked to spend as much time as possible in Florida. After some more discussion, Allison mentioned a price of $700,000. Rick didn't blink at this but acted as though he could easily put down such a sum if he decided to go with the deal. He asked for time to make a survey to find out if the price was right, just as though he had the money in his pocket. The way Rick handled this was bound to please Allison. If Allison knew Rick had no money, he would admire his bluff, and if he thought Rick had Detroit cash in hand, he was willing to let him examine the goods. He asked whether a thirty-day option would be satisfactory, and Rick agreed.

Rick didn't have to do any serious research to determine that the Indianapolis Speedway at $700,000 was a bargain. The buy would include 320 acres of ground, and the city was growing out that way, making profitable real estate deals entirely possible. But most valuable of all was something intangible that could be listed only under good will — the tradition of the Decoration Day 500-mile race. In the days since Rick had won in California, New York, Texas, Iowa, and other states, but never managed to keep his mount in one piece at Indianapolis, that race had become an institution. Rick decided this was too good to finance out of Detroit. Everything would be easier to manage if the money came from Indianapolis. He started to make inquiries in that city's financial circles.

This proved to be a mistake, for all Rick succeeded in starting around Indianapolis was excitement among real estate men who planned to pick up the option and cut the 320 speedway acres into developments. Rick hurried to Jim Allison and assured him all was well, but suggested that another thirty days of option time would be most helpful. Jim Allison bit off a piece of eating tobacco and smiled. He said something like, "Eddie, why don't you go back to Detroit and put this thing through? Yes, take another thirty days."

Rick got to see Frank Blair at Union Guardian in a hurry. No one had to tell Blair the speedway option was worth money. The only question was how far to extend Rick's line of credit. Blair said he thought he could float a speedway bond issue, but this couldn't be done overnight. The bank's lawyers would have to draw up the wording, the attorney general of Michigan would have to approve, and the bond department would have to sell the paper. Although that last requirement shouldn't take long, it all must happen before Rick could have his money. Frank Blair suggested that the bonds pay 6.5 percent. Rick was in no position to bargain. All he asked was a prompt completion of the business.

Blair set wheels in motion, and Rick had the by now familiar experience of waiting for others to make arrangements that, though they had vital importance for him, were out of his control. Three weeks went by, with the bond issue grinding through legal machinery. On the last day of the fourth week, when the option had one more hour of life, Blair called Rick and told him everything was all right. Rick immediately telephoned Jim Allison to report that the money was available and that he was leaving for Indianapolis the minute the bank finished making out a certified check. What it amounted to was that the bank had arranged for Rick to have his money at 6.5 percent, retaining 49 percent of the stock as its fee for floating the bond issue. The other 51 percent was in Rick's name, and he took control of the Indianapolis Speedway on November 1, 1927.

In view of his instinctive understanding of the region, it might have seemed that Rick had found his natural home and would never leave the city where he now controlled a famous racetrack. But just as he had politely withdrawn from Columbus, Rick placed Indianapolis on his list of cities to be visited only when business made it imperative to do so. He arranged to draw $5000 a year from the speedway corporation; in return, he would devote the month of May in each year to promoting that year's race. With this effort he expected to make profits from his speedway stock. He appointed Steve Hannagan consultant for publicity, and Hannagan suggested calling the speedway "the world's greatest outdoor testing laboratory for the automotive industry." Hannagan also suggested that they invite the president of the newly formed National Broadcasting Company to the first race under Rick's direction, on Decoration Day, 1928.

Merlin Hall Aylesworth watched a splendid race in which a rainstorm at 475 miles brought out the caution flag. Then the rain blew off across the cornfields, and Louis Meyer, driving a Miller Special, nipped in first with a nerve-racking close finish. This took place before the age of television, but it was all that "Deac" Aylesworth needed to see and hear. Back at NBC headquarters in New York, he called the production department and ordered it to start planning full coverage of the Indianapolis Five Hundred. And beginning in 1929 the race was on the air. It made a good broadcast, with announcers at various points around the track and the sound effects of the roaring engines. This alliance with broadcasting was one of the best things Rick arranged for the greatest testing laboratory. In the eleven months that he spent away from the track, he continued to hunt for an occupation in which he could express himself with all his talents combined to bring about a single result. During the years of the late 1920s, Rick often gave evidence that he felt the pull of aviation and discerned in it the ultimate satisfaction of his needs and wishes. But the matching of right place and right time continued to elude him.

For the present, Rick had to stay with automobiles, and he

went to Detroit for a solution to his problem. The founding of
Rickenbacker Motors had put him on that level at which a man
can always have another job, no matter how badly he has
messed up his last one. Auto sales was still Rick's game, and
they invited him to play it at General Motors. There can be no
doubt that Mr. Sloan was pleased to see Rick's car off the market, and he had made no move as leader of the industry to correct the lies of the Studebaker brake advertising. But as far as
Rick was concerned, Sloan harbored no ill will, and did not object when GM created a $12,000 job for Rick as special assistant
general sales manager for a new car that the Cadillac division
had brought on the market. This was the La Salle, in the
upper-medium price range, with a V-8 engine under its hood.

News of Rick's job at General Motors attracted attention in
the business world, and he received many congratulatory letters. Some were anything but subtle. An example is the letter of
a man named C. S. Lee, who was Washington lobbyist for the
asphalt trade. Lee wrote that he had just toured New England
and Canada in a Rickenbacker car and "passed Buicks on the
hills." Slighting reference to Buick was not a happy touch, since
it was a General Motors brand. And it didn't occur to the man
that Rick might prefer not to hear any more about the car
worthy of its name. Lee bumbled on that he wished to congrat-
ulate Rick on achieving his post, and enclosed a folder of literature about asphalt. When people pack this sort of material in a
kit, you can throw it away with one toss to the wastebasket. Rick
did so, but added Lee's name to his mailing list.

Before he started on the new General Motors brand, word
came down to pull Rick off La Salle and put him on Cadillac.
They were saying at GM headquarters that Cadillac had run
into sales resistance. The most expensive car in the GM line
wasn't selling. Orders were for Rick to find out what had gone
wrong and to inspire the dealers at the top of the merchandis-
ing structure, the middle rank of sales executives known as

closers, and, most important of all, the floormen who had first contact with potential buyers as they wandered in off the street. Away went Rick on a sales trip that made his lecture travels look like a leisurely tour of the Lake District by a professor of English on a sabbatical year. Rick visited seventy-five cities in eighty-one days, and harangued Cadillac sellers with the intensity of Paul addressing members of the early Church. As he had done when preaching Rickenbacker sales, he brought stenographers to the meetings, so his talks have been preserved exactly as he improvised them. There was identifiable Pauline fervor and mystery in his message to the Boston Cadillac organization on March 22, 1928:

> . . . I say to you all that, if you go after your business tomorrow morning on the basis of the capital you are using, being your capital, that you have no connection whatsoever with any other department of your business, you haven't anybody above you to keep you at work on your problems, you will learn more than you ever knew in your life was possible to know about running a business; and I hope that the ambition of every man connected with the service station or any part of a new-car organization to make something of his life beside staying where he is, will not lead him so far astray as to assume too many burdens, and the worry of them, and, if you want to appreciate that, just get in the boss's shoes and assume the boss's responsibilities, gentlemen. . . . Take your used-car business. I say, as you say, that is a business of itself. . . . I pledge you my word, gentlemen, that during this trip I have found in our organization reputable distributors who have used Cadillacs to sell for $1,000, $2,000, or $3,500 and storing them in some ramshackle place, in the basement, upstairs above the new-car salesroom, a Buick behind, a Chrysler here, and I say that, to me, is criminal. Why, I know and you know men that have the courage of their convictions to such a degree that they go down on your business highways and they buy, lease or rent a store, buy your used cars that you haven't the courage to display in your salesroom, put them on their floors, sell them and make a

profit, and their chance of success as compared to the used-car
department of any new-car institution is a thousand to one in
their favor . . .

Rick had good understanding of economics when he
preached that secondhand sales should be handled by the automobile industry rather than by free-lance operators who
worked under canvas or on entirely roofless lots strung with
light bulbs. He perceived that these rogues were taking money
from the system and putting none back. At the same time, the
local floormen and closers of the Cadillac organization may not
have fully understood Rick's economics, for his thinking was
not easy to follow. But it was sound.

He had grasped a theory of values which stated that the
manufacturers as a whole sold their product twice every time a
used-car buyer found what he wanted and put his money
down. Part of the money this buyer paid for his secondhand
car went back into the manufacturing cycle, *provided* the sales
were made by franchised distributors who paid taxes to Detroit.
The distributors' profits from used cars paid operating fees to
the same system that provided new cars, just as distributors put
a good part of the value of their efforts in selling and maintaining showrooms into the central enterprise. This cash flow had
such importance on the books, both at the distributors' offices
and at Detroit, that the men on the floor were empowered to
sell any make of used car, even the dreaded Packard. Drawing
their minds back from the immediate scene far enough to see
the entire automotive industry at once, Rick and those who
held his views saw that it was all one thing, an even greater
combination of suppliers than Mr. Sloan had built in General
Motors. When financial troubles disposed of weak links in the
chain of supply and demand — such as the Rickenbacker car —
the chain grew shorter, and it also grew stronger.

Holding the position of sales exhorter at General Motors did
not prevent Rick from continuing his hunt for companies to
buy on credit. Shortly after Rick got control of the Indianapolis

Speedway, Jim Allison made his last trip to Florida and dropped dead from a heart attack. Rick asked the executors what was to become of the Allison Engineering Company, and learned that the property would go at auction to the highest bidder. He noted that "just about everybody in the aircraft industry or who wanted to get into the aircraft industry was after the company." Friends in a position to know kept Rick informed of the amounts that were bid, and he stayed $5000 ahead until the company was his for $90,000, which he did not have. He told the executors that he would show money right away, and then called on the Indianapolis bankers who had turned him down when he was negotiating for the speedway. This time the bankers liked what he had to tell them. They took special interest in the possibility of selling the acreage that surrounded the plant. They would immediately open an account for $90,000 in the name of Edward V. Rickenbacker. He signed a note, and so acquired Jim Allison's high-quality machining business. But in a few days Rick began to wonder how far he could carry this thing. It was time to go back to Detroit. And when Rick talked business there, he found that interest in aviation was increasing every day.

Aviation was under discussion at Fisher Brothers, whose influence came from their automobile body works. The company had set up the Fisher Investment Trust, and here Rick told his story of a high-grade machine shop in Indianapolis with a navy contract. Who owned this interesting company? It belonged to E. V. Rickenbacker, who was frank to say it was getting too heavy for him. The moneymen's decision was instantaneous. They called downstairs for a check, and an old office messenger in a baggy linen coat brought it right up. They put it in Rick's hands, he signed a memorandum of agreement, and his worries about Allison were over. But it seemed to Rick that he ought to have compensation for his time and trouble and for putting Fisher Investment Trust on to a good thing. They told Rick to stay calm and say nothing. Something would be done for him; they could see the outlines of it right now; and they would let him know. A few months later, Fisher Investment sold Allison to General Motors, and obtained a finder's fee of approximately $9000 for E. V. Rickenbacker. Everyone came out ahead.*

On December 21, 1928, Rick started his custom of sending a letter of greeting in prose to all his friends. It was a form letter, and Rick did not worry about sensitive persons who might feel something patronizing in a copy of a personal letter that reached an indefinite number of people. His first annual letter was admirably brief:

> My dear————,
>
> With the closing of another year,
> we are reminded of the fleetness of
> time, which brings with it the thought
> of old friends and new.
>
> It is my sincere hope and wish that
> you and yours will enjoy the Holidays
> in the spirit of youth, and the New Year
> will bring all that I might wish for
> myself.
>
> > Yours in Yuletide,
> > *Eddie*

Such was the force of Rick's personality that many recipients treasured these letters and preserved the entire series as he issued them at increasing length throughout his life. The first-name signature was disarming, and the "My dear" salutation indicated cordiality. If you had questioned him about the Christmas letters, Rick would have told you he had so many friends, there wasn't enough time to write to each one as an individual.

* The mighty Allison engine powered the P-38 and the P-51, among others, during World War II.

# CHAPTER V

# Common Carrier

RICK'S PERFORMANCE in the matter of the Allison Engineering Company made a good impression at General Motors. Early in 1929, he got a call from Charles E. Wilson, the executive vice president who later became head of the company. Wilson spoke in confidence, and what he had to say justified Rick's previous feeling that aviation was becoming important in the business world. Wilson said that GM "planned to take a position in aviation." Sloan and his aides had decided to acquire the Fokker Aircraft Corporation as a start. They wanted Eddie to look into it and arrange the sale. It was strange that planes designed by Anthony Fokker had given him a close call in the war and now he was to look over the Fokker Aircraft Corporation of America company with a view to doing business.

Fokker was building a tri-motored commercial ship, the F-10. Linen covered the steel-tubed fuselage, and the wings were formed by laminated wood. Rick decided the F-10 would be a success, and he brought Fokker and Wilson together. This time Rick's fee was a job instead of money. General Motors offered him the chance to get out of auto sales and into aviation. And he was delighted to become vice president in charge of sales for Fokker as a division of General Motors, with his office in New York. Here was where he belonged, in his real home town, which remained so through all his travels for the rest of his life.

At this time Rick made one more large corporate sale, by finding purchasers for the Pioneer Instrument Company, a maker of aircraft equipment. It became the Bendix Aviation Corporation, but Rick never liked to talk about his contribution to the deal. "It can't be mentioned" was all he would say later on when persons interested in his career would come to this short chapter of it. What happened was that for a brief time Rick was the legal owner of Pioneer, and he remarked in putting down the confidential source material of his life story that "I saved the boy who sold it to me a million dollars in the tax field." It turns out that financial sleight of hand was involved, and Rick's commission for arranging the sale was 2400 shares of Pioneer stock. He sold enough of this at $95.00 a share to retire the outstanding amount of his loans in behalf of Rickenbacker Motors. Somehow Rick managed to freeze out the tax collectors, for which one can give him nothing but applause. Like all honest men, he had an instinctive hatred of tax gatherers, and so decided to draw a curtain over the Pioneer deal, while at the same time he congratulated himself for settling his personal loans on behalf of the Rickenbacker car. No one was able to make up the losses of Rickenbacker stockholders, and Rick himself was a big loser along with the others, if you figured the stock that he held in his own company as money even though he hadn't bought those shares. After all, they had been payment for his ideas and salesmanship and for his name. The idea that stock certificates were better than money had a firm hold on the financial community in 1929. But on November 1 of that year, the great bull market lay dead.

In December 1929, Congressman Robert H. Clancy of the Third District of Michigan had decided it was time for Rick to receive the country's highest military medal. This award was called the Congressional Medal of Honor because the legislators at Washington had to confer it by vote. Clancy wrote to

Rick about what he was trying to do, and revealed that the task was not so easy as one might have supposed. The recommendation might originate in either house, but had to pass both. Clancy thought it better to start things in the lower house. He was a popular legislator and did not expect anyone to torpedo his sponsorship on personal grounds. But Clancy feared the "drys," the name by which people generally called supporters of Prohibition. There was no hiding the fact that Eddie patronized bootleggers and went to convivial parties. Clancy knew the ropes, and started around the Capitol in a sure-footed way, talking to various men. Things looked bad at first; then Clancy made certain commitments and the dry opposition vanished. He now saw that the trouble would be in the Senate.

Leaving that bridge to be crossed when he reached it, Clancy got the approval of the House Military Affairs Commitee for a bill to authorize and direct the Secretary of War to award the medal to E. V. Rickenbacker, "formerly Captain in the Air Service of the United States," for "displaying unusual heroic courage and skill as an aviator during the World War." Specific deeds would be listed after consultation with the War Department. With the drys whistled back in their kennels, the bill passed unanimously in February 1930, and Clancy went over to the Senate to find out how matters stood.

Here, fellow legislators told him to see two American Legion officials from Connecticut, who knew how the land lay. The news was that Senator Hiram Bingham of their state "unalterably opposed" giving Rick the medal. Bingham was a respected man with a background of nonpolitical achievement. He had been a college professor and an explorer in Brazil, and his distinctions included a life membership in the National Geographic Society. The senator held two grudges against Rick. The first was that he thought Rick had commercialized his war record. But that complaint was a smoke screen. Bingham, who had been a ground officer in the air service, was commander at Issoudun field from August to December 1918. This put him in the ranks of desk officers for whom Rick had never tried to conceal his lack of unquestioning respect. Bingham had heard what Rick said about the denying of parachutes and had not forgotten it. And recently there had been Rick's appearance at the Mitchell trial, where "he had talked about superior officers" on the witness stand. Rick had called big generals and admirals cowards and stupid asses. Give our Congressional Medal to that fellow? Not on your life, said Hiram Bingham.

Clancy ran into more trouble when he asked the War Department to have a citation drawn up. The department also remembered Rick's remarks at the Mitchell trial and had not forgotten what he said about parachutes. They shunted Clancy around as much as they dared, hoping that bureaucratic delays would wear him out. Because of legislative schedules, Clancy hoped to get the medal approved in the Senate by March 4, but the department managed to delay him until after that date. Representative Clancy now enlisted support from Governor Fred W. Green of Michigan, who seconded the American Legion in recommending favorable action. Clancy said Rick had won the medal "a hundred times more justly than Lindbergh, Byrd, or Bennett, even if he did take such pride in his insigne as to put it on the car, and even if he did attack superiors for deficiency in supply."

A considerable amount of public interest made itself felt in Washington, all of it on Captain Eddie's side. The Republican strategists decided they didn't wish to appear to be insulting a popular hero by denying him recognition. Certain persons spoke to Hiram Bingham, and he withdrew his public objections. And Clancy at last obtained a specific citation from the War Department. For conspicuous gallantry and intrepidity above and beyond the call of duty against the enemy, the department selected events of September 25, 1918, when Rick had attacked seven enemy planes and destroyed two of them.

Rick finally got his medal on November 6, 1930, at Bolling Field, near Washington. The chief general of the air corps read the citation and President Hoover conferred the medal, lifting the ribbon over Rick's head in the traditional way. Hoover looked preoccupied as the cold wind fluttered the turned-up collar of his overcoat. His statement ended with these words:

> Your record is an outstanding one for skill and bravery, and is a source of pride to your comrades and your countrymen. Although this award is somewhat belated I hope that your gratification in receiving this Medal of Honor will be as keen as mine is in bestowing it on you. May you wear it during many years of happiness and continued usefulness to your country.

All who could hear Rick's answer in the stiff breeze agreed that his voice shook with emotion as he gave his prepared reply. It was brief, its main point that the medal was a tribute to his "comrades in arms, soldiers and sailors, living and dead." After an air show as they rode back to town Rick tried to put in a word with Hoover about the unified air service that Billy Mitchell had recommended. Rick found the President courteous, but realized that military aviation came far down on Hoover's list of current worries. The Depression was getting worse and people were losing hope. Since Hoover had earned the world's admiration in directing war relief and acting as food administrator, not to mention his performance as Secretary of Commerce, the country expected him to solve national business and employment problems by using his authority and prestige. The conscientious Hoover accepted this responsibility and, at this time, still believed he could meet it. A cold morning at Bolling Field and a medal to Captain Eddie meant only an interruption in unceasing labors at the White House, where, bent over his desk, he tried to find a way to better times. Rick meditated, as he later wrote, that the nation's leaders were not ready for military preparedness, especially in aviation.

Having now turned forty years old, Rick had reached the age when most men in business are still among the candidates outside the door that leads to permanent rank. Most of them fail to gain admittance. But Rick had passed that point and had exorcised the word "failure" when he pulled out of the motor car company and got the speedway under his control. More than most, he was ready for the decade of the 1930s, that silver period of recent history which was so kind to a few Americans while it subjected many to physical and emotional trials that would have been impossible to imagine in days of triumph immediately after the Armistice. Framed at the start by the end of easy prosperity, and at the finish by the beginning of another war, the 1930s were peculiarly Rick's time. The troubles and demands of those years fitted his strengths, and they prepared him for personal and national disasters in the 1940s as well as for a third of a century of extraordinarily active living after 1940 until he died in 1973.

After Rick and Adelaide adopted the boys, they moved from their Jefferson Avenue apartment in Detroit to a house in Grosse Pointe. He bought the place and its mortgage from a man who had come out loser in a deal involving motor cars. Rick said this man had fallen so low that he was "selling on the street from a briefcase." The house was a bargain, and Rick turned a fast and lucrative deal on the property in the summer of 1929. Four months later he would have had to take a loss on the Grosse Pointe mansion. What it amounted to was a trade for another large house in Bronxville, an expensive Westchester County suburb just north of the New York City lines.

Rick also rented a permanent room at the Roosevelt Hotel for nights when commuting to Bronxville by train or car was not convenient. Adelaide was patient about this, recognizing that Rick was an unusual man; life with him was exciting and rewarding, but also demanding at times. Only a strong woman could handle it. Sometimes Rick accused himself of selfishness in his married life, but he knew he wouldn't change. And sometimes Adelaide thought it was better for him to stay over in town than drive a car to Bronxville after a convivial meeting at a speakeasy or club.

One night he came home after a drinking bout and went quietly to bed. Later he got up and, by mistake, opened the French doors to the balcony, toppled over the rail, and fell to the lawn, breaking his collarbone. Rick explained that he had dreamed he was sleepwalking and that his taking the wrong turn and falling off the porch was, in fact, sleepwalking. Rick never attained the grade of complete professional drunk. But for years he maintained a place among those who could be said to drink a good bit. He also smoked cigarettes like a testing machine in a cancer laboratory. Often enough, Rick saw pall-bearers carrying out heavy boozers and cigarette burners from among his friends. He attended the funerals, filed away the obituaries, and kept on living.

Rick's life in 1930 began to strike rough spots just as he thought he had put his affairs into satisfactory shape. The difficulty came because Rick was ahead of his time in the matter of changing residence to conform with corporate planning. It was characteristic of Eddie that after acting as pioneer in the acceptance of company locating when he moved from Grosse Pointe to Bronxville, he then rebelled against the practice and never afterward allowed anyone to tell him where to hang his hat. This brought him to one of the rough spots. Financial panic had struck before aviation yielded profits to GM, and consolidation was in order. In 1930, the head office moved Fokker from Hasbrouck Heights, just beyond the Hackensack Flats in New Jersey, to merge with other plants, near Baltimore, under the name of General Aviation Manufacturing Corporation. On December 8, 1931, General Aviation announced that sales would remain in New York, with Captain E. V. Rickenbacker in charge. Then word came from Detroit: "Get Rickenbacker to

Baltimore." They made one error when issuing that order, which was not to find out in advance if Rick would obey it. He would not. He didn't like the sound of Dundalk, Maryland, where the factories were, or of Baltimore, where General Aviation had set up its front office. His address would continue to be New York City and its environs. He summed it up, "Once again I left a good position with a good future."

Although he had abandoned a job with a good future, Rick had by no means turned his back on commercial aviation. He was one of the knowledgeable men in the field, qualified to analyze rumors of new ventures that constantly developed on the financial pages of the newspapers and in conversations around town. And the question was not whether there would be money in the future of aviation, but how to connect with the new industry, to find the ground floor. Rick knew that Averell Harriman and Robert Lehman had formed a holding company for this purpose. It is hard to define a holding company except to say that the holdings are supposed to yield profits like the seed sown on good soil in the parable, some of it, as we read in Mark, returning from 30 to 100 percent. Harriman and Lehman put out seed money for something called Aviation Corporation, or AVCO. Fledgling airlines had appeared across the country, and AVCO combined a number of them into American Airways. This looked fine on business pages in the *New York Times* and the *Herald Tribune,* but the promoters found less agreeable reading in American Airways' operating accounts. No matter how you phrased it in bookkeepers' language, the thing was losing money. Rick also had an eye on American Airways, and since the owners happened to have been keeping *their* eyes on Rick, it was not regarded as miraculous that, within a month after leaving General Aviation, he became vice president of American Airways, out of sales at last and into general management of the firm.

One of Rick's most important duties was to be a lobbyist in

Washington. His efforts, as he put it, were "to develop and maintain government good will." He flew to Washington from New York whenever possible. The cities were connected by a barnstorming operation called Eastern Air Transport, which flew when weather permitted. The planes were lumbering Curtiss Kingbirds, which struggled into the air, rattling and groaning, from the field near Newark. Passengers assembled in a shed at the middle of wasteland in the heart of the New Jersey industrial area, with the stubby skyscrapers of Newark a mile to the northwest as you got off the ground and the pilot picked up the line of Pennsylvania tracks for the Delaware River and Philadelphia. On the ground there seemed to be grim-looking wire fences everywhere. Going out to Newark Airport made one think of going to a concentration camp, and getting into a Kingbird or a Ford tri-motor brought to mind the mounting of a gallows to be hanged.

Rick would have lost little time aboard the Congressional Limited, and would have been comfortable on the way, but he passed up the "Congo" whenever Eastern Air Transport was willing to take off. As one of the first businessmen to fly regularly, Rick set the pattern for executive travelers. He carried a fat briefcase, mulled over papers, made notes. There are views of the eastern seaboard in the slot between Philadelphia and Baltimore, with marvelous colors to be seen in the off-shore waters. But Rick liked to make the planes his flying offices; he would take papers out of the case, look at them, scribble on them, and put them back again. But he was always conscious of the creaking sounds that came from the fuselage, and the engine's drone told him how things were going with the power plant.

The basic anxiety of flying never left him. It never leaves anybody who takes off in a plane until the thing is back on the ground. And a few minutes of additional nervous tension always came at the end of the flight, while the pilot was solving the problem of getting onto the Washington airfield without landing in the Potomac River. The New York landings were easier to approach, but Newark Bay and the Passaic River looked uninviting, and there was no place to land in Elizabeth, which stood between the pilot and his target at the end of the northward run. When Rick got out at Newark and carried the briefcase toward his parked car, he had to admit to himself that he was dedicating his life to something that was dangerous and unnatural. Still, aviation was the transport of the future.

Transport east and west was the business of American Airways, whereas Eastern Air carried people north and south, and got them all the way to Florida, when conditions were right. Its busiest months, therefore, came in the winter. As a transport man, Rick had interest in the problem of moving vacationers from north to south and bringing them back when they were ready to come home. Railroads were doing this in a satisfactory manner, as the hero of Ring Lardner's "Golden Honeymoon" had told with painstaking detail. Nevertheless, Eastern was getting good business during Florida vacation seasons.

As Rick pondered the question of Florida tourists, he noted the national traffic pattern, which gave American Airways its busiest times in the spring, summer, and fall. It was obvious that "merging American and Eastern would give them a year-round peak." Best of all, planes could be transferred between the lines when needed. Rick began to think how he could bring about a merger of the companies. As he himself said, "Dealings in high finance are never simple." North American Aviation, a holding company similar to AVCO, numbered Eastern Air Transport among the elements under its control. A man named Clement T. Keys owned the majority interest in North American. But he took hard blows as the Depression grew heavier, and word got out in 1933 that Keys was through. Rick told Lehman and Harriman to get ready for fast dealing. Their respect for Rick increased when Keys threw in the towel and asked the courts to declare him bankrupt. Rick's principals immediately began negotiating with receivers to buy North American and thus gain control of Eastern Air and its north-south routes from the metropolitan area to Florida.

Things now began to happen which showed that Rick was right when he said nothing of this sort ever came out in a straight line. For now there appeared the well-known and energetic entrepreneur Errett Lobban Cord, who also had caught the scent of Keys's difficulties. E. L. Cord had first entered the world of commerce by playing a hose over auto bodies at a carwash stand in Los Angeles. He rose rapidly because he understood the principle of "buy low and sell high." In addition, Cord brought out the Auburn automobile and the famous advanced model bearing his name, which Frank Lloyd Wright hailed as the most elegant design on the market.

Like Eddie, Cord had now turned from engines on the ground to engines in the air, and he acquired a small barnstorming outfit called Century Airline, in the Northwest, which he sold to AVCO in return for stock. This move by the dollar-students Lehman and Harriman might have been compared to the famous error of the Arab who allowed the camel to get his head into the tent. For openers, Cord used his privilege as a stockholder to shake down the AVCO books, and what he found aroused interest. He discovered that the holding company had a kitty of money in New York and Boston banks, $30 million in cash, all earmarked for development of AVCO properties. Cord thought it would feel good to have the money in his own pockets. Lehman and Harriman were controlling AVCO with only 7 percent of the stock. Cord sent his runners to buy all the AVCO stock they could find, while at the same time he suggested a number of new companies as AVCO possibilities to promoters, hoping in this way to increase the value of the stock after he acquired it. Such manipulations were beyond ordinary understanding, but the maneuvers seemed plain enough to Eddie, who took counsel with Harriman and Lehman. There now existed a possibility that they might find themselves outside their own company, with E. L. Cord pocketing their money and looking around for more.

Rick suggested that they pay for the acquisition of North American Aviation with money to be realized by issuing two million shares of new AVCO stock. This would leave the cash reserves untouched and would "have the effect of reducing Cord's interest." That is, if Cord bought the new shares himself, he would be paying for North American, and if he did not, his current AVCO holdings would be diluted. When Cord heard about this, he threatened to give AVCO the treatment that Samson inflicted on the Philistines: he would tear the whole structure down on their heads. Rick's assessment was "Cord was so angry he threatened to put not only this particular controversy but also the airline situation in general before the public."

Rick said, "I hope you don't do that, E. L." He went on in a reasonable tone to explain why the move was unwise. There had been sharp practice in the aviation industry; no one could deny that. But if a man of Cord's stature made a public fuss about the merging of airlines and the manipulating of stock, everyone concerned would be a loser. The reason was obvious: the government in Washington was growing at a monstrous rate, and anything that attracted the government's attention was bad. Rick pleaded that "the industry was becoming mature, and capable of clean and efficient operation." This would make no difference to bureaucrats who had nothing to do but interfere in other people's business and cripple those who had actual work in progress by making them fill out thousands of forms and spend hundreds of hours explaining themselves to petty officials. Rick said that, though the new Roosevelt administration had restored confidence throughout the country and relieved much misfortune by welfare payments and by putting government funds into public works, the administrative apparatus was bound to become topheavy, and would not go away when the need for it had disappeared.

Although he himself had suggested undermining E. L. Cord, Rick now realized that his own interests lay in merging airlines to serve the American people, as he piously put it, rather than protecting Lehman and Harriman from financial harm. He therefore assumed the role of peacemaker between the two factions. The negotiations kept him away from Washington for a while and brought him to the new Waldorf-Astoria, a huge building on Park Avenue through the block to Lexington Avenue in the rear. Part of the enormous hotel was called the Waldorf Towers, and here the management rented permanent suites for persons of wealth. Former President Herbert Hoover gazed morosely on his collection of blue and white china in a Waldorf Towers apartment, and in the elevators he might see Henry R. Luce or Rick's employers, Lehman and Harriman, or E. L. Cord himself. Rick became familiar to the courteous, silver-haired Irishmen, retired members of the New York Police Department, who unobtrusively inspected all comers in the small private lobby off East Fifty-first Street, where tenants and visitors entered the Towers. He could talk to Harriman and Lehman and then get quickly to Cord under the same roof. It looked as though the trouble was going to quiet down, as Cord became noticeably less belligerent in talking to Rick.

This was a deception. Cord was using Rick to lull his enemies while he prepared to make a sweeping solicitation for AVCO proxies. Cord knew that Rick had been postponing a trip to Los Angeles. He convinced Rick it was all right to leave New York, then called some telephone numbers from his suite, and the battle began. Harriman and Lehman called for Rick in California by long-distance telephone. He left Los Angeles on the transport of the future, and the weather of the present marooned him in St. Louis. When he got off the train in New

York and walked past the newsstand in the Pennsylvania Station, Rick saw the headline E. L. CORD IN PROXY RAID OTHER HEADS DROP.

Up in the Waldorf Towers, Rick took off his coat and went to the telephone while Harriman and Lehman paced the floor. Rick did what he could in the way of persuading friends not to deal with Cord, but it didn't work out. Next day, Cord was in control. He ousted the AVCO directors and put in his own. Conceivably, he could siphon off the AVCO kitty before Harriman and Lehman could get to their lawyers. Rick said that he went to Cord at the end of the business day on which the takeover was announced and offered his resignation from American Airways, but Cord decided that Rick should stay on for a couple of months. A face-saving excuse for Rick's official departure would be found in the removal of the home office to Chicago. Rick announced that he didn't want to leave New York, but he told everyone he and E. L. Cord were the best of friends. The date of his resignation was to be February 28, 1933.

Once again, Rick was without a job. And he might slide back from the transport of the future to the automobile business, and from a position on the planning staff to the strawboss role as exhorter of salesman, which he had held with General Motors. But he would be able to extract benefits from his time with AVCO, which had not yet run out. He must keep cool and give no sign that he even entertained the possibility of not continuing toward the top of airline operations. This he was prepared to do, for Rick was now a veteran of campaigning on the personality market.

The proxy fight over AVCO left North American Aviation on the shelf. While Cord and Rick's principals had battled for AVCO proxies, accountants for receivers had shaken down the North American books and revealed stock holdings worth taking over. Among the plums were securities of Pan American,

Transcontinental & Western Airlines (TWA); and, in addition to Eastern Air Transport, which had first inspired Rick's interest, North American appeared to be in control of the Sperry Gyroscope Company.

Once again Rick played for the high stakes of selling where the price tags read in millions. While still working at AVCO, he got in to see Ernest R. Breech, a moneyman at GM, and told the tale. Breech was in the second line of GM officials, but said he would speak to Mr. Sloan. Meanwhile, Rick talked to John J. Raskob, who kept an eye on things from his big office at GM. Raskob then talked to William S. Knudsen, and he also dropped in at Mr. Sloan's office and brought up the subject of North American Aviation. Mr. Sloan said, "What would you say to our taking thirty percent?" General Motors acquired control of North American with this amount of stock. Ernie Breech went in as president, and Rick became vice president. The announcement came on the date of his resignation from AVCO — February 28, 1933.

The faultless timing of the shift was proof that Rick was fast on his feet and capable of landing safely when seismic shocks were felt in corporate foundations. Now he turned his attention to building up the elements of North American that showed promise and closing out those that did not. It was possible to guess wrong. Rick never ceased to regret the disposal of Sperry Gyroscope, which GM sold at a bargain-basement price. But it was more harmful to GM and North American — it was deplorable — that what Rick had feared in relation to E. L. Cord came true: Cord's attacks on the AVCO management caused unfavorable publicity, which stirred up the government in Washington.

The stories that Cord had told of AVCO people trying to drop him into a financial hole caused talk about how something called Wall Street, not precisely defined but quite sinister, had invaded the field of aviation like an octopus in a cartoon by

Thomas Nast. Underwriting and borrowing from banks were accepted procedures, but you could make them look bad if you questioned the motives behind the organization of every new company as it came along. Then there were complaints from disappointed people, such as old Tom Braniff, who ran a small hedge-hopping airline out in the boondocks of Oklahoma and Kansas. Braniff tried to get a government mail contract and said his failure to obtain it should be charged to villainy in Washington. It is impossible to say whether there was anything in this, but it looks plausible, for politicians and bureaucrats, just beginning to realize how their powers were expanding, seldom missed a chance to steal or to collect graft. Some people went so far as to imply that Postmaster General Walter F. Brown, of the Hoover administration, had been on the take. Rick spoke of this with the righteous tone he later gave up, remarking that he "believed Brown and the Post Office Department were primarily interested in furthering a dependable air mail service all over the nation." This was hogwash, and Rick must have known it, but he could speak high-corporate jargon as well as the next man, and it was expected of him at the time. Mr. Hoover did not steal, and he did not have to. He had made a fortune as an international mining engineer.

An investigation of newly fledged air transport had already occupied a congressional committee. The aircraft industry must be important, with money in it, or politicians would not have chosen it for a target. Rick pondered the lesson in his orderly mind, and by January 1934 decided that the administration he had helped elect was going to commit a monumental error in the flying of U.S. Mail.

It is possible to document more than one approach to the air-mail dispute, but there is no way of escaping the conclusion that official persons concerned in the affair sacrificed human lives to politics, red tape, and vanity. President Roosevelt had called in an air force general and asked him if the army could

Elizabeth Basler Rickenbacher, husband William,
and son Eddie.

Eddie as a factory hand, third from left.
Promoted to salesman, below, Eddie gives William Jennings Bryan a ride.

Wind distorts Eddie's face during speed trial
*(Indianapolis Motor Speedway Official Photos).*
At center, Eddie with Tom O'Donnell, who
died in a wreck *(Indianapolis Motor Speedway
Official Photos).* Below, Eddie in his Maxwell.

Sergeant Rickenbacker goes to war.

Eddie in the Spad fighter plane *(U.S. Army Signal Corps).*
Below, mother and son reunited after World War I.

Adelaide Frost Rickenbacker in 1922.
Below, first president of Eastern Airlines, about 1935.

Affinity for birds is shown
in Venice, above. Owl made
Eddie's acquaintance
in New York.

Eddie and General William Mitchell. Below, Eddie poses in duplicate of Pacific raft. Original gray hat is in Smithsonian Institution.

*All pictures not otherwise credited are reproduced courtesy of David E. Rickenbacker.*

fly the mail. Nobody knows what went on in the general's mind, but it appears that he gave the sort of answer that Napoleon liked to hear from his marshals: "Nothing is impossible if you command it, Sire." Orders came out: all air-mail contracts were to be canceled at midnight, February 19. This was at the height of the worst flying weather in the year. Young pilots just out of training were not so well prepared to go through blizzards over mountains as the veteran civilians who had been carrying the mail. Charles A. Lindbergh telegraphed the White House, advising further thought on the question. And Rick had something to say when reporters came to his New York office and asked for quotes. Now a veteran at furnishing newspaper copy, Rick knew what the "newspaper boys" wanted to hear. The newsmen had visited him on a dismal foggy afternoon, and he looked into the drizzling street as he said, "The thing that bothers me is what is going to happen to these young Army pilots on a day like this. Their ships are not equipped with blind-flying instruments, and their training, while excellent for military duty, is not adapted for flying the air mail. Either they are going to pile up ships all the way across the continent, or they are not going to be able to fly the mail on schedule."

Rick added notes to this that showed he was speaking truth as well as furnishing some interesting quotations. Though the airlines had only recently come from primitive beginnings, their operations were meeting high standards, and the pilots knew their business. The lines were covering some 200,000 miles every twenty-four hours. Captains or first pilots had to log 4000 hours' flying time before taking the left-hand controls. And every man had to present certificates for at least 1000 hours of commercial flight before he could take the right-hand seat. Even then, he had to ride shotgun, as the pilots put it, for at least one year, perhaps up to five years, depending on how much time he had brought to the airline. This kind of experience, plus blind-flying instruments and the two-way radio,

made commercial aviation a different thing from the hazardous flights of military pilots in light combat or observation
planes. And the airlines had 7000 ground technicians supporting the men in the air. Rick found out the army had assigned
200 officers and 334 men to ground support. He noted, "I considered the whole thing shocking and I said so."

North American Aviation controlled Eastern Air Transport,
and, after the air-mail controversy died down, a decree from
Washington renamed it Eastern Airlines. It was in poor shape,
and the men in Detroit thought the case might be hopeless, but
perhaps Rick could save the property if he worked on it full
time. In December 1934, he accepted their offer to become
general manager and responsible head of the line. Rick said he
wouldn't make promises, but he'd give it a try.

He had found the right place for his talents and technical
knowledge. At the start, fewer than 500 employees operated
planes along routes that totaled no more than 3500 miles. Making something of this required his traveling all night and working all day. He preached what he called "the gospel of pitch in
and help," and carried baggage to the claim area, along with
the uniformed freight hustlers. Word would go out by the jungle drums of minor employees that the Captain had moved in
to help when needed. He also would step behind ticket
counters and lend a hand when he saw rush-hour delays. The
remarkable part of it is that Rick managed to make the employees accept him as a disinterested helper, not as a boss trying to make them look bad. Rick accomplished this with the
kind of sincerity that cannot be faked.

He was now an aviation man, but Rick did not refuse to acknowledge his connection with automobiles when chances for
public appearance came along. Rick gave an example of this
early in the days of his airline adventures, after press agents invited him to the new Chrysler Building, a center of attention in
New York. With the nearby Graybar and Chanin buildings ris-

ing in well-kept magnificence, the Chrysler, with its fantastic spire, made people believe for a while that midtown New York would give the world an example of metropolitan civilization and style. Perhaps Rick didn't notice that the excuse for celebration was the unveiling of new Chrysler and De Soto cars. Therefore he was in danger of public embarrassment when the emcee called him to the mike and asked for a few words. The business-magazine publisher B. C. Forbes wrote to Mr. Sloan about what happened next. Forbes reported that he had been eager to see how "Eddie" would handle the situation, and that it amused him when Rick convulsed the audience by closing his remarks with congratulations to Walter Chrysler "on being the second-largest manufacturer of automobiles in America." Forbes said it was so delightfully neat that he could not refrain from telling Sloan about it.

Although the Forbes letter read as though it had been written by Robert Benchley, it showed something more important than business humor. What it revealed was the fact that, though they couldn't push Rick around and give him orders, moguls of General Motors constituted the commercial power behind Eastern Airlines. And what counted in business was profit or loss. According to Rick's reading of the books, Eastern lost $1.5 million in 1934 and made a profit of $38,000 in 1935, his first full year in control. In 1936, the line reported profits of $168,602. As long as Rick was in charge, there were no more losses.

In the year 1935, when Rick was turning Eastern around and directing it toward profits and growth, the speedway at Indianapolis paid only $78,575 in prizes. This was $16,575 less than in 1929, and showed that the New Deal had not yet completely restored the prosperity that supported such luxuries as sporting events and purses for racing drivers.

Rick went to Europe in 1935 to find out at firsthand how the aviation industry was getting along over there. The big event of this trip was Rick's visit to Germany. He had last seen the Germans at home in 1922. Although he had appeared to be down on his luck, Goering had harangued Rick about German plans for building an air force and winning the next round of European war. Rick regarded the German nation as a kind of nuisance springing from natural causes, like all other calamities of nature. But he admired the Germans for technical skill. He believed that the French, not the Germans, were the most odious people on earth.

When he met them at Tempelhof Airport in the fall of 1935, Rick was surprised to see how Goering and his colleagues had come up in the world. Whereas Goering had previously made a shabby appearance, both he and Ernst Udet were now in splendid uniforms. They wore caps like those of circus bandsmen, with badges all over them, and carried swords. Goering had gained so much weight that he resembled a sausage in its skin, and his attitude was one of unlimited authority as he barked at the police who respectfully attended his party. He swept Rick and Adelaide off to a grand luncheon at the new Air Service Building. Rick remembered this structure as being a block long with a roof of concrete six inches thick. After a luxurious meal with the drinking of many toasts, Goering drew Rick aside for a confidential chat.

Goering asked, "Herr Eddie, do you remember what I told you about the future of our air force when you visited us in nineteen twenty-two?" Rick said he remembered it well. Goering then said that he had given Ernst Udet the mission of showing Rick how it had all come true. They would conceal nothing, and Goering was willing to guarantee that Rick would be impressed, to put it mildly. It was Nazi policy at the time to give these tours. Charles Lindbergh got the same treatment, as did the military attachés of the United States, Britain, and France.

This flaunting of air power was the first move in Hitler's

campaign against everyone who wasn't a German of certified genes. As a man, and even as a politician, Hitler seemed third-rate. His critics explained away the political successes by saying that nobody but Germans would accept his orations at face value.

Rick knew what was going on, and when it seemed that Ernst Udet, as a former ace, felt privileged to criticize Hitler, Rick said, "You keep talking like you're talking now, Ernst, and you'll get your goddamned head shot off. They'll put you against a wall." He recalled an American embassy party at which "there was a violent argument about the Hitler anti-Jewish campaign. I moved away from it. I couldn't imagine that there was no one of Hitler's Gestapo there, and I didn't want to engage in the row. There were quite a number of Germans present, with eyes and ears at work. They seemed to pay special attention to Udet."*

As soon as Rick and his family saw the sights in Germany, they went to London, where the elder Rickenbackers attended a dinner party at the home of the former William Maxwell Aitken of Canada, now Lord Beaverbrook and a powerful newspaper publisher. Robert Gilbert Vansittart, Undersecretary of the Foreign Office, was the highest-ranking guest. He drew Rick aside after the first cocktail and asked for news about German air forces. Rick said he thought the Germans would be ready to fight in from three to five years. The jittery and gloomy Vansittart said he thought the Germans could be at war in two years. After the guests sat down, Beaverbrook acted as bear-leader, putting Rick on to recount what he had seen in Germany. Rick tried to tell them, but the other guests were hitting the wine pretty hard and were an opinionated lot. It seemed that each Britisher had his own ideas, and when the

---

*It was reported that Ernst Udet died of a mysterious gunshot wound in November 1941. Rick was inclined to believe reports that Udet actually lost his life while testing an airplane that had been tampered with by the Gestapo.

wine took hold they got to fighting among themselves. The playwright Frederick Lonsdale looked on with a satiric gleam in his eye. Rick gave a mental shrug and thought, "What's the use?"

In a few days, he went to Washington with his report that Germany was building a war machine. It didn't seem to make an impression. Rick said he thought the indifference he met with was due to "social-climbing lounge lizards who were too busy going to cocktail parties to do their jobs." Even the air force seemed unable to act. Rick told his tale at a meeting with General Henry Harley "Hap" Arnold and other officers. When he got to the account of how the Nazis were training cooks, mechanics, and chauffeurs to fly airplanes, his audience became restive. They told him one couldn't make pilots out of mechanics. Couldn't be done. Rick said that he had been a mechanic and had learned to fly and "did all right." They said that was a special case. Rick wrote, "Our military leaders had their own ideas of training, and anything that did not conform to those ideas could not be allowed. I could not awaken them to the danger. They continued on their placid way."

Rick discovered about this time that he had a beneficial effect on friends who were confined in hospitals. When he visited them, he seemed to bring an extra supply of vitality, some of which he left with the sick person when the call was over. An old friend needed this treatment in 1936 at Doctors Hospital near Gracie Square. Rick would go up to Billy Mitchell's room and say something like "What's going on here?" Then he would sit by the bed. Billy Mitchell was worn out at fifty-seven, and nothing could lift his gloom and depression. A telegram caught up with Rick out of town — Mitchell was dead. He hurried to New York in time to join the small group of friends who walked with Mitchell's sister, escorting his coffin to the express car that took it to Milwaukee for burial. Undertakers brought the coffin to the back of Grand Central and put it on a truck.

The mourners followed through catacombs of underground freight yards, footsteps echoing in the cold dark place. Rick found the scene hard to take. He thought it demeaning to Mitchell, a bad end to an unselfish career. Baggage men pushed the door shut, and Rick walked off toward the Commodore Bar. He was shivering from more than the cold.

Rick had supported Roosevelt for the first term, in 1932. During the next few years, Rick was often in Washington, and he did not like what he heard and saw. He opposed Franklin Roosevelt in 1936. Thereafter he became strongly anti-Rooseveltian, and so had to endure being classed with "Neanderthals." Rick could not understand the denunciatory tone with which liberals and New Dealers called on him to start thinking some other way and to stand corrected. His brand of politics was simple. He thought business would be better with Republicans in charge at Washington, and he said so.

The time machine travels with less celerity and efficiency in going back a few decades than when we send it off across centuries. It might be that good and evil weighed at balance in 1936, but many thoughtful persons felt in their bones that war was on the way. It was not really to be a new war; rather, it would be Act Two of the old original war, which had closed temporarily in 1918. And it was frightening to reflect that well-made plays had three acts — beginning, middle, and end. An obvious overture to the middle part was the Spanish Civil War, in 1936, after a military uprising against the government in which a combination of parties shading from the center to the left had won a majority. Taken as a whole, the Spanish conflict needed Goya for its horrors, Mark Twain for its folly.

Such developments gave a fatalistic air to the United States that permeated the thinking of those who had regained their luck in the 1930s, and even affected those who had never lost their luck in the Depression. One remarkable thing was the decision of educated young people. The young men said that when war broke out, they would go. And their sisters said they would get into war work. That was Rick's natural position, and since 1919 he had been talking about aviation as part of national defense. And yet he opposed war itself. He began talking along the lines of becoming so strong that no one would dare attack us. Those who agreed with Rick would be known as isolationists. Many were prominent citizens, and they formed an influential America First Committee, to discourage our national identification with the Allied cause.

But there was no question about the good news conveyed by the books of Eastern Airlines in 1936. After the accountants had shaken these books down, a profit of $168,162 appeared.

Rick got the purse at Indianapolis up to $82,525, and saw one of those dreaded Packards rolling around the track as official pace car, with Tommy Milton at the wheel. But that was the last time Packard enjoyed such advantageous promotion, for the car was fading in popular esteem while Mr. Sloan was filling the country with GM automobiles and establishing popular belief that Cadillac was the equal of any fine European make.

By this time, Rick had perfected his skill as a public speaker and had learned to charm audiences with his lower register, in what a friend called his "underslung" voice. Rick also commanded a higher register and could reach a clear yodeling tone when he wanted to. He had taught himself to speak distinctly and not swallow the consonants, the test of anyone who wishes to make himself understood. It was now an instinctive reaction for Rick to wait until he had the attention of his audience and to speak slowly, with plenty of pauses. Rick said he had boiled it all down to one rule, which was "Talk to the last man." If that man in the last row could hear, so could everybody else in the hall.

In 1936, Rick made numerous informal talks and six major addresses. He started in January, speaking in Washington to the Women's Patriotic Conference on National Defense. On December 2, he gave his last important speech of the year at a luncheon in New York in memory of Dr. Rudolf Diesel. He had addressed reputable audiences in between: societies of engineers, Junior Birdmen, and persons who had gathered to honor Charles Kettering, of General Motors. And those who had Rick's interests at heart noted that the Christmas letter of 1936 did not exceed reasonable bounds.

Life in the United States ran on very well in 1937. The Pulitzer award in fiction went to Margaret Mitchell for *Gone with the Wind*. A farce called *You Can't Take It with You*, by Moss Hart and George S. Kaufman, won the drama award. Rick had Miss Mitchell's simplicity of approach, but little in his nature that would respond to the frivolity of Hart and Kaufman.*

Americans might relish comical doings on the Broadway stage, soon transferred to movies, but out east something dangerous and disturbing took place. The Japanese fired on and sank an American gunboat, the *Panay*, killing two sailors. The *Panay* had gone up the Yangtze River into a war zone to protect American tankers delivering oil. Apology and payment of indemnity did not erase the fact that this was an ominous event. But Rick's temperament was such that he was able to continue his busy life while convinced that war lay somewhere ahead. Rick felt that strengthening the aviation industry was a contribution to the country's future defense. He certainly was improving the fortunes of Eastern Airlines, for he pushed the profits up to $197,000 in 1937, and in the following year the books showed $354,000 on the profit side. Also in 1937 and 1938, he managed to drum up more than $92,000 in prize money for each of the races at Indianapolis.

Now that Rick had Eastern Airlines making money, he attracted

---

* Some years later Rick left the theater during a performance of *Oliver*, a musical based on *Oliver Twist*. He said it disgusted him to see children being taught to steal.

attention from men who thought it would be worthwhile to get control of the company. One of these was a man named John Hertz, a Chicagoan who owned the Yellow Cab Company. General Motors bought the cab line, and Hertz stood high with Mr. Sloan. While Rick was riding his airline and drumming up trade, Hertz was secretly talking to bankers and getting ready to make his move. But Rick had a friend in the Hearst newspaper chain, who called early in 1938 and said he heard John Hertz had bought an option on Eastern Airlines for $3 million. All Rick could say was that he had heard nothing about it.

Rick was not able to resist voicing complaint, although he did it in private. Here he had turned Eastern into a profit-making concern, and the managers at GM were going to sell it out from under him for $3 million. He later wrote, "It was I who increased the value of this property, and to more than three million in my opinion — and my reward was to be kicked out on my ear. There was no love lost between John Hertz and me."

Rick went into action, and the first man he talked to was Henry M. Hogan, the GM house lawyer, who worked in the company's New York office. Hogan said that Hertz was to have Eastern, Rick to step down. Rick asked if he could see Mr. Sloan, and Hogan said he'd find out if it was all right. He left the room, came back in a few minutes, and told Rick he could call Mr. Sloan's office for an appointment. Rick got Sloan on the wire and said he had to see him right away. Mr. Sloan, "All right; if it's really important, come right now."

Rick had his petition firmly in mind by the time he sat down beside Sloan's desk. It was still "Mister Sloan" and "Eddie," but Rick's attitude was not that of a man who had come tugging his forelock, with cap in hand. His recollection was that he recited his grievance firmly, in a tone that did not invite argument as to whether or not he had been treated right. Rick said he had worked hard to start the airline in the right direction, and felt that he had as much right as any outsider to bid for it if GM was putting it up for sale. Mr. Sloan listened quietly and then said, "Let me look into this, Eddie. Perhaps we can work something out." That was as cordial as Mr. Sloan ever got. In the morning, he gave orders to hold up the Eastern deal for thirty days so that Rick could get something on the table at showdown time.

When he heard the good news about postponement, Rick also learned something that put him in shock. His old and dear friend Ernie Breech had been preparing the double-cross. It became known that Breech was hand in glove with Hertz. Breech had been at the head of North American Aviation since 1933, and Mr. Sloan liked the way he set up balance sheets and handled the money and stock issues when he was folding the assets of General Aviation into North American, with the skill of a fry-cook making a Western omelette on a hot griddle. Sloan wanted Breech to have a higher place at General Motors, but old Bill Knudsen, the executive vice president, wouldn't hear of it. Knudsen had worked on shop floors, and he held Breech in contempt as nothing more than a bookkeeper in the back office.

Knudsen was Rick's pal. He warned Rick to beware of Breech, and suggested that he find out from Sloan exactly what Hertz had agreed to do. At a second interview with Sloan, Rick discovered that the price of Eastern Airlines was to be $3.5 million and that Hertz was to get it for $1 million cash, the rest in notes. But nothing in this world is certain. Rather than a drawerful of notes signed by John Hertz, wouldn't Mr. Sloan prefer cash money for the entire $3.5 million? Of course he would rather have money. If Rick could put $3.5 million in cash on the table before the option ran out, he would be the owner of Eastern Airlines. Showdown day would be early in March.

Three and a half million dollars was real money in those

days. And when Rick went downtown to raise it, he recalled his trip in search of funds for the motor company, which had resulted in a great deal of chagrin and no money. But he plucked up heart when he realized that the situation was not the same. The other time, he had been in search of help for an ailing corporation; now, he was talking about a concern that had shown profit under his management. He went to see a friend at Smith, Barney and Company, a firm that bought and sold money in a dignified, high-class manner. They sent him on to Kuhn, Loeb and Company, where the partners said they might be able to make a practical suggestion. Translated, this meant that Rick would have his money. A few bankers talking quietly in a paneled room with a portrait of James Loeb* on the wall made the decision that released Rick forever from decisions reached by other men. He had finally broken into the altitudes of absolute independence.

There were formalities to go through. For one thing, Rick had to get approval from the board of North American Aviation to submit his offer. He talked to these men at the General Motors Building in New York, and they wouldn't say yes and they wouldn't say no. It appeared that Breech thought he could keep Rick's offer in limbo until Hertz got money down; then Rick would be outside looking in. Rick telephoned Bill Knudsen in Detroit. He told Knudsen to call New York and warn Ernie Breech to stay out of his way. While talking to Bill Knudsen, Rick was angry enough to have given Breech a few punches and possibly a couple of kicks. But he restrained himself at the University Club, where the meeting was to continue after dinner. Knudsen had called men at the GM office in New York and told them to keep Breech in the background. They took two big private dining rooms on the third floor and

* Generations of students have blessed James Loeb because, in 1910, he founded the Loeb Classical Library, which provides texts and translations of classical literature in convenient pocket size.

started to wrap up the deal. Rick and the Kuhn, Loeb men gathered in one room, the North American crowd in the other. Rick's lawyer would go over and hear what was said, then come back and report. Then he would take a message from Rick and his backers to the North American room, and so on, until three in the morning.

Rick thought it would work out all right, but still the suspense was terrible. His anxiety increased when he realized that it was now Friday morning; the option expired on Sunday at six in the afternoon. Hugh Knowlton of Kuhn, Loeb told Rick a check would be ready for him when he needed it, but Rick couldn't help wondering how the bankers proposed to raise $3.5 million on such short notice. The fact was that Frederick M. Warburg of Kuhn, Loeb could sign a check for that amount any time he felt like it. Discussion ended at dawn, when Henry Hogan led in a group of directors and announced that GM had accepted Rick's offer. Then everyone tottered off, looking for bed.

This late session left Rick all Saturday in which to worry about actually getting his money down. He recalled, "By Saturday night I had fretted to the point of desperation." There was nothing for it but appeal to Mr. Sloan. Rick telephoned at about eleven that night and said he had to have an interview on a vitally important matter. Sloan's voice always came over electronic equipment in a strange way. Somehow its timbre flattened into a peculiarly nonresonant croak. Without enthusiasm he said, "All right, Eddie. Come on over."

Sloan himself answered the bell in robe and pajamas when Rick came to his door. Rick's anxiety was so great that he made no apology, but immediately told his tale. He feared the bankers would be late and that John Hertz would pounce with a million of ready money. Therefore, he asked the boon of a ten-day extension. Mr. Sloan wouldn't go into that. He merely said, "I don't think you have any reason to worry. Everything will be worked out." In spite of this assurance, Rick got no sleep for the rest of the night.

In the morning, Frederick Warburg called Rick and asked, "Where and when do you want the money?" Rick asked him to wait, and called Mr. Sloan. When could he turn over the check? Mr. Sloan said, "Monday morning will be fine, Eddie." Warburg delivered a certified check for $3.5 million in the Eastern hangar of Newark Airport at eight the following morning. The publicity setup was scheduled for two hours later, when Rick placed the check in Mr. Sloan's hand. As always, Sloan was cool and collected. He said, "Congratulations, Eddie. I wish you every success in the world."

Working overtime the lawyers constructed a new corporation with Rick at its head to operate the airline. Rick's friends downtown had a hand in it because the money they advanced was not an ordinary bank loan. They had service fees, and Rick paid those in stock. This business of using stock certificates in the way ordinary people used money was easy to get accustomed to, and Rick liked the feel of it. A block of shares went to Kuhn, Loeb. Smith, Barney also got something for their trouble. Rick found that a member of the Rockefeller family had taken an interest in the deal. Laurance Rockefeller was five years out of college and had stated that the two men most influential in his life had been the paleontologist Henry Fairfield Osborn and Rick. He therefore subscribed to the Kuhn, Loeb syndicate, starting a long relationship with Eastern Airlines.*

It pleased Rick to have it known that a Rockefeller approved of what he was trying to do. But the recognition did nothing for operating funds. This till of ready money had to contain at least $500,000 so that Eastern could have its daily feed of gaso-

---

* See Collier and Horowitz, *The Rockefellers: An American Dynasty* (New York City, 1976). The authors state that Laurance "increased his investment . . . availing himself of stock splits and options, until he was the largest individual stockholder and a primary influence on the board of directors."

a year, the lowest of any man heading a railroad or airline in the United States. The profits went back into the company for new equipment and payments to stockholders. Everyone in aviation knew that Eastern paid the lowest salaries, and the traveling public was aware that the line skimped on amenities. Rick had the instinct of the common carrier, which was to sell nothing but transport from here to there at times convenient to customers, on reliable schedules. Rick never reconciled himself to expensive competition between airlines in providing luxuries that were actually nothing but talk. He had ridden the big trains and the last of the ocean liners, and he knew that first-class travel was impossible on an airplane. You were locked up in a metal tube and hurled into the air. The insult to the law of gravity was so great that the plane had to generate about 80 million foot pounds of energy at the time of landing to keep from striking the ground so hard that it would disintegrate, while framework and passengers' bodies absorbed the shock of its fall. He knew that a plane ride was, in fact, a bus ride with the miracles of takeoff and landing at start and finish. There was no way to tie it up with the lobby at the Plaza or the smoking room on the *Berengaria,* and he didn't intend to try.

By 1939, Rick's problem of competing with the railroads was beginning to solve itself. There was something wrong with the way the railroads kept their books, and politics also got into it. In 1940, the trade-paper editors counted up 108 railway lines in receivership. Ten years before, only 30 lines had gone bankrupt, and 87 gave up in 1935. It wasn't long before the railroads began deliberate discouragement of passengers, and of course Rick and the other airline managers harvested the travelers who had to fly to get where they were going unless they could drive in cars or endure the tedium of intercity buses. The airline advertisements started to emphasize speed and the saving of time. No one took much interest in the question of energy production. Apparently the firing of fuel had no limit, and the traveling public began to accept the idea that common carriers would hurl them through the air at increasing speeds, in the name of progress, while the questions of thermodynamics received no answers.

Rick is not a candidate for blame because he did not study theoretical physics and mathematics in 1940. But, like his competitors, he did examine the facts that came to view where physics and economics intersected, and had the satisfaction of passing the million-dollar mark for the first time that year, when the accountants reported $1,575,000 in profits. The spring of 1940 found Rick making effective propaganda not only for Eastern, but for the entire industry. He had further developed his predictions, and gave a lecture at the airlines terminal on Forty-second Street. He said the time would come when a flight from New York to England would take only seven hours. He pictured a *Queen Mary* of the air, a dirigible one mile long, which would stay aloft for years at a time. This airship would visit the principal ports of the world, being fueled and provisioned by smaller ships that would come and go as needed. Rick explained that once you put a ship that large in the sky, you would have to keep her up there, because landings would be too expensive and dangerous. There was a hint of the permanent artificial earth satellite in his thinking. This was far different from the cramped, buslike airplane of the present, and would permit the comforts of a large hotel. Indeed, the ship was to be a "floating sky palace" of dance floors, movie theaters, and luxurious living quarters with ample private balconies.

On the military side, Rick said he saw the United States training 500,000 pilots a year. Most of these would be in the reserve corps and, along with millions of civilian pilots of private planes, would make the air so thick with traffic in twenty years that some kind of red and green sky signals would have to be provided. The radio commentator Gabriel Heatter made admiring comments on these predictions to his national audience, and exclaimed, "You can't beat vision like that!"

The vision, the imagination, the showmanship that Rick displayed in preaching air transport also benefited his rivals. Juan Trippe, of Pan American, was another airline president with a talent for catching attention, but he did it by refusing to speak or appear in public. Trippe and his associates tried to make the planes themselves objects of romantic interest, and somewhere in their shop a good idea sprang up when they named their Pacific passenger transport the *China Clipper.* Rick then called his overnight line to the south the Great Silver Fleet. People in the news, and most of the important big-deal operators in any field, were now traveling by air at least part of the time. Business was improving at a rapid rate for all airline men, and Rick begrudged the prosperous times only to old Tom Braniff, running his string of Lockheed Electras down in the Southwest.

There is no telling what would have happened if Rick had ever happened to catch up with old Tom. Rick gave a good idea of what it might be when he addressed a group of businessmen in Montgomery, Alabama. Rick cried:

> I say this to you, that Tom Braniff — I'm sorry he is not here, because I would like to look him in the eye when I say these things — is specifically responsible for stopping us, and in a way that is anything but what I consider manly. First, because there never has been a man in this country who was more responsible for the air mail cancellation than one Tom Braniff. Tom Braniff was interested not in serving this country or a trunk line; he was interested in getting long-haul business for himself; that's his business, but it is not fundamentally sound.

For years, Rick had trouble in the Southwest, where they suspected him as a New York man.

The spring of 1940 also brought Rick the anxiety that Eastern and all other airlines would have to go on short rations of new parts and planes when war finally broke out. The time to buy new equipment was right now. Again he raised cash by sale of stock, and again the events of unfolding European history gave him bad moments. Some financial advisers told Rick he did not need to have the stock issue supported by bankers, but he disagreed, and made a deal that the shares should be underwritten seven points below the market price on a fixed date. Three days after the issue, the Germans moved into Holland. The market reacted as usual, and Rick recorded, "I had my money at $32.50 a share, and within a week's time it was down to $25. I couldn't have sold it for $15. My money was in the bank. I just got under the wire by the skin of my teeth."

In spite of his realistic approach to the probability of war, Rick continued to urge that the United States keep clear. He wrote an article for the *American Legion* magazine entitled "Keep America Out," broadcast the same message on the Blue Network, and repeated it in other speeches and informal talks. The radio speech began, "Men and women, fathers, mothers, sons and daughters, young and old in every part of this great land, I come to you tonight without political ambitions or self-ish motives. I speak for myself alone as a private citizen who loves his heritage . . ." Rick argued that we should spend our money on eliminating slums, multiplying highways and airways, and improving life in general, and that it would be gross folly to "regiment our boys and girls." He begged all hearers to work for such statesmanship as would "prevent posterity or future generations from condemning or indicting us as having legalized wholesale slaughter, murdered the flower of our youth, and massacred democracy."

In a speech at Kansas City, Rick said:

We can stay out of war if we want to . . . We fought for democracy. What did we get out of it — destruction, starvation, depression, and plenty of it. I think you are going to see Communism the world over. I don't see how you can stop it. I have two boys. The Lord spared me in war — I don't think they'd get through. I can't see what good they would do. I have tried to raise them the same as you have your sons and daughters, to live beyond me, and leave something behind them, make good citizens out of them so the country can carry on what our forefathers gave us — our heritage. And yet some people think we should send millions over there. Think in terms of your family — we can stay out of war if we try hard enough. I am not going to let my sympathies be the cause of millions of young men being maimed and murdered and billions of our wealth being squandered. No. War is meant for one of two things — the destruction and ruination of material things, and the destruction and ruination of human beings — men, women, and children. There is one thing certain, ladies and gentlemen, that both sides, when the war is over, will be losers, and you and I don't want to be part of that picture.

What he took to be an unusual sensitivity to coming events worried Rick from time to time. His experience in France when he had precognition of two fliers' deaths remained with him and strengthened his feeling that all he could do was endure whatever the luck should bring him, or, in another favorite mode of speech, whatever the good Lord decided was right. Some said this was a strain of Irish in Rick's nature, though where it could have come from, nobody knew. Rick seemed to have a feeling for weather, and in the airline business bad weather could mean hazardous flying and the possibility of wrecks. Although the controlling factors are not clearly understood, Rick's emotional responses might have come from changes in atmospheric pressure, which precede changes in weather and may be responsible for them, and on February 26, 1941, Rick was exceedingly nervous.

He never forgot that the day in New York was "a bleak, rainy Wednesday." Miss Shepherd also remembered the day, for the Captain had been restless all afternoon. He had other reasons to be disturbed than those which might come from air pressure. Skilled as he was in apportioning time, he had managed to get into a position where he wanted to be in two different places at once. A group of businessmen in Birmingham had formed an Aviation Committee to increase air traffic into their city. They scheduled a luncheon meeting for February 27 so that important men could hear about the plans. Rick wanted to support the Aviation Committee because he saw the chance to link Birmingham to Chicago and Miami by Eastern Air. On their part, the committeemen wanted Rick as a star attraction. Interests appeared to be identical, yet Captain Rickenbacker turned them down. The Eastern directors were meeting in Miami on February 28 and, much as he regretted it, Rick saw no way to appear in Birmingham the day before.

The committeemen put pressure on Rick, and the mayor added a personal touch. He couldn't help thinking that Rick must consider himself too important to visit Birmingham. Reproach did what argument had failed to do, and at the last moment Rick agreed to attend the luncheon. There was rejoicing in Birmingham and a nervous reaction in New York, where Rick stared out the window, paced the floor, and called to see how weather down south was developing. He told Miss Shepherd he might take the train. But that wouldn't do. He couldn't travel to promote aviation and have photographers and reporters greet him in a railroad station. At last, he packed his papers, went home for a small bag with clean linen, and had himself driven to Flight 21 of the Great Silver Fleet. This was a sleeper plane leaving at 7:10 P.M. for Mexico by way of Washington, Atlanta, Birmingham, New Orleans, Houston, and Brownsville. At the time, there was heavy promotion of sleeper flights, with berths for passengers, and Rick's presence on Flight 21 would be a good thing from that point of view. After the lunch at Birmingham, he would take an afternoon plane back to Atlanta and fly on to Miami that night.

The plane took off from Newark in the dark, with rain spitting at windows, and wings shuddering in the wind. Rick established himself in the sky lounge next to the cockpit. Like a good executive, Rick spread out his papers and settled to work. He looked up when he saw First Pilot James A. Perry, Jr., at his side. The pilot said, "Captain Rickenbacker, the weather in Atlanta isn't too good. We may have trouble getting in." Rick had long since reached a decision about his relations with pilots on the line. They were in charge of the flying, and he never made suggestions as to what they should do. He told Perry to use his best judgment about coming down in Atlanta or going in at Charlotte, the alternative stop. Perry went back to his controls. After a while, the plane began the approach to Atlanta. Flight Steward Clarence Moore sat down next to Rick for the landing. Rick peered through the scud and saw lights below. The plane rolled as the left wing dipped for a turn. Then Rick heard the wing hit a tree.

All on Flight 21 felt a tremendous crash, everything seemed to burst open, and they found themselves caught by twisted metal, in darkness, under a sprinkle of rain. The one woman on board was Mrs. H. A. Littledale, editor of *Parents'* magazine. She lay trapped, with a section of fuselage converted into nippers that held her left foot bent. The pain was dreadful and she couldn't help breaking into sobs. Her husband's voice came from the darkness: "There, there, old girl. Don't do that. Save your strength." Mr. Littledale was helpless with both legs broken. Then Mrs. Littledale heard Captain Rickenbacker's voice. He was yelling, "For God's sake, don't strike matches! Don't strike matches!" He added, "I'm awfully sorry this had to happen to you boys." What had happened to Rick himself was bad enough. When he heard the wing strike, he had jumped to his feet, thinking he would go up the aisle to the tail, the safest place when an airplane crashes. This showed that Rick's nervous reactions were as fast as they had been in his racing and fighting days, but the disintegration of a large airplane slamming into a piny hillock was even faster. Rick had a clear recollection of things that happened almost instantaneously:

I had just jumped when the pilot felt it, and yanked it the other way. The right-hand wing hooked on a big tree, took it off, then the plane went up on its nose. I was bouncing around in there and got my hip broken by landing on the steel arm of the seat. I came down on that, you see, on my left hip. We turned over, put them out [killed them] on the nose, both pilots, then went back over and broke the tail off, broke it in the middle, then went up on the tail end of the front end of the ship, about midways, and wound up and twisted. It was just as a kid would blow up a bag, you know, and twist it to hold the air in.

Meantime, Rick fell on the deck after hip-smashing collision with the chair arm, and the steward fell on top of him. Rick's recollection went on, "My first thought was fire, and I was prepared in my mind to inhale a lot of flames. That would be a quick way to get it over with. It burns your lungs out, you see." No fire came, but there was agony in the hurts Rick had sustained. He had broken twelve ribs, cracked his nose, and wrenched his left knee, dislocating cartilage and straining tendons at the back. The elbow of his left arm was broken and locked. There was a dent in his skull almost half an inch deep. But his worst injury was the broken hip. He thought to himself, "If you have to die, you might as well die trying to get out as lying here and letting things happen."

He couldn't push up with his left hand because it was "paralyzed and horribly painful." His head was edged between the bulkhead and a gas tank. His record says: "I had room to move my head just about an inch. In my madness to break loose, every now and then, a little jagged piece of aluminum on the bulkhead cut my left eyelid right through and cut the muscles, and the left eyeball when I came out that morning was sitting on my cheek. I couldn't move my hip, of course. I had about a six-inch movement of my foot. I would come around here and pull hell out of my left hand to try to ease the horrible pain I had." He could hear "the old ribs crackling" when he tried to move.

Presently, a voice in the darkness said, "Let's start a fire and try to keep warm." This was when Rick first shouted his warning about lighting matches. He called the warning from time to time until daylight, and thought he was conscious during the entire time. At one point, he realized that the steward whose body lay across him was dead. Rick said that the pain got so bad that he prayed God to end consciousness, "but that did not happen." Toward dawn, he was sure he heard rescuers trying to get through underbrush lower down the hill. He tried to yell loudly enough to attract attention, but his voice was weak. "I didn't yell half as loud as I thought I was yelling, and they didn't hear me, which was really an act of fate, because if they had found us they could not have gotten to us without lanterns, which would in all probability have set fire to us."

The first alarm had gone out shortly after the plane ended radio contact with the ground. The pilot's last words to base had been "Over Stone Mountain at eleven thirty-seven, eighteen hundred feet." Assuming the plane was down, the flight controllers knew it could be on the ground at any point in an area of two or three hundred square miles. At the moment, they had no way of knowing that it had struck in wooded, hilly terrain about five miles north of Jonesboro and ten miles south of the city line.

Two passengers crawled away from the plane, seeking help. One fell into a ravine and got no farther until rescue came. The other was J. S. Rosenfeld, treasurer of a New Orleans clothes-manufacturing firm. Staggering, falling, and crawling, he managed to go a little over two miles in about three hours. At last he came to a farmhouse. The dogs went crazy when they heard him crawling under the fence. Out came the farmer with a shotgun. When he heard what Mr. Rosenfeld had to say, he called for a young Negro farmhand, the best rider on the place. The man jumped on a horse and took off for the nearest telephone, his mount running flat out in the dark, belly to ground.

This report gave newspapers, police, hospital people, and airline employees a point to make for. The thrilling and inspiring word "rescue" was in the air. Ten ambulances went hurtling over muddy roads at top speed, sirens wailing. Closer to the wreck, word spread among farmers: plane's down north of Jonesboro. They shouldered pickaxes and coils of rope, took down first-aid kits, flashlights, and lanterns in toolhouses, and set out, on courses according to the best information they could get. There had been no pillar of fire in the night, but one farmer had heard an explosion, and they lined up on his place, aiming toward where he thought the sound had originated. Women went with them, some carrying food and hot drinks in vacuum bottles.

The woman aboard the wrecked ship had heard her husband's voice grow fainter; his calls of encouragement had stopped by the time dawn came on. Shortly after, Mrs. Littledale was able to see outlines of trees in gray light, and she found herself looking up at the figure of a woman with a shawl over her head, silhouetted against the sky. It was like a photograph by a WPA photographer. But it was real. This was Mrs. C. L. Murphy, from the hamlet of Morrow. Three young men appeared beside her. They were three of the five Murphy sons. Mother and sons bent above Mrs. Littledale, comforting her, while Mrs. Murphy held her hands and the young men carefully pried apart the flanges of metal imprisoning her ankle. Then they carried her down the hill. There were ambulances in a muddy turnaround at the foot of the hill. Other rescuers brought Mr. Littledale down, and a doctor said he would live. Clara Littledale was lightheaded when they started for town. She recalled, "In the ambulance was a bassinet, which I thought was a lovely touch, and so appropriate for the editor of *Parents'* magazine."

The indomitable Mr. Rosenfeld continued on his way to New Orleans by air. He said, "They promised me a reservation." But Captain Rickenbacker was not by any means in such good shape. When they got him to Piedmont Hospital, in midtown Atlanta, he looked so bad, with his caved-in chest and dislocated eyeball, that they put him aside among the dead. A priest saw signs of life and asked Rick if he was Catholic. Rick replied, "Hell, no! I'm a Protestant, like everyone else around here."

The chief surgeon, Dr. Floyd W. McRae, actually was an old friend. He had first met Rick in Paris, when he operated on Rick's infected mastoid bone. The mathematical probability of encountering Rick again as patient was so small as to be negligible, and yet, like many improbable occurrences in Rick's life, it happened. He looked closely and saw that the supply of life in Eddie Rickenbacker had not yet given out.

The first thing the doctor had to do was care for the eye. He ruled out anesthetic because it might deaden muscle reaction and cause him to make an inaccurate repair of the eyelid. We blink our eyes thousands of times a day, and if Dr. McRae cobbled the lid out of synchronization with its mate, Rick would have had trouble with the vision of both eyes. Accordingly, McRae called a strong intern and told him to keep the patient immobile. Rick heard his ribs grinding as the intern pushed his shoulders down, but this eye repair proved to be successful. At the same time, McRae straightened and taped Rick's broken nose. Rick called this a much-needed cosmetic repair. He said the nose had been off center because of six previous breakings. Correcting this seventh one left the nose in classic perfection.

Rick had his own ideas about what was good for him, one conviction being that narcotics were dangerous to his nervous system. He said they "made him wild." He also thought highly of osteopaths, who had not yet gained the standing they have today in comparison with medical physicians. He started calling for an osteopath the minute they got him into the operating room. Rick told McRae he would be out in three days with osteopathic treatment. The doctors gathered round. Rick was not talking sense at all times, and one doctor measured the dent in his skull and suggested that they make a hole to relieve pressure on the brain. Rick heard them discussing his smashed ribs and broken pelvis. The ball of the left hip joint had crushed the socket and ridden on top of it, so that the left leg was four inches shorter than the right. As though they were talking behind a curtain, Rick heard them debating whether to operate on the hip or leave it alone. He thought Dr. McRae said, "Well, gentlemen, we may let him die on our hands, but we'll never kill him."

The doctors could see Rick as a difficult patient in more than one sense of the word, but to newsmen he was a heavenly gift. The dean of their corps in Atlanta acknowledged the importance of the wreck when he went out at dawn to cover the story, along with many other newspaper and wire service men. This noted journalist was Ralph McGill, editor of the Atlanta *Constitution,* whose voice was influential in Washington and throughout the South. At the scene of the wreck, McGill saw Rick's lips move in the bloody face, and leaned down to hear him mutter, "Hello, Ralph. The boys are doing a great job getting them out of the plane."

The story was to have prominent space in all the country's papers for days and weeks to come, but first reports of the disaster took the entire front page of the Atlanta *Journal,* when the afternoon paper made its appearance in the middle of the day, and the *Constitution* would devote almost all its front page to the story on the following morning. In the *Journal,* two eight-column lines told it in nine words: SEVEN KILLED, RICKENBACKER HURT IN AIRLINE CRASH NEAR HERE

Beneath in six columns ran one of the ugliest air-wreck photographs ever published, showing the plane crushed and twisted as Rick described it. "The huge Mexico Silver Sleeper crashed in a pine thicket near Morrow ten miles south of Atlanta," the main story began. In another column, feature writer Bill Key gave a prose version of the photograph: "A great ship had come to journey's end . . ." Later that day another passenger died, bringing the death list to eight. Of these, five were the first fatalities to passengers — three of the victims were crew — that had ever occurred on Eastern Air.

Adelaide and the boys had reached Rick's side on the afternoon he arrived at the hospital. Rick said, "I'm mighty sorry I interrupted your work." He referred to the Women's War Defense organization in which his wife was active. Adelaide said the important thing was for him to get well. Rick said, "Well, honey, you'll have to shoot me to get rid of me."

Doctor McRae knew that Rick had ordered the doctors to give him no more pain-deadening drugs, but they disregarded his instructions and kept him under sedation as much as they could for the first week. They had to get a plaster cast on Rick that extended from his shoulders to his toes, and the pain was excruciating, even with the drugs. He talked wildly. A turn for the worse came, and McRae called Adelaide at her hotel and told her the end might be near. She asked the state police to intercept the bus on which the boys were going back to their school, which was in Asheville, North Carolina. The police got the boys off the bus, and stopped for gasoline at a roadside pump. They told the attendant they were in a hurry because the boys with them were Rick's sons, on their way back to the hospital. The attendant said, "You don't have to hurry now, the Captain just died."

When the boys came into the hospital room, Rick was hallucinating. He thought he saw fruit growing over his bed and asked Adelaide to pick some. David was old enough to understand that Rick was delirious, but Bill thought he had lost his mind, and asked his mother if "Daddy would always be like that." Rick then went into a bad week, and the hospital became a communications center, with thousands of telegrams and telephone calls coming in. There were so many flowers that the room couldn't hold them all.

Rick said it was like the time when they had opened a blood

vessel in his throat during the tonsillectomy, years before. Giving up and sliding out of life seemed so easy, and, what was even more dangerous, it seemed natural, rational, and right. He said he continually thought of "a lovely land where there was no pain." That feeling, said Rick, was "the calling card of death." The orthopedists decided that his injured leg would have to be pulled on to make the ball and socket joint function properly. They bored a hole through the thigh bone above the knee and put a bolt through it, then attached a cord to the bolt and weights to the cord. Next, they put a steel brace on Rick's knee to keep it from moving out of line.

During a lucid interval, Rick asked McRae how long he would be in the hospital. The doctor said he couldn't tell for sure, but Rick should "count on at least eight months."

Word came from Los Angeles that Rick's mother was too ill to be told of the wreck and its results. She was in Beverly Hills with her son Dewey. Meanwhile, the Atlanta wreck continued as a center of public discussion. In Washington, some said there would be a congressional investigation.

By March 6, the papers were able to report that probers had decided the wreck was due to the plane's flying too low. Certainly the *Mexico Silver Sleeper* was flying too low when it struck the ground. And a few feet of altitude, or the pilot's turning a little farther out, would have saved the ship at the time it brushed the tree. The *Journal* consulted an expert, who said the instruments could not have misinformed the pilot. According to this authority, there were two altimeters, and it wasn't possible for both of them to go wrong. But the wreck had destroyed the instruments, so the cause could never be named. Rick said later he thought it was the pilot's fault. If so, it was partly Rick's fault, for his insistence on meeting schedules was known in the trade. A veteran airman said, "Eastern's pilots have a long-established reputation for pushing weather. They are very good and very tough to follow."[*]

[*] Ernest K. Gann, *Ernest K. Gann's Flying Circus* (New York, 1974), p. 78.

The *Journal* recapitulated figures showing that nobody escaped without harm, listing eight dead and eight injured of sixteen on board. Congressman Hale Boggs escaped with a minor injury, to die twenty years later, when a small plane in which he was flying disappeared from the sky over Alaska. The account reported even the indomitable Mr. Rosenfeld as having sustained a hurt, but did not say what it was. Rosenfeld and the passenger who crawled to the ditch showed the freakish way a crash can disseminate its forces. In coming years there would be more examples of men and women escaping alive and unharmed with every button in place, though passengers sitting across the aisle might be torn to pieces. Also frequently to be found in the wake of bad wrecks were people who had left ship along the way, as the famous columnist Drew Pearson had done in this case, or canceled flight for one reason or another, sometimes just a hunch. As we know, Rick suffered anxiety about Flight 21 and had joined it only because of business reasons.

Rick's instinct to direct affairs and assign men to their positions did not abate merely because he lay helpless in a hospital. He insisted that the doctors admit Eastern executives to his room, and frequently conferred with Paul H. Brittain, first vice president, from the New York office; Sidney Shannon, from the Miami office; and Beverly Griffith, a publicity man who enjoyed Rick's confidence. Rick made no claim to being a calm, cooperative patient. He demanded a lot of attention, and the hundreds of letters, cards, and telegrams from friends and strangers helped him like medicine. Steve Hannagan wired: GET UP OUT OF THAT BED. YOU CAN'T DO THIS TO ME. A telegram that read I KNOW THE INDOMITABLE RICKENBACKER SPIRIT WILL PULL THROUGH was signed John Edgar Hoover.

Coincidences so extreme that the laws of probability would rule them out as impossible had a way of occurring in Rick's career. One of them took place at the hospital, and Rick became aware of it when they told him that another transportation magnate, also the victim of a wreck on his own line, was recovering in a room a few doors down the hall. The patient was Rick's friend Ernest Eden Norris, president of the Southern Railway system. Norris resembled Rick in his belief that a man selling transport ought to get out on the line and visit customers. He also resembled Rick in going downtown to buy money. When the Southern needed $30 million for new equipment, Norris called at the partners' room in the House of Morgan. Soon afterward, the Southern started ordering new engines and improving roadbeds, which hadn't received attention since they cleaned up after General W. T. Sherman. Bad luck lay in wait when the private cars *Virginia* and *Carolina* lunged into a ditch. Ernest Norris sustained injuries that took a long time to heal, and he moved to a New York hospital shortly after Rick arrived at Piedmont. As they began to improve, the two friends exchanged hospital banter by telephone.

They discharged Rick in early summer, four months and two days after the crash. He took a cottage at Candlewood Lake, in Connecticut, and started a weekly regime of three days in town, four days at the lake. Here, he rowed a skiff with the boys, who delighted in seeing their father. A masseur worked on Rick every day, easing muscles that injuries had pulled out of place. Rick limped with his bad left leg and could not get comfortable in the orthopedic shoes that were supposed to correct the limp. He also found that because of the trouble he had in lifting his foot, he couldn't operate the clutch of an automobile. Rick noted, "That was easily taken care of — I gave up driving." He never touched a steering wheel again. He had never in his life taken out a driver's license.

Rick hadn't been out of hospital long when he read in the papers, along with his fellow citizens, that the U.S. Marines had occupied Iceland, on invitation from that country. There were airfields and radio installations up there that would be useful for enemies attacking Canada and the United States. Of course, these enemies would be Germans. Americans were resigned to fighting Germans; even the America Firsters had privately accepted the coming war. And from start to finish Rick was one of them. He felt all the emotions that the imminence of war had released, and they reacted on him by causing an even greater consumption than his already generous rations of whiskey and gin.

The fatigue of long days traveling or in the office — for he was now back on full time — and the continuing pain in his bones contributed to Rick's increased drinking. A doctor who knew Rick both as friend and patient wrote to a member of the family that there was a delay in muscular development and that Rick should not set his heart on speedy recovery. As for alcohol: "To tell a man who has been a rather active drinker all his life to stop would probably accomplish no good." But Rick was extremely fond of people, and "like all of us" he enjoyed being made much of. The doctor thought Rick's drinking was due to conviviality rather than to nervous craving or addiction. Maybe the trouble was centered in Miami. There were associates down there who did Rick no good, and perhaps his family and friends ought to look for ways to improve matters. The suggestion was that certain unnamed people might be transferred so that Rick wouldn't run into them when he hit the southern end of his airline. This was a counsel of perfection, and nothing was done. Rick liked to attend mechanics' picnics in Florida, where beer and whiskey flowed freely. He would drink all evening, kneel in crap games, and join in barbershop harmony. In spite of everything, his body held up and mended its hurts from the Atlanta wreck.

Rick had heard the news of Pearl Harbor at his office, that Sunday morning of December 7, 1941. He returned to his East End Avenue apartment and talked late with Adelaide as they listened to the radio, which added little to first reports of surprise attack. Next day he found out how bad things were from EAL people in Washington, where insiders talked of nothing but disaster.* Some said California was in danger. Deciding that he must become physically fit for whatever lay ahead, Rick went to his houseboat in Miami.

He had a smaller boat rigged for deep-sea fishing, and would go out wearing nothing but trunks and a wide-brimmed hat, "soaking in the salt air and the sun" and stretching his leg muscles. But he could not get rid of the limp. The orthopedic shoes prescribed at the hospital seemed to do nothing for him but make walking all the more painful. Then one day he put on a pair of shower clogs and accidentally got the elastic under his left heel. This suspension gave him the support he wanted. Rick got several pairs of clogs and experimented, cutting the rubber until he found a length that suited him. He demonstrated this rig to makers of special shoes, and it served him well for the rest of his life. Most days the support kept pain in reasonable bounds, and he felt that his limp was scarcely noticeable. But Rick did not like his special shoes to be photographed, and only a few pictures of the ankle-high boots got into circulation. Except when he was seated with trousers hitched, the boots looked like the kind of handmade oxfords he had been wearing for years. They were neat and black, with the kind of toes only British shoemakers can produce, and both the high and low editions of Rickenbacker footwear were the farthest possible advance over the shoes that had drawn mockery in a Columbus schoolyard.

As walking became easier, Rick noticed another improvement: the dent in his head began to fill. But his hair had become thinner, and he was beginning to have the look that he carried in his closing years, an appearance that put one in mind of battered metal.

*Rick closed the Indianapolis Speedway for the duration, and sold it, in 1946 to Anton Hulman, Jr., of Terre Haute.

So for a few weeks Rick absorbed sunlight, testing his improvised foot supporter and squinting across blue water on Biscayne Bay. Like other men of his type, he was utterly preoccupied with the war. How would he get in it? What could he do? General Hap Arnold of the air forces started the sequence of events. His voice came down the wire from the Pentagon: "Eddie! I have a job for you. When can you get to Washington?" Rick said, "At once," and called for Adelaide to lay out town clothes and alert the chauffeur for an airport run. Rick didn't know where he was going, but he was happily on his way.

# CHAPTER VI

# Peril on the Sea

When Rick had first met him in the 1920s, Hap Arnold had been a captain in a service where money was scarce and hopes of advancement few and dim. But things began to improve after the Mitchell affair, and now Rick found his friend in a huge office behind a desk the size of a billiard table. As commanding general of the army air forces (not yet a separate arm), Hap Arnold was under pressures of great responsibility. Two men were above him, the elderly but capable Secretary of War, Henry L. Stimson, and Franklin D. Roosevelt, in the White House.

All men in positions as lofty as that Hap Arnold occupied feel the need of confidential information gathered for their eyes alone. It was to help fill this need that Arnold had called in his old friend Captain Eddie Rickenbacker. He asked Rick to visit all the airbases in the United States and bring back a report on how the equipment looked to a combat veteran, and what the pilots in training thought about things in general. There had been rumors of disaffection. Some thought that communists might be at work, but this was wrong, for the Stalinist line was to encourage anyone fighting Germany. Rick was to find the truth of these matters, under cover of such morale-raising visits to student pilots as he could give. When should he start? Right now, if possible.

Rick was still pulled out of shape from the battering in the Atlanta wreck, so he received the boon of taking along his favorite osteopath and a masseur, who would do what they could for his aching bones and muscles after each day's travel. It was as exhausting as any travel Rick had ever attempted, but apparently did him no harm. He said that with his cane he got along all right, but his body would stiffen when he stopped moving, either at the end of the day or flying between bases.

Rick sat up all night to compose a preliminary report after visiting six airbases. He called for more flying time and gunnery practice, better maintenance, faster replacement of defective machinery, and a more effective training program for the complicated gun turrets on bombing planes. Rick also put in a word for a squadron of Negro pilots who had not yet received their commissions. This complaint went straight to Hap Arnold, because Rick was working outside usual channels. Otherwise, it would have circulated, perhaps forever, in the lower reaches of air force administration. But when Arnold read Rick's note, he began grabbing telephones and punching buttons. And Rick recorded that "the nation had a new crop of second lieutenants."

It was a big day when Rick got to Long Beach, California, where Squadron 94 was training. He told the student pilots they wouldn't believe the changes he could see all around him. For example, the old 94th flew 100-horsepower planes. The P-38s of the present 94th drummed up 2400 horsepower when running right. And one of these P-38s mounted more firepower than the entire old 94th Squadron. But there was one thing lacking. The authorities had ruled out the hat-in-the-ring emblem, though nobody knew why. The bureaucrats who erased the emblem obviously had no idea how important tradition could be for military organizations. But Arnold concurred in returning the hat to Squadron 94 even though it had appeared on the Rickenbacker car. After visiting forty-one flying groups in thirty-two days, Rick concluded his mission at Mitchell Field on April 13, 1942. Within a week, he gave Hap Arnold an enlarged version of the early report.

General Arnold now asked Rick to call a confidential meeting of all the airline operators and make plans for putting the lines into wartime service. Rick gathered them in Washington, and, as a result, half the civilian fleet came under government lease, and technical men, such as dispatchers and weather predicters, entered the military forces or took government jobs under contract. Thus began the Air Transport Command,* which set up many famous routes, including the run that carried passengers, mostly War Department officials and staff officers, from Miami to Chungking. When the ATC announced it was going across the mountains to China, in the opinion of the world transport aviation came of age.

Shortly after June 1, Arnold asked Rick to come in and see him again. In addition to gaining newspaper space, Rick had accomplished actual good in his surveys of supply and transport problems. But General Arnold was uncomfortable. He told Rick that people were writing to their congressmen about the quality of aircraft that were being supplied to fighting pilots. Arnold felt that the criticisms were too severe and that many came from uninformed people who took rumor and gossip for fact. He would feel a good deal happier if someone could turn off the heat and focus attention elsewhere. Would Rick take on the job of straightening this out?

What Arnold wanted was that Captain Eddie go before the American people and "tell the truth about the Air Force." And when Rick got the promise of a free hand, he accepted the job. At the time, the B-29 bomber was still a secret, in the planning stage, and the public's interest centered on the B-17 (the Flying

* This command later became the Military Air Transport Service (MATS).

Fortress) and two pursuit planes (the P-38 and the P-40).

Rick made a survey, using what he called "confidential, trust-worthy information" from pilots and mechanics. He used this material in writing three reports to the nation, delivered over NBC radio and originating in the East, the Midwest, and on the Coast. In each case, NBC gave Rick the national network, and Rick's messages to the public had an air of truthfulness that made them different from government propaganda. He spoke of the P-40. which had seen the most combat of any model we then had in use:

> How does the P-Forty compare with the Japanese Zero? The Zero is an excellent climber. It is very maneuverable. In these two respects, it surpasses the P-Forty, but only in these two. The P-Forty has more firepower, heavier guns, and carries more ammunition than the Zero. The P-Forty has protected gasoline tanks. The Zero has none. The American incendiary bullets turn it into a flaming coffin . . . Yes, the Japs have added armor to their latest Zeroes . . . But, we still knock them down. In Japan, it's a great thing to die for your country. In America, it's a great thing to fight and live for your country — to fight another day.

Rick was aware of basic air force strategy; he called it the original Billy Mitchell doctrine. The plan was to send bombers over the enemy with an escort of fighters. These escort planes needed armor and the capacity to carry fuel for long-range flights. Thus they were heavier than the British Spitfires, which did not fly far from base because their purpose was to defend the island. Another fighting plane that served the British well was the twin-engined Mosquito. Critics wanted to know why our P-38 wasn't as good as the Mosquito. The Canadians were turning out Mosquitos built of plywood, right across the river from Detroit. The planes were cheap and plentiful, and would fly up 25,000 feet in the air.

Rick said not to worry about the P-38, but it was giving trouble in 1942. What Rick couldn't reveal was that the "P-Shooter" was due for drastic improvements, and it would be able to take its twin fuselages to 35,000 feet, and fire cannon and fifty-caliber automatics up there to make the heights dangerous for anyone who came along. The P-Shooters could get up so high, you couldn't see them from the ground, and then they could drop like hammers on aircraft lower down or troops and trucks on roads. They could dig a ditch straight down the middle of a road when they came strafing, and blow up a truckload of ammunition with one cannon shot. They also learned to hunt at night, coming in on the tail of a train and swooping the length of it, battering with guns every foot of the way, and leaving a wreck on the railroad. Knowing what was in store for the P-38 right up to its combat tactics, Rick did not have to feign sincerity when he said, "This one is going to be among the best."

Another warplane that Rick examined and found good was the P-47, the bee-bellied, swift fighter named Thunderbolt. The 'Bolts went well in formation, and climbed to 40,000 feet, where they kept hawklike surveillance. There was a secret in these high-altitude fighters, another thing that Rick could not talk about. This was the turbosupercharger, a new engineering development. A man who was so good at salesmanship, which did not depend on truth, was overpowering in conviction when his material was strictly true. Many an American decided to trust his government, and in particular the leaders of its war in the air, after some exposure to Rickenbacker addressing the nation on the subject of our fighting aircraft.

In the middle of September 1942, Rick got a letter from Secretary Stimson that began with a paragraph of praise for his work in the spring, "a magnificent job." Stimson went on to ask if Rick would go overseas to look into conditions among American airmen. The best line in the letter was the last: "On return to this country, you would report to me directly."

Stimson gave Rick a secret intelligence mission, and did so in an impressive manner. He called Rick into his office at the Pen-

tagon, ushered him to a seat beside the desk, and leaned back
in his great chair. Rick listened with such concentrated attention that he remembered every word. Stimson said he wanted
Rick to keep his eyes and ears open for subversive activity.
"Whatever you observe or hear along these lines, do not write it
down. Rather, report it orally to me and to me alone. Don't
breathe a word of these final instructions to anyone, Eddie,
because we must never let anyone suspect that you are doing
intelligence work for me. To everyone but you and me, your
duty is to evaluate the aviation progress and equipment of the
enemy, our allies, and ourselves."

Soon Rick was in England, where a friend told him about the
secret development of a pursuit plane for the British. Rick got
a chance to see it, and when the secrecy came off, he was able
to praise it as enthusiastically as he had once extolled the Rickenbacker car. This new fighter was the P-51, the Mustang. He
caused unhappiness in Washington when he remarked that red
tape would have stopped the Mustang at the Dayton proving
ground like a shell from a Nazi cannon. On Rick's recommendation, the army air forces bought half a dozen Mustangs. Rick
then told Arnold it was essential that we make the planes in
large numbers over here, ship them without engines, lashed to
Liberty ship decks, and have the British mount Rolls-Royce
Merlin engines, developing 1600 horsepower. Shortly after his
return, Rick visited his old haunts at Allison and urged the
managers to make their 1450-horsepower engine even more
powerful.

On October 13, 1942, Rick handed in his report to Stimson,
along with a duplicate set of plans for the invasion of North
Africa. When Rick had called on General Eisenhower, just before flying back to the States, "Ike" had entrusted these papers
to him, remarking that two copies had already gone, by a navy
cruiser and an army courier. Ike said he'd appreciate it if Rick
carried his third copy as insurance. He knew that Rick would

put his copy straight into Stimson's hands. Rick had no grudge against Eisenhower and was glad to help him. Stimson liked Rick's own report so much that he called him in for another confidential assignment.

What Stimson had in mind was that Rick should carry his warrant as consulting inspector into the Southwest Pacific and see what he could see. So much would be on paper, and Stimson's chop meant that no local commander could get in Rick's way and that nothing was to be hidden from him. But there was more. Rick was to visit General Douglas MacArthur in Port Moresby, New Guinea, and give him a message from Stimson "of such sensitivity that it could not be put on paper."

MacArthur held command over the Southwest Pacific Theater, which included Australia but not much else at the time. He was making big noise in his small theater by way of dispatches and press releases, but Admiral Chester Nimitz ruled over the Pacific Ocean, many square miles larger than MacArthur's domain. And he refused to bow down before "Dugout Doug." The nickname, which appeared to indicate scant respect, was the sobriquet for General MacArthur among troops of the line; he was probably the most despised of all high commanders in our military establishment. The derisive nickname failed to find a mark in MacArthur's courage, for he had been noticeably cool under fire on more than one occasion. According to his press officer, MacArthur's brave bearing "had galvanized the spirit of resolution of the Philippine people, and confirmed the faith of the American people in their armed forces." Such was the man to whom Rick was bringing a message so important that it couldn't be written down.

Arnold ordered Colonel Hans Adamson to travel with Rick as military aide, and Rick enjoyed Adamson's company for fifteen hours as they flew, on October 12, 1942, from San Francisco to Honolulu on an uneventful trip by Pan American. This time Rick had not been able to bring along a masseur, and found it hard to keep from stiffening, which he avoided to some extent by his own system of twists and turns. Rick was not a good physical candidate for a long wartime journey, and he knew that after he left Honolulu he would be riding military aircraft, which afforded no comforts. He limped out at Hickam Field for a day-long inspection of the base and all air force units around it.

Rick showed endurance by choosing to go on without a night's rest in Honolulu. The commanding general picked up Rick and Adamson in his car and drove them to the field, with sirens howling and air police darting ahead on motorcycles. As they climbed aboard the B-17D, the general saluted and turned away in the consciousness of a job well done and a visiting fireman off his hands. One can understand his dismay as he watched the 17D blow a tire just before takeoff and lunge left, heading for the hangars. Then the plane swung in a ground loop, which sent up a cloud of dust, and stopped a few feet short of the bay. The next B-17D was ready a few minutes past midnight. It took off in a routine manner, and Captain William T. Cherry, Jr., said he expected a smooth, quiet flight. During the early hours, the engines settled to a steady humming beat like the drone in bagpipe music. There was nothing to see except the moon at three-quarters riding thin clouds. The dark Pacific Ocean seemed like infinite empty space below. Rick moved to the cockpit, where the instrument panel lit the pilots' faces. Captain Cherry had the plane on automatic. Every once in a while, he would reach up and turn a little wheel to trim ship. Otherwise he had nothing to do.

They were heading 1800 miles southwest for Canton Island, then known as Island X, where a small secret airstrip broke the journey for Port Moresby and Australia. Ten hours of flight should bring them down. At dawn, they saw nothing in any direction but water, which looked like gray metal. It was like the Ascension Island leg on the Air Transport Command flight from South America to the Gold Coast. You found yourself thinking about the navigator. On this flight, he was First Lieutenant John J. De Angelis, and he kept scribbling on a pad and shooting the sun with his octant. The copilot was First Lieutenant James C. Whittaker, who had worked with small planes as a civilian. By now Rick had met the crew, which consisted of Sergeant James W. Reynolds, the radio operator; and Private John F. Bartek, the mechanic. There was another passenger, Sergeant Alexander T. Kaczmarczyk. He asked Rick to call him "Alex," because his last name was hard to pronounce. Alex had just been discharged from hospital in Honolulu, where doctors had treated him for jaundice and taken out his appendix. He was going back to his outfit in Australia.

The crew had put cots in the back for Rick and Adamson. Rick got up early and enjoyed drinks from a cold bottle of orange juice, and a hot bottle of coffee. At 8:30 A.M. Cherry began letting down, and straightened out 1000 feet above the sea. Everyone looked ahead for the island. Nobody saw anything. Two hours went by. Rick asked Cherry how much gas he had. Cherry said. "About four hours."

Rick thought it seemed likely that they had overshot the island. Cherry said they had been running before a tail wind of ten miles an hour. The tail wind had added thirty-one miles an hour to their speed. But this would have meant only an earlier arrival if they had been aimed right. The radio direction finder had turned balky and refused to answer its crank. And Lieutenant De Angelis reported that there might be something wrong with his octant. The ground loop in the other plane had thrown it against a bulkhead. Captain Cherry said, "We're lost."

Lieutenant Whittaker concluded their trouble had come from missing rather than overshooting the island, going either northeast or southwest of it. Sergeant Reynolds had raised Canton, and now the emergency justified his calling to ask for radio guidance. It was to be hoped no Japanese were listening.

But the island operator answered that he did not have the gear to bring the plane in. Cherry told Reynolds to ask for an island where they did have homing gear. Reynolds learned that this was a thousand miles from Canton, and they had fuel for only 750 miles. All they could do was swing low and hope to find Canton by luck.

Rick's face looked expressionless to the pilots, but he nodded agreement when Cherry proposed to box the compass while they peered at the ocean. This maneuver called for their going west for forty-five minutes, then north, east, and south. There wasn't enough fuel for all four legs, but at least it was something to be decided on and to start doing. Rick didn't know at the time, and may never have found out that the crew, with the exception of Sergeant Alex, had received orders the previous day to fly a Fortress to the United States. Then the orders were canceled and they had been told to use that Fortress to carry two visiting firemen to Port Moresby, had ground looped the first plane — and here they were. Whittaker reported that they had felt better about the change in orders as soon as they learned they were carrying Rickenbacker, for they believed that he would have something important to do. There were things worth dying for and things not worth dying for. And the chances of survival grew less each minute the Fortress ground on. Yet the engines spoke gravely to Rick and sounded as though they would never stop.

The sea was blue, without whitecaps, but wrinkled in a way that meant heavy swells were running. Rick suggested that Cherry call Canton and ask them to fire antiaircraft shells to burst at 7000 feet. The men in the Fortress might see them above the moderate cloud level that had built up since early morning. If there were planes on Canton, they might come out for a look. Reynolds hammered his key, listened to the answering chatter of Morse, and reported that Canton would be firing shells and sending planes. But the men on the B-17D saw nothing. Cherry said, "In one hour we'll have to set her down."

He cut the two outer engines, thinned the fuel mixture to the others, and climbed for a last search of empty seascape. Anyone who had taken a personal interest in overseas flying knew that the "landing" of a four-engine plane on water could result in immediate death for all on board. Hitting water was like hitting a brick highway, and after the impact, big planes seldom floated for more than sixty seconds. Assuming those on board weren't killed by the force of the crash, or exploding fuel, they had no more than one minute to launch the rafts, get into them, and pull clear of the sinking ship. In that time they would have to get survival gear set up, rafts outboard and inflated, emergency supplies and equipment properly stowed. It couldn't be done.

Cherry said to Reynolds, "Mayday." This meant to call for help with the repeated signal of SOS, which Reynolds proceeded to grind out, over and over. Rick handed him a slip of paper. Reynolds stopped the SOS sequence long enough to send FOURTEEN HOURS SSW OAHU MAY HAVE OVERSHOT ISLAND HOUR'S FUEL RICKENBACKER. Then he picked up again with Mayday. Nobody answered. Rick, Adamson, Bartek, and Alex went aft and opened the bottom hatch, through which they passed everything they could get their hands on. Out went mail, cots, blankets, Rick's new Burberry topcoat, his suitcase (a gift from Eastern employees), and his briefcase. They put aside some cartons of emergency rations and several vacuum bottles of drinking water, coffee, and condensed milk. All this they carried back to the radio compartment and stacked near its overhead hatch, through which they planned to leave the ship after it struck water.

Some time went by, the two faithful engines still muttering away. At last Cherry called out, "We'd better pack up to crash." Rick knew more about hard landings than anyone else on board, and he supervised the packing. Bartek, Alex, Adamson, and Rick lay down with their heads toward the tail and their feet against a bulkhead. They used parachutes for padding. Reynolds remained at his key, pounding SOS. De Angelis, Whittaker, and Cherry were strapped to seats in the cockpit. Rick propped himself on his elbows so that he could see a small slice of wing and sky and water. Adamson remembered Rick's "calm, conversational tone" before they hit: "I'd say we were now at five hundred feet. Four hundred. Two hundred. About a hundred feet to go. Fifty feet. Here she comes."

Cherry had come down under power so as to keep the plane in control. He had seen that the swells were twelve feet high. When the ship made contact, the men felt and heard a tremendous thump. Rick knew that it was louder than the Atlanta crash. A box of tools from the tail broke loose, and metal whizzed like shrapnel. There came a second crash and a third. The plane settled. Cherry had bounced from the top of a swell into the trough, lowered the tail and then the prow. The plane held together. Rick recalled that the window beside him cracked apart and the green Pacific Ocean poured in. But Rick knew how airplanes could twist, fold up on themselves, or break in two at the shock of crashing. As far as the ship's holding together was concerned, this was better than Atlanta.

Rick wasn't hurt, and he stood up on deck, heaving in the swells. They had two injuries here at the start. Adamson had wrenched his back. Reynolds had stayed at his post, and the crash had knocked his face into the radio panel; he was bleeding from a cut over the nose. The three officers hustled in from their cockpit. Water came to their knees. Bartek pulled the release cord and called, "The rafts are loose." Officers and crewmen boosted Rick and Adamson out first, because they were passengers. Rick still had his cane, and the gray fedora sat tight on his head. He and Bartek helped pull the others out on the wing. One moment they would be in a trough with solid-looking green blue water rising above their heads; then they would feel the wing rising, and they would look out over acres of ocean, with a bright sun throwing splinters of reflected light into their eyes. Water rolled on the wing and pulled at their ankles.

Rick now saw that another man was hurt. Bartek had ripped his fingers on a piece of jagged metal in trying to release the rafts, which had been expelled from under the fuselage when he pulled the cord. His blood stained the water. These two automatically ejected rafts were supposed to have room for five men each. The smaller raft, which they had launched by hand, had an official carrying capacity of three men. This meant that thirteen men presumably could sail away in the three rafts. Practical experience immediately showed that eight could scarcely find room.

The rafts were floating. Rick and Bartek pushed Adamson aboard a large one and climbed in after him. Rick threw away the cane. He had wound a sixty-foot line around his waist. In his pockets he had a map of the Pacific, a book of traveler's checks, and several packs of cigarettes. He also had a leather folder with a crucifix that a child had given him in 1917. This was a descendant of the charms that once attracted good fortune on the racetrack. Reynolds, Whittaker, and Cherry climbed into their raft. De Angelis and Alex took the small raft. When they climbed in, it tipped, and both men went into the sea. They managed to clamber back, Alex swallowing sea water in the struggle. All this happened fast, much of it simultaneously. Now they felt a stiff wind blowing them away from the plane, which still wallowed in the swells. Somebody cried out, "Who has the water?" They discovered that the rations and bottles of water and coffee were still in the plane. Then they saw its tail point to the sky, and it slid down out of sight. Rick's watch, on Honolulu time, registered 2:36 P.M.

They decided to use Rick's sixty feet of line to keep their fleet together. Cherry was captain of the ship and in command of the party. His raft took the lead, Rick and Bartek with the injured Adamson followed twenty feet behind, and De Angelis and Alex, at the same distance, brought up the rear. They now started to take stock of the situation.

The inventory of food and water showed that Alex had half a dozen chocolate bars, but sea water had ruined them. Cherry had four small oranges, which they decided to hoard for the time being. As long as they had these four oranges, they weren't destitute. Rick warned that no matter how thirst might torment them, they must drink no salt water. It made you more thirsty than ever; it could kill you. Alex had taken in a bellyful when the small raft tipped, and had not brought all of it back up. They were sick from the heaving swells, except for Eddie, who never got seasick, and, though Adamson suffered most pain, Alex seemed to be in the worst general condition. It was at this time that Rick found out Alex had just left the hospital. He began to doubt that Alex would pull through.

Most of the men were smokers. The cigarettes they carried, like those in Rick's pockets, had spoiled in sea water, and they threw them away. They passed the rest of the first afternoon adjusting their minds to what had happened and trying to ignore the thirst that had already begun intruding to the conscious level. As the afternoon wore on, they talked about the danger of sunburn and tried to think of some way to tell where they were drifting. Then they noticed a convoy. They saw long shapes trailing a few feet below the surface, and realized that the creatures were sharks. Rick thought the smell of blood from Bartek's cut hand might have attracted them.

By the time night fell, the raftsmen had discovered that the only way their situation bettered the Black Hole of Calcutta was that they could breathe fresh air. The claim that the rafts were big enough for five men would not have been correct even if the men were midgets. Inside dimensions were six feet nine inches by two feet four inches. In Rick's raft they put Adamson lengthwise. He was tall and heavy. This left one end for Rick, sitting with his knees over the flotation roll, his feet in the air. Bartek fitted himself on the bias, with his head toward Adamson and his feet behind Rick. It was worse in the third raft, where De Angelis and Alex were so cramped for space that they had to sit facing, each with his legs over the other's shoulders. As darkness came on, it got cold. Mist rose from the sea. They kept a Very pistol and flares ready in case they should see the lights of a plane overhead. No light appeared.

All night long sharks continued to escort the rafts, sometimes bumping them from underneath. The mist began to lighten before dawn. At last it lifted and they saw the sun of their second day afloat. They also learned why the sharks bumped the rafts. When one of them surfaced, Rick saw a parasitical growth on its head. The creature had been trying to rub it off. The sharks looked black under water, gray when they broke surface. They had minnowlike swiftness in darting, and there was no use trying to kill them with pistol fire.

On the mainland, news of Rick's distress message had come in at San Francisco, and in the morning he was on the front pages. The Los Angeles *Times* was typical, with black letters across eight columns: RICKENBACKER'S PLANE MISSING

The navy started to hunt for the castaways, but they had gone down in such a forbidding, empty space that searchers said there was little hope of rescue. Editorial writers and cartoonists took the cue and decided we had seen the last of Captain Eddie. Within a week, the New York *Daily News* ran an editorial headed, "Good-Bye Rickenbacker." On the same page was a cartoon by C. D. Batchelor, showing a wreath floating on waves. The caption was "So Long, Eddie." The New York *Journal-American* published a cartoon by Burris Jenkins, Jr., entitled "End of the Roaring Road?" It showed an old-time racing car fading in the distance.

The popular sportswriter and versifier Grantland Rice looked out over the Hudson from his study window at 450 Riverside Drive, and wrote a set of verses to commemorate his friend. Rice called the poem "Rick," and showed that its subject evoked poignant emotion:

> Danger and Death have always been your mates,
> The pals you loved — above all else in life . . .
> Danger and Death — you took them hand in hand
> With that quick smile we all remember well
> Through flaming air, above some flaming land,
> Along the path to heaven. Or to hell —
> You never bothered much about the ride,
> As long as your two pals were by your side.

Speaking as deputy of the public voice, Rice continued to develop the idea of a man in love with death and danger, until he reached his elegiac vein:

> Here at the Inn tonight we lift a glass . . .
> We stand — heads up — with fog-bewildered view,
> Happy to know the human race had you . . .
> So, Happy Landings! Flying clean or blind,
> We'll break no faith with what you left behind.

Some might feel uncomfortable with Rice, but none could deny the directness and simplicity of the anonymous writer in the *Sun* of Durham, North Carolina, who headed his lines "Hope":

> Captain Eddie Rickenbacker
> Our No. 1 ace of World War No.1,
> Is missing somewhere in the Pacific.
> America, accustomed as it has grown already,
> To the grim losses of war,
> Is stunned by the news.
> Not only has Rickenbacker been a war hero,
> But he has been one of our great heroes,
> Of peacetime, civil aviation.

He is especially beloved in Durham,
For his fine character and presence,
His idealism and energy,
And for his interest in our own airport.
Durham and the Nation have not yet given him up.
Perhaps we have only hope left,
But, ever a hopeful people,
We shall hold fast to that,
So long as we can.

Having escaped the quick death that Rice and other friends thought they could not have avoided, the castaways began their ordeal with a concerted effort to be cheerful about it and to exclude despair from their minds. Adamson recalled that his moods of hope and despair were to come and go with the regularity of tides. In spite of his pain, he tried to joke when, waking from a confused nap, he saw the Captain hunched against the flotation ring, the trademark gray fedora jammed on his head. Adamson said, "What are *you* doing here?" Rick answered, "I just came along for the ride."

But when the sun burned off the mist, the men found themselves so stiff from the cramped night that they could hardly move. Rick talked with enthusiasm and hopefulness he did not feel. He said it was just a matter of time until someone flew over and saw them, and he would give a reward of $100 to the first man who spotted a plane. Whittaker, for one, understood this as an effort to cheer them up, and thought it was good of Rick to make the effort. But hope was absent. Rick's private thoughts were bleak: "We were the only ones in the whole world who knew we were alive. It might be days, even weeks, before we were picked up. It might be never . . ."

They decided to eat one of the four oranges. Adamson was entrusted with cutting the orange into eight segments, which gave each man a few drops of juice and a little pulp and peel. By eleven o'clock, the sun neared zenith and the rays came straight down. "Molten metal" was the phrase that came to Whittaker's mind to describe the heat. They made sunbonnets of shorts and undershirts. The thirst was bad now, and they couldn't help thinking of shaded wells, woodland brooks, tin cups brimming from picnic springs, milk shakes, and various cold fruit juices. The wind began to bang the rafts together. Cherry rigged an undershirt as sail on an aluminum oar, and steered his raft ahead so that all three fell into line. The sun plunged toward the horizon, and the chill of their second night came fast. That night they shot one flare, but no one saw it.

Next day Rick noticed Bartek reading a small canvas-bound New Testament, the sort that chaplains supplied, and suggested that they pass it around so that those who wished might read passages aloud. For this, they pulled the rafts together. From time to time a shark would bump the underside of a raft as Captain Cherry prayed and recited the Twenty-third Psalm from memory. The sun made its swift disappearance, and they tried to settle down. Cold damp mist, the presence of sharks, and relentless discomfort from cramped space made sleep impossible. When daylight came, Rick saw that Reynolds' legs had begun to blister. There had been no healing in the cut across his nose, which still oozed blood. He had cut two fingers to the bone; Rick applied iodine from the first-aid kit, but the frequent splashings of salt water washed out the iodine, and Rick's impression was that "the salt would eat into the open flesh. Salt was everywhere. It dried in a white, grainy crust that covered everybody and everything."

Next morning the sun came up on the fifth day with its impersonal glare and quick rise above the surface, which could be identified only as a straight line of division slipping down the sun as it moved into the sky. For the first hours until mists cleared away, sky and sea were the same. Then the bite of the sun began to sink into exposed parts of the men's bodies. There have been differing reports about the amount of conversation from raft to raft. But there is no question that they used their voices at the Scripture readings. Each time, according to survivors' memories, Cherry led in prayer. And once Rick offered a prayer, in which he addressed what he called "the Power Above" in a reasonable tone. His point was that the Lord helps those who help themselves, and they had done that. Now it was the Lord's turn. All of the religious speaking was sincere. They would also try an occasional hymn, deriving comfort from Newman's immortal words to "Lead, Kindly Light," and drawing psychic strength from Sir Arthur Sullivan's marching measures to "Onward, Christian Soldiers," with its words by the Reverend Sabine Baring-Gould, which have entered every Protestant's bloodstream. The Roman Catholics, De Angelis and Alex, joined in, but Alex seemed to be getting worse by the hour.

Adamson looked over the available reading matter, which was a waterlogged issue of *Reader's Digest.* The only pages not ruined by sea water described how Santos-Dumont made a balloon flight over Paris at the turn of the century, eating a lunch of chicken, lobster, ice cream, and champagne as he sailed around in the sky. The castaways had now learned that the heat was at its worst from 11:00 A.M. to 4:00 P.M.; during those hours they had almost nothing to say, and drifted in silent misery as sharks scraped backs on the raft bottoms. Whittaker in his recollections thought that they had reached a daily routine by this time, which consisted of trying to shield themselves from the sun and sitting in stupor until it went down. During the night some dreamed that they were at home, pouring water from cool pitchers, or sitting down at tables loaded with food. Rick dreamed that he was talking to Adelaide, and he called to Adamson, "She'll be right over with the car, Hans." All reported that waking after a good dream and realizing that it had been a dream gave a feeling of unbearable desolation.

On the sixth day they found that, since their stomachs were

not yet shrunken from lack of food, the hunger pangs were ag-
onizing. This made them think with frustrated fury of the
thieves who had stolen the hardtack, chocolate, and concentrated rations from the rafts. The supplies were standard
equipment, but greedy natives or Americans had carried them
off, either from Honolulu warehouses or from planes at airfields. They still moved under power of the sail-rigged shirt on
the lead raft. Opinions as to their location differed, but Rick
and Cherry later verified their estimate that the rafts were
floating between 400 and 500 miles from the Gilbert Islands,
which were held by the Japanese.

The thought of capture by Japanese caused some hesitancy
about firing the flares. The consensus was that they should take
the chance, and the Very pistol cracked on each of the first five
nights, sending up a cartridge that exploded a dazzling crimson
light shining from its small parachute over the ocean as far as
they could see. Then they discovered that the remaining shells
were duds.

On the sixth day the great event had been eating the second
orange. The fruit was almost entirely dried out, and no help
for thirst. They chewed the fiber and peel for a momentary
illusion of having something to eat. After another night of torment in the crowded rafts, they ate the third orange. And on
the following day, their eighth at sea, they decided to eat the
last orange, which was wrinkled, dry, and beginning to rot.
That seemed a sensible decision, but Rick thought it a mistake
from the emotional point of view. The last orange had been a
symbol of something to look forward to. Now they had nothing
left. In a similar frame of mind, Whittaker looked over his
mates. He thought Rick inscrutable and probably indestructible. Whittaker decided Colonel Adamson had lost hope.
Cherry and De Angelis were noncommittal, trying to shade
their faces and eyes from the "beating" of the sun. Bartek was
suffering from his unhealed cuts. And every morning, Alex

had looked worse; on this day, the others could see that he was very sick. As for Whittaker himself, he "was beginning to weigh the possibility that our situation might be hopeless."

The matter of command among castaways is interesting to sociologists, anthropologists, and all students of human nature. To the world at large, the drifters were "Rick's party," and newswriters fell into the habit of presenting the group as a military unit, under Rick's command from the takeoff at Honolulu. This was not the fact. Like the captain of a ship, Cherry was in charge of passengers and crew aboard his plane and also of survivors riding in rafts. Whittaker was second in command. Rick never disputed this. What happened was that Cherry and Whittaker took Rick on as adviser, because he had been in tight places before, and he had not put himself forward, but just sat there under his fedora, making a suggestion from time to time and seeming to pass each day and night without worry or fear. The two younger men were glad to have Rick in a partnership of responsibility, for there was no questioning the dignified strength of his presence.

Rick also served as a provider, in a way that was later to catch the world's imagination and to rank with many as a miracle and proof of divine mercy. The occurrence in itself was prosaic. It happened on the afternoon of the depressing eighth day, two hours after the consumption of the last orange. They drew the rafts together and someone read a passage from the Book. Captain Cherry prayed for deliverance. Whittaker recorded that his prayers were sincere; Cherry was a Texas Baptist, and he addressed the Divinity as "Old Master." After his plea for relief from hunger, lassitude descended on the drifters. Rick sat like a stone carving, the hat pulled over his eyes. He was dozing off when he heard a flutter and felt something press on his head. He told himself it was a seagull. He simply knew this, but could not say how he knew it.

In fact, it was a sea swallow, a bird about the size of a well-grown crow. Rick could see the others gazing at him, afraid to make a sound. Slowly, he raised his hand until it was level with the top of his hat. Rick decided against making a grab, but moved his hand, very slowly, until he felt that it was close to the bird's feet. Then he closed his hand and felt legs in it. He pulled down the bird, flapping and squawking. In his account of the experience, Rick said it took no time at all to wring the neck. He pulled out feathers, gutted the bird, laid guts aside to use as bait. Then he divided the rest into eight portions and served them out. They ate bones and all, finding the bird's flesh tough to chew and fishy to the taste. But they took heart from Rick's windfall. It put strength into them. And that was not all. Cherry and Rick tossed out fishing lines, baited with the bird's guts, and pulled in a small sea bass and a mackerel about twelve inches long. Rick carved the mackerel, and each man ate his portion, again chewing up bones and all. Everyone was aware that he had obtained the food shortly after Cherry's prayer for relief.

Even the two sick men felt better, and Cherry decided to thank the Divinity for this food that had reached them on the sea. After rendering thanks, Cherry added a request for water. And when the sun went down, a low-lying haze suggested that rain was on its way. Later they awoke and smelled rain under a black sky with no stars. They took off some of their clothes and set them aside to soak up water, which they could wring out. They put out empty Very cartridges to catch rain. The fresh smell continued, and after two hours Rick and the others felt the touch of small drops falling. Then the rain began to fall steadily. They threw back their heads and let rain into their open mouths. The rain fell on their heads and faces and was cool.

In the distance lightning flashed at the center of the rain squall. They grabbed aluminum paddles and started pushing toward the thunderhead, where the rain would be thickest. When they entered the squall, wind sprang up and tore at them, the waves grew violent, and, in Rick's phrase, "flashes of lightning etched them against walls of darkness." Thunder sounded as it does in storms at sea: flat cracks without echo or resonance. Then they heard De Angelis yelling for help. The small raft had broken loose and was about to capsize. They couldn't find it in the dark, but then a wave rolled white foam against which they could see the raft. They paddled to it and secured the line. Cherry's raft turned over. Rick and Bartek held it while Whittaker, Cherry, and Reynolds managed to scramble back in. Suddenly, the rain stopped and daylight came. When they took stock, they found that they had filled two buckets and a few cartridge cases with water and had defeated thirst by swallowing a satisfactory amount during the storm. Since there was no telling when another rain squall might come their way, they decided to ration the stock of water at one ounce a day to each man.

Now came the ninth day. They ate the other fish, the sea bass, and then Whittaker cast a hook and pulled in a small ugly shark. Cherry leaped on it and gave it the knife in the head. They tried to eat its flesh, but it tasted too horrible. Alex looked so bad, they gave him extra rations of water, but he kept getting worse. They discovered that he had an infection of the gums and lips, which was rotting away his mouth. On the third night after that, Alex died.

The following morning, they pulled the rafts together, and Cherry, Whittaker, and Rick examined the body for signs of life. Cherry took Alex's papers. There were orders, a couple of letters from his parents, the photograph of a girl. They recited the Twenty-third Psalm and the Lord's Prayer, and De Angelis said what he could remember of the Catholic burial service. Whittaker's recollection was that "Johnny Bartek fastened the zippers of Alex's flying suit. We said the Lord's Prayer again and put him in the water. He did not sink, but floated away. I could see him for a long time."

In New York, they now were reporting on Rick every day,

but in brief stories amounting to no more than "still no news of Rickenbacker; believed lost." The reports implied that he was lost forever, but the papers didn't like to say so. Marguerite Shepherd, however, was not going to fly any flags at half-mast. With four secretaries under her direction, Miss Shepherd continued to operate Rick's office at EAL in New York as though he would step in at any time and attack the papers winnowed out for his attention. Every morning they threw away the water in his vacuum jug and replaced it with fresh. The sharpened pencils and clean note pads that he liked to have near at hand were ready. Miss Shepherd said, "Don't give up on Captain. He may surprise you." Adelaide and the boys said the same. And the Café Louis XIV, across the street from the office, kept Rick's usual table reserved. It was a table for two at the balcony rail, where he could see everyone who came through the entrance downstairs. Every day, the management set out crisp linen, sparkling glassware, and a fresh carnation in a slim, silver vase. Joseph, the balcony waiter, said, "He'll come up that stairway. You wait and see. He'll come walking on his cane." In the past, whenever Rick appeared at the cloakroom, a swift signal would go to the upper service bar, and the dry martini would be waiting when he sat down.

Far from the Café Louis XIV, days and nights ran together after Alex's death. Adamson failed to gain a protective tan, and his swollen arms and legs gave pain every time he moved or touched the canvas, or if someone brushed him when trying to turn over. The pain from his wrenched back continued. Rick began to estimate that he, Rickenbacker, would outlast them all. The reason was that he had passed four months in the hospital less than two years before, and during those days had worked out what he considered to be a mental and spiritual technique of survival. Rick wrote in his autobiography that God had shown a purpose by keeping him alive in Atlanta: "It was to help the others, to bring them through. I had been saved to serve. It was an awesome responsibility, but I accepted it gladly and proudly." Rick was a hero-maker, using himself as material and subject. The heroes of romance had a common attribute: service to others. It should be noted that the reign of King Arthur ended in catastrophe and the Round Table broke up when Lancelot disregarded this rule. Rick was not going to make that mistake, either in his actual life or in the epic that he told in his last years. On the rafts, he would keep the others from surrendering to fatigue and losing their vital grip. He pictured himself as sarcastic and harsh, but keeping them to the mark. And if this did not save them Rick figured that Adamson would be next to go, Reynolds next, then Bartek. De Angelis and Cherry were about equal in stamina, he thought, and would last a while. As to Whittaker, Rick sized him up as unusually strong in mind and body. He and Rick might be the last men alive in the rafts.

It doesn't decrease Rick's stature to note that he did more for the party by example than by scolding and that his most useful contributions to the common good were catching the sea swallow and the fish. The men couldn't tell that to Rick, and, as people so often will do for strong-minded individuals who like to say the last word, they played to Rick's assumed role when he hectored them to hang on. He was building his legend against the day of deliverance, if it should come. A rational view of their plight would show that survival did not depend on what any one member of the party might say, or in what tone of voice he said it. Rick could have yelled at Alex of the rotting face until the sharks heard it, and not extended Alex's life one minute. But that is how myths come into being.

On the rafts, the two Colt .45 pistols corroded, and the owners threw them away. Occasional rain squalls at night refilled the stores of water. The sharks kept alongside. They looked strong and healthy, but continued to bump the rafts to rid themselves of parasites. A school of mackerel came along, and the sharks rushed them. Two mackerel jumped into the rafts and made rations for two days. Another food supply turned up when Cherry, Whittaker, De Angelis, and Rick discovered that they could catch the small fish resembling freshwater minnows that sometimes gathered, nosing the rafts. The trick was to grab the creatures and toss them aboard. Each fish made a small bite, and the men ate them whole.

They passed the eighteenth day drifting in stupor until Cherry called out, "I hear a plane!" The plane came out of a cloud, heading away from the rafts, kept going, and flew out of sight. Rick pointed out that where there was one plane there must be more. He called on every man to hang on and wait for the break that must be getting closer. During the night, they plucked up heart, going over Rick's argument and refusing to see flaws in it. On the following day, the nineteenth of their ordeal, two planes went by in the distance, kept on steadily, and vanished. Next day, four planes passed a few miles away, flying in pairs. But if the pilots weren't on the lookout, the chances of being seen were negligible. Cherry and Whittaker thought they would all have a better chance if the rafts spread out. Rick thought the opposite, but did not oppose Cherry's authority as commander of the party. Adamson thought that since he was a colonel, he was actually ranking man and holder of final authority. But he was technically wrong in thinking that anything bound Cherry to take his orders. Rick found it regrettable that there were words spoken, the sort that are best forgotten. Adamson talked about "direct orders," and it was unpleasant.

Cherry had boarded the small raft and paddled off alone for about 100 feet when a plane came over, flying low enough for them to identify it as a navy Kingfisher. But the pilot did not see them. Whittaker took Reynolds, who was semiconscious and barely able to move, and De Angelis into the other large raft, and prepared to move off. As the plane disappeared, he paddled alongside and said, "So long, Rick. I'll be seeing you." Rick said, "Good-bye, Jim. Good luck." Adamson said, "I forbid you to go, and I'm still senior officer." Whittaker answered, "And you're still wrong. As copilot, I'm second in command." He paddled away without further argument.

Rick was alone with Adamson and Bartek. The emotional stress of trying to keep the rafts together had worn Adamson out, and Bartek was very weak. The sharks followed them through a long night. The next morning was their twenty-first at sea. Rick dozed. He felt Bartek tugging at his arm and heard him say, "Captain, I hear planes!" Two patrol planes passed over but gave no sign of recognition, and flew on. In about thirty minutes, two other patrol planes passed directly over the raft. Rick waved the old fedora and saw one of the pilots wave back.

In less than an hour, a Catalina flying boat came back and stayed, circling. Rick kept waving his hat — for three hours, as he remembered it — using strength that came from the mysterious source of strength that keeps flowing after it should all be gone. It is not possible to improve on Rick's description of the final hour:

> Darkness was approaching. The plane kept circling. I kept waving. The pilot fired two flares, a white one and a red one. In the distance I saw lights blinking; the pilot had signalled a boat. Now that the boat had our bearings, the pilot came down and made a marvelous landing on the choppy sea. He taxied to within a few yards of us, and then shut off the engine. I paddled the raft to the plane and grabbed the pontoon. The radio man came down to give me a hand, then the pilot. They were the finest-looking young men I had ever seen.

When they got to the island, navy corpsmen carried Bartek and Rick on stretchers to the one-room hospital. Rick lay on his back and looked up at the moon shining through the tops of palm trees. They had already brought in Adamson; he lay with plasma tubes attached, and they added diabetes to his other troubles after a full examination on the following day. As to Rick and Bartek, their clothes fell apart when the medics started to undress them. There were sores on their legs and arms, which the doctors bathed in disinfectant. Soothing ointments helped to make them comfortable. The chief navy doctor said Rick could have two ounces of water every two hours. But later that night, Rick emptied the jug within one hour. It did him no harm and made him feel better. Then the burned and ulcerated places on his body began to make themselves felt through the analgesics in the salve. They hurt worse than they had when Rick was under the sun, but at last he went to sleep.

Meanwhile, planes had spotted the Cherry raft, and a PT-boat brought him in. Whittaker, De Angelis, and Reynolds had landed on a small island, and they too had been seen from the air and picked up. Whittaker had rowed the raft for seven and a half hours to reach shore, a remarkable feat for a man forty-one years old who had gone almost entirely without food and water for twenty-one days. Rick, eleven years older than Whittaker, had also paddled a raft with two passengers. Between them, they proved that stamina cannot be measured by age, and they brought to mind interesting speculations as to the nature of will and the power that comes from exercising it.

Cherry, Whittaker, De Angelis, and Reynolds came ashore the next morning from their rescue boats. When Whittaker saw Eddie, he said, "What's the matter? Have you been sick?" and Eddie held out his thin arms. They had shaved his beard, and his face was white and gaunt. He understood Whittaker's joke as an example of service humor. Whittaker said later that day, "I hope if I ever have to go through hell like that again, Eddie Rickenbacker or someone like him will be along."

By this time, the public at home had decided that Rick would never be seen again, so the headlines, like those in the Los Angeles *Times*, reflected excitement and joy: RICKENBACKER FOUND ALIVE! The words filled eight columns across the front page of an extra edition. Preachers and editorial writers immediately went to their desks to compose homilies, and, as details began to emerge, hundreds of folk artists sat down to write poetry about the events that had taken place in the Pacific.*

The navy considered the story its property and released the news in Washington, but General Hap Arnold was fast on his feet and immediately announced that he was sending a special plane to take Captain Eddie wherever he wanted to go. He hoped the public would forget that the air force had lost Rick and the navy had found him. All America felt that something fundamental and astounding had occurred. Even the writers of formal wire service stories let themselves go, and something that nobody ever thought to see came over the teletype out of Washington. This phenomenon was the appearance of editorializing in wire copy, when the main Associated Press story referred to Rick as "the country's embodied proof that you can't keep a good man down." The Boston *Globe* ran a picture of Rick with the caption "The Great Indestructible."

Other wire services also put opinion into news copy. Hearst International News referred to Rick as "the death-cheating pioneer of the world's airways." And the United Press called him "the man who always comes back" and "iron-man Eddie Rickenbacker." Rick was in Samoa when he read what was being said about him. The American newspapers got there only a few days late, and the Jenkins and Batchelor cartoons, which had run shortly after his disappearance, gave him an especially good feeling. It was like attending your own funeral and hearing good things said about you. Soon he had the pleasure of seeing Batchelor's picture of the floating wreath reprinted, with

---

*Grantland Rice was pleased to write another poem about his friend who

    . . . whipped the Pacific and shoved Death aside
As part of the job that he takes in his stride,
While grinning at Charon who knows how to pick —
So I'll stick with Rick.

"Beg pardon, Eddie" scrawled across it in the cartoonist's crayon. He also read that as soon as Adelaide got the news from Washington, she telephoned Mrs. Adamson and said, "They're found!"

Rick got a message through to Secretary Stimson, reporting that he was all right and would proceed on the mission to MacArthur as soon as possible. In two weeks, he regained twenty pounds and was up and around the island, looking at everything his hosts could find to show him. His diet had been large quantities of fruit juice, plus hearty meals at the officers' mess. The navy doctors thought Rick was a fine specimen for his age or any age. They marked Cherry, De Angelis, Whittaker, and Rick as fully recovered, though not yet back to desirable weights. Reynolds and Bartek were getting better, but Adamson remained a sick man. He was one year older than Rick, and, although he hadn't known it, was unfit for hazardous travel when he left Washington for Honolulu. The Pentagon was supposed to give thorough physical examinations to all War Department officers going overseas. How they managed to overlook Adamson's diabetes remains a mystery, but this man nearly died on Samoa. He got pneumonia, they gave him one of the sulfa drugs, he reacted badly, and they were about to give up when three blood transfusions saved him. It was obvious that Adamson couldn't go on with Rick, and the doctors did not want him to risk a trip back to ZI, or Zone of the Interior, as military language called the United States. So he stayed in a hospital bed on Samoa as Rick boarded a B-24 Liberator early on the morning of December 1, 1942, to complete his interrupted hop to Port Moresby.

Once again, Rick could stare down at the Pacific while he listened to the growl of four engines and became conscious of their basic rhythm. The main thing on his mind was the message he had to deliver by word of mouth to Dugout Doug. His recollections of MacArthur were unpleasant because of the

Billy Mitchell affair, and he knew that the words of Secretary Stimson, which Rick had orders to repeat, would put Mac-Arthur into a bad humor. Rick resolved not to say anything "derogatory or argumentative" on his own account. The plane snored on. During a stop, he was surprised to see a B-17 Flying Fortress drawn up, and to hear that MacArthur had sent it to bring Rick on the last lap. MacArthur had said that he couldn't allow Rick to make this last part of his flight in an unarmed plane. Perhaps the bristling guns of the B-17 were to impress Rick with the proximity of fighting to the Port Moresby headquarters.

When he got out at Port Moresby, Rick saw a group of officers marching toward him, with MacArthur himself in the lead. The tall general embraced the captain and pounded him on the back. Obviously, MacArthur wanted to forget the acrimony of the Mitchell hearings. MacArthur at that time had a peculiarly strained relationship with the front office in Washington. He had managed to make himself a symbol of future victory and had become a political figurehead, with many people fashioning a national bandwagon on which MacArthur might ride to the White House. This was why Stimson had closed the door and given Rick the secret message for Mac-Arthur's ears only. The message was simple enough: MacArthur was to ease up on personal publicity, stop complaining about the Joint Chiefs of Staff, and stop fighting with Admiral Chet Nimitz. Stimson knew Rick could be trusted to speak the piece and keep quiet afterward. An authority on MacArthur has deduced that the words were "stinging,"* as indeed they must have been.

MacArthur continued to treat Rick with respect, and told him he could go anywhere in the Southwest Pacific Theater. Rick had orders cut to take him back to Australia and then to

* D. Clayton James, *The Years of MacArthur*, vol. two, p. 859, note 39 (Boston, 1975).

Honolulu by way of the Solomon Islands and Guadalcanal, which was not declared secure until about a month after Rick's visit. He saw the slit trenches and foxholes that the ground crews had dug around the airstrips, and heard Japanese automatic weapons stuttering near enough to make him reflect on the consequences. Airfields were dug out of the jungle, and Rick said it made him nervous to see "young men with shiny wings" putting large planes down on those short, narrow, rough runways.

Almost six months of ground fighting had gone into the victory that was now being tidied up. Two marine divisions, two army divisions, and an additional army regiment had taken bad losses. The roughness of terrain added to the horror of it. "Godforsaken" was the term that came to mind when one examined the 1100 square miles of Guadalcanal, as Rick did from the air. He compared the living conditions with his experience in France. Squadron 94 had not been pampered, but the pilots had slept dry and had eaten decent food. On Guadalcanal, constant rainfall kept fliers and ground crews wallowing in mud day after day. Hideous parasitical creatures, including oversized leeches, flourished in the steamy swamps. Malaria knocked out many a man, and every week the breakbone fever struck a number of them into fits. Rick saw the problem as that of trying to wage modern technical warfare on a tropical island fit only for prehistoric forms of life. And if the air force had to live like this, the sufferings of the infantry must be indescribable.

At this time, one of the guiding ideas of Rick's later life began to take form. He wrote: "Suppose our civilian leaders back home, especially those men concerned with labor and war production, could be brought to this godforsaken spot to spend one day living the way our boys in uniform lived all the time. I bet things would soon be different back home." Rick talked to men on flight lines and discovered that their overwhelming desire was, not to leave the tropical swamp from which they were fighting, but to receive more supplies with which to fight. From this he developed the idea that not enough of these things were coming out of factories back home. Without going into the possibility that delivery to the front rather than production was at fault, Rick exculpated the leaders at home and began talking about workers in the factories.

Rick got back to Samoa on December 11 and took off two days later for Hawaii, with Adamson and Reynolds coming along as stretcher cases. Adamson's lung had been operated on for an abscess, and Reynolds was still thin and weak. They had their private doctor with them, a navy commander. This shows Rick's power. Men not associated with a celebrity who was also a vicar of Henry Stimson would have stayed on Samoa and received routine treatment with no frills. They arrived at Hickam Field on the 14th, and at Oakland on the following morning. He tried to telephone the East End Avenue apartment, but the operator told him the number was out of service. There had been so many calls from cranks and psychos, the family had put on an unlisted number. He managed to reach the apartment-house manager, and soon Adelaide's voice could be heard. Rick was overcome, and stammered that he hoped he would never again make her endure such an ordeal.

The doctors said Adamson should rest for twenty-four hours. During that time, Rick went to Los Angeles and saw his mother. Rick said, "It was a wonderful reunion, for Mother has always been the greatest inspiration of my life." Adamson felt better after his rest, and they got to Washington on the morning of December 19. General Hap Arnold came to the airport, escorting Adelaide, Dave, and Bill. There was something good in that scene for everybody, because all those present were genuinely glad to see Rick safe and sound. It went beyond symbolism and public relations to honest love for Captain Eddie.

The next thing Rick knew, he was in Secretary Stimson's office

for a press conference. One might have compared it to the
reception of the prodigal in the Bible, except that Rick had
wasted no substance. The most extraordinary part was that
Stimson said, "Captain Rickenbacker, the chair is yours." As the
swarm of reporters pressed around, Stimson moved aside, and
there was Rick, behind the official desk.

Photographers blazed away with flash bulbs, and reporters
applauded, which they seldom do. Then Rick told of hours
looking for the island, crashing on the ocean, scrambling to get
away, days and nights of suffering. He went on to tell how
Sergeant Alex had died and of the men's feeling that all
chances for survival had disappeared. Rick's low voice became
eloquent when he turned to the conclusions he had brought
back after three weeks afloat and his visit to Guadalcanal. He
spoke about his idea of the salutary effects that might come
from transferring the positions of combat soldiers and factory
workers, and presented his idea that production would be dou-
bled in thirty days. Rick's purpose was clear. He wished to state
that the average American at home was shirking and letting
down the boys at the front. This would be true if you took patriotism seriously and went by the book, but there was no way
to equate civilian life with combat on a tropical island. There
were pickings for all in the ZI, and, though the workers took
home good pay, the managers and government officials were
enjoying life as never before, relishing the excitement of struggling to meet production schedules, using the share of crowded
transportation reserved for them, making speeches, and finding zest even in the feel of wartime strain. National defense! By
now Rick had been a front-office man for so long that apparently he could not imagine how the world looked to factory
workers. And he was having such a splendid time as a special
emissary, at no financial profit to himself, that it did not occur
to him that he ought to criticize managers as well as working
folk.

On December 20, technicians ran a wire into 130 East End

Avenue, and Rick talked on a national network. He told those who listened that they should make more efforts to help win the war and that they could not imagine "the sacrifices our men were making on the battlefronts." Among those who heard the talk, some of Rick's admirers felt uncomfortable at his tone. This wasn't Captain Eddie at his best. His endurance on the Pacific had been admirable. But the average man and woman thought Rick had been in command of a bombing flight, when in fact his mission had had no combat significance, even though it endangered six crewmen and killed one. The sad part was that Rick had started reading his own publicity and, what was even sadder, had started to believe it.

Evidence of how Rick was beginning to see himself came in the Christmas letter for 1942. With unusual syntax in its opening sentence, he wrote:

My dear————,

With the coming of Yuletide, our Nation passed another milestone with its first year of all-out war, the consequences of which most of us are not aware . . . So while we are enjoying Christmas at home, let us not forget our loved and dear ones in the four corners of the world and share with them the spirit that makes us proud and glad of our heritage, trusting that 1943, or the not too distant future, will see them home again with us — happy for the privilege of having served.

To you and yours goes my wish for as happy a Holiday Season as the grim war will permit.

Sincerely,

In Shangri-La
No Signature possible
Dictated by E.V.R. before starting on his Pacific Mission.

Rick had planned an old-fashioned Christmas at East End Avenue. Then he would attack the work that was waiting at the office. He had speeches to make, interviews to give for magazines and newspapers, and the writing of the preliminary account of the Pacific adventure. Rick said that he had not only escaped the Grim Reaper, but had brought six others through. This was a good thought for Christmas Eve, but his rest at home ended when the telephone rang and he heard Helen Adamson speaking from Walter Reed Hospital. "Hans is dying." Rick seldom refused a sick call, and he answered, "I'll get there as fast as I can." He arrived at Walter Reed a few minutes before midnight. Hans Adamson was indeed in terrible shape. Rick talked to him for an hour and a half. As Rick saw himself, "The old tough Rickenbacker was gone. The boys on the raft would not have recognized me that night." He got back to his New York apartment at five in the morning. Later that day, he called the hospital and heard that Adamson was better and that vital signs now pointed to recovery. With his flair for dramatic structure, Rick remarked that "on Christmas day, the Pacific ordeal ended." He said that he was sure Alex was among friends in Heaven.

And there was no doubt that the country as a whole rejoiced to see Rick safe. The wave of affection that washed over him created an undertow like that which had carried MacArthur into political waters, for Rick also was soon being mentioned as a presidential candidate. Political experts who favored him included both Democrats and Republicans in Ohio, who sent word that they were ready to give him a start. In New York, he attracted the attention of a man who had specialized in popular journalism for many years. This was Captain Joseph Medill Patterson, founder and publisher of the *Daily News* tabloid. Patterson and his wife invited Rick to lunch and told him there was enough support among influential people to start a Rickenbacker-for-President drive. They urged him to get into the race immediately. Rick had opened his mouth to reply when the cartoonist C. D. Batchelor came into the publisher's dining room, carrying the original of the "So Long, Eddie" cartoon with its apologetic superscription. After thanking Batchelor for the drawing, Rick also thanked the Pattersons. He said they did him honor by thinking of him as a possible President of the United States. Then Rick adopted a businesslike tone and said, "You know I couldn't possibly win. I'm too controversial."

Controversy had developed around Rick in spite of the affection that people felt for him. Shortly after his return, he had acquired a champion who had influence throughout the Midwest, but stood in low esteem among the opinion-makers of the East. The advocate was Colonel Robert R. McCormick, editor and publisher of the mighty Chicago *Tribune* and Captain Patterson's cousin. Another cousin, Cissy Patterson, owned the Washington *Times-Herald,* and the three made war on Franklin Roosevelt, who was well able to defend himself. Rick looked especially good to the embattled publishers because Roosevelt disliked him.

McCormick had ordered a handsome obituary notice for Rick when it seemed that he was lost at sea. Written under the publisher's eye by managing editor J. L. Maloney, the article filled six galleys of type and was the longest newspaper notice to commemorate Rick's supposed death in the Pacific. Rick talked to McCormick and Maloney in the publisher's office, high in his tower above Michigan Avenue. They gave Rick a clipping of the obituary. Then McCormick turned the conversation to the future and discussed what Rick might accomplish in government and politics. The first thing would be to take a big war job. The publisher talked for an hour and a half, and Maloney observed that Rick's body had stiffened so during the long interview that he had to rub his legs before he could get up. Rick then hobbled to the door of McCormick's large and ornate office with the help of his cane, stamping his left foot on the floor as though not certain of the feeling in it.

Next day, the *Tribune* hit the streets with an editorial that recommended putting Rick in charge of American military and ci-

vilian aviation. Production, procurement, training and operation of the fighting forces, all were to be under Rick's
command. It was a good idea. Rick would have done well in
that job if it had been created. In his way, he was another Stimson. Like Stimson, Eddie had an impeccable record from the
war that had taken place when he was of fighting age; since
then, like Stimson, he had shown the combination of sincere
patriotism and common sense that was necessary to lead this
country in war.

The editorial might place Rick in the position once occupied
by Billy Mitchell. Mismanagement of aviation had become scan-
dalous; Rickenbacker was the man to put things right. With
recommendations like this appearing in print, the reaction was
such that the leaders in Washington decided Rick must be handled with care so that another MacArthur might not be conjured up. Here was where the controversy around Rick's public
position began to interest Stimson, Marshall, and Roosevelt.
Labor unions were now so powerful that their members could
speak out against a hero if they wanted to, and many did, while
Rick kept making his speech against workers who failed to appear every day on the assembly line, those absentees who were
letting down the boys on Guadalcanal.

By now, Rick was receiving hundreds of letters a week, and
as opposition to his remarks about workers in war plants began
to develop, many who wrote did not pay tribute to his patriotism. Others tried to say that they could not make up their
minds as to how they felt about Rick and his relation to things
in general. Such was the dilemma of a man who wrote:

> What in hell is going on anyway? Just who is behind this plan to
> get the War Department to keep sending you out on one hazard-
> ous journey after another until you finally get killed while super
> patriots like Phil Murray and Bill Green* dine at the White House
> cursing you and your kind and plotting ways to reap the windfalls

*Murray and Green were union chiefs.

of war. I'm a Catholic but I don't expect God or the Pope to protect me if I let someone else send me off on a jackass mission when my family needs me at home . . .

Talk had emanated from the White House about limiting wartime salaries or profits of executives to $25,000 a year. This was big money at the time, but Rick said he couldn't agree to government limitation on what a creative manager could make for himself. Rick thought of front-office people as superior to *Untermenschen* on assembly lines. But a workingman wrote to ask, "Why do you oppose overtime for working men and also oppose limiting the salary of bigshots to $25,000?"

Another union man made a direct attack, giving his opinion that

Just as soon as a man gets so big he loses the common touch, he goes into a tail spin . . . You have led a spectacular and most interesting life, and are here to tell the tale. Why be selfish, others would like to enjoy life too . . . You have gone completely out of your head, giving Stalin credit for being a good business man, because he pays the best wages to those who produce most.* Our former President, Herbert Hoover, who will go down in history as next to the worst we ever had, also shed bitter tears for the boys who were in the trenches during the last war, but I don't want anyone shedding crocodile tears for my boy, because I know that should he come out of it all right, and he went to Washington after the war, and you were President, you would probably kick him out the same as Hoover did.

Rick answered with a form letter that said he did not oppose honest union members and leaders, but could not condone racketeers who had insinuated themselves into the labor movement. As far as Russians were concerned, Rick explained that he wanted to recommend piecework with no time limit in

* Rick had expressed approval of the Stakhanovite system of encouraging "shock workers" in Soviet plants.

American plants making war supplies. This would result in higher wages.

Rick touched the emotions of people who opposed him in a way that caused some to descend to a level of controversy on which they belittled his Pacific ordeal. One of these wrote in December to call the raft flotilla "the best publicity stunt Steve Hannagan ever pulled." This letter was written in strokes of the pen that bit into the paper. And it was one that Rick decided not to answer. From his home state came a letter which showed that he had failed to make a friend. Writing from East Liverpool, Ohio, a man complained:

> Your sponsors, the American Manufacturers' Association and the U.S. Chamber of Commerce, can not lead we Americans down the road followed by France . . . I have seen wars start in America, and each one has been passed on to the poor devils that done the fighting. Damn few of those that benefit financially in our wars do much of the battling . . . You attack the workers in their various positions and think you are in a "fox hole." Your fox hole days are over . . . You spoke tonight of your humble origin. That's a part of we Americans. Most of us come from lowly parentage, and most of us change when *luck* comes our way. You did very suddenly. Yours was a fast rise in those racing cars. That's old stuff to those of us 50 or 60 years old . . .

The disturbing aspect of the letters from strangers was that so many of the critics seemed to have more sense than the givers of praise who attributed a mystic authority to Captain Rickenbacker. Some of the detractors talked like old-fashioned Americans and made observations that would be hard to refute if Rick had met them in formal debate. A woman wrote from Moline, Illinois:

> When you were lost at sea I felt very bad, and when the news came that you were found I was like the rest of the people overjoyed, but after reading what you had to say about time and a half

for overtime, I think the same as a lot of people, it's just too bad you didn't drowned.

I am the mother of four and number five is on its way my husband has been making very little it was between $25 and $30 a week, of course you don't know a thing about having to try to get along . . . My husband is now home sick and will lose a week or two, and that puts us back about 2 months, did you ever have to worry about Dr. hospital food bills and so on? No you always have enough, they talk about hoarding I couldn't if I wanted to we just live week to week . . . It's always the guy with money that can tell the poor what to do . . .

In spite of the erroneous accusation that Rick had never known poverty, the woman's hopeless anger carried the urgency of truth, for it recited the old story of poverty and bad luck. No matter how often Rick might say that he understood what it meant to be down and out, there would be such voices raised against him, crying that he didn't care what happened to his less-gifted fellow citizens who could not know the taste of personal victory or the joy of rising to the top.

Members of the Communist party identified themselves by the wooden style of their letters. One such writer hailed Rick with "Do be careful, old darling. It is so easy to do an injustice, to sow confusion, to slip up in orientation and coordination. Every last American of us has just been on his toes cheering your heroic American performance — don't make us gasp now at any blind spots . . . Do be careful, Eddie."

On May 1, 1943, the communists sponsored a rally at Yankee Stadium. When speakers mentioned Rick's name, the crowd groaned, and yelled "Boo-o-o . . ." as though an unpopular player had come to bat. Communist papers took up the chorus. It should be noted that the American press was picturing Josef Stalin as a jolly, pipe-smoking old chap, something like a favorite uncle. He had long been a hero with gullible American intellectuals, some of whom fancied themselves fellow travelers or close sympathizers of the Stalinist machine. Rick made no claims to being an intellectual, but he saw the resemblance of communism and fascism plainly enough. If Stalinists attacked him, he thought that showed he had the right enemies.

Although his opponents wrote in an emphatic manner, they were outnumbered by writers who commended Eddie for his rebuke of shirkers. The encouraging messages came mostly from middle America and the South. These letters often expressed belief that God had saved Rick so that he could carry on his work of warning and inspiring the country. Rick intended to reach as many Americans as he could by the sound of his voice at the forum of meetings and over the radio, drawing on the emotion of his patriotism and his personal charm to move listeners. To high officials, he would talk in confidence as a professional consultant. On this basis, he labored over a report on the Pacific mission that reached Stimson's desk on January 25, 1943. It contained a paragraph on logistics: "The ever changing technique in aerial warfare demands that engineers think in terms of designing artillery, automobiles, tractors and airplane parts with the idea of disassembling and reassembling them quickly for transport by air. The day will come when all cargo and weapons will be transported and will have to be by equally fast cargo planes to keep us with the combat planes in any maneuvers or moving from one place to another." Uneasy syntax obscured Rick's conclusion: land and air weapons should move together by air, heavy stuff to be broken into components for assembly near point of use. And nowadays, that is exactly how it's done. Stimson read the report and bucked it down the line.

Rick had already started improvement in the design of rafts. The finished product, called the Rickenbacker, carried two-way radio gear, adequate rations, and apparatus to distill sea water.

In the first three months of 1943, Rick spent two weeks resting at home. He divided the remaining time between reviewing

the condition of the airline, which had made a profit of
$1,886,000 in 1942, and touring the country to speak before
citizens' groups and at factories. It took courage to face workers in the plants. Against their hostility Rick started by proclaiming himself friend of all good working people. He had
nothing against unions; he dealt with them at the airline. He
respected labor and worked as hard as any man. Rick said that
what he detested was the racketeering element that had crept
in among union organizers. He would then proceed by means
of entertaining anecdote, and by the sincerity of emotions rec-
ollected from the Pacific disaster, to draw listeners close and establish the idea that they stood together in a crusade. The audiences seldom failed to respond by the time he had finished
speaking. Rick would then ask them to pledge "greater effort,"
which they promised with applause and cheers. Communist
strawbosses in the labor force never settled to a consistent line
on Rickenbacker. They wanted to belittle him as a member of
the American ruling class, but had no objection to his Stakhanovite recommendations for increasing war production, which
they hoped to see employed on a second front in Europe, as
Stalin was demanding.

Rick gave a comprehensive statement of his views on war
production at a gathering where one would not expect to hear
the discussion of serious subjects. He stated his ideas to
the banquet of the Baseball Writers Association, on February 3,
1943. On this annual occasion the writers wanted nothing more
than a jolly stag dinner, and for the address of the evening, a
talk by a humorous Tammany judge or witty Shepherd of the
Lambs suited them well. They were surprised but not offended
when after preliminary pleasantries, Rick began talking in a
serious tone. His point was that if we register men for military
service, we should also register everybody, women included,
for producing the materials of war. Records should be kept so
that no one would be able to escape making the proper con-

tribution. And, of course, this argued for undeniable higher authority in the government, and the end of individual choice as to wartime occupations.

Rick was not the only prominent American who thought we should see that everybody toed the mark. Eleanor Roosevelt had said all citizens should consider themselves under military command, and ways should be found to give them clear instructions on what to do. Opponents said Mrs. Roosevelt was interested in building a power base at the White House and that Rick wanted to weaken the unions by setting everyone, including returned soldiers, to compiling work records under government supervision. The two unlikely allies were very capable of defending themselves. Mrs. Roosevelt said nothing in the universe could be so important as the defeat of fascism, and Rick bristled in personal defense, giving the baseball writers the gist of what he repeated many times afterward:

> Yes, I know I have been accused of being the representative of the National Association of Manufacturers — the automobile industry — the America First Committee — and even accused of being a Fascist. Frankly and sincerely, I represent no person or persons — group or groups — color or creed — nor have I any political ambitions. I speak for myself alone, but echo the sentiments of millions.
>
> And again, I frankly state that I much prefer to break bread with Henry Ford — the Fisher Brothers — the K. T. Kellars of Chrysler — and the Charlie Ketterings of General Motors — for here are men who have come from the soil and given the world one of the greatest gifts humanity has ever received in history — *the automobile.*
>
> Yes, I would rather sit down with these men than with those who are living in the laps of luxury at the expense of the sweat and toil of millions of honest men and women.

Rick then said that racketeers fattening on union labor didn't declare their incomes for taxation and that Congress should do something about that. He went on to his usual disclaimer of any malice toward honest working people:

> I have been laboring for forty-odd years — since I was twelve years of age — in many lines of endeavor. I come from humble parents. I know the value of honest labor . . . For believe me when I say there is nothing under the sun that any of you have on the face of this globe that I want, and yet I pray that I may have another ten years of life with my physical and mental faculties — and only God can give me that.

The baseball reporters thought it was great. Here they had a man who could eat with Charlie Kettering or Henry Ford sharing their dinner and taking them into his confidence with a fighting speech. The belligerent close went over especially well. Rick liked the defiant sound of it and failed to detect the ungracious note of a man telling a group of listeners that not one of them possessed anything he would like to have. It was complacent, and in print appears to express a monstrous egotism. Here we meet the danger of oratory reduced to cold type as opposed to words as they are being spoken. Rick's face, the old underslung voice, the simple hand gestures, all were there to soften the severity of what he proposed.

Granting the importance of the war and admitting that sacrifices fall with unequal weight, one doubts that our condition would improve if an army of inspectors and petty officials began keeping records of what we did and did not do. And the probability is that Rick was not altogether serious in presenting this plan. He himself detested regulation and official persons sticking their noses into his affairs. He may have thought he and his high-ranking colleagues, the people he said he would always be glad to dine with, would not come under the authority of the omnipotent recorders. And sometimes one recommends drastic measures that cannot be adopted, simply to make a point, which may have been Rick's purpose when he electrified the baseball writers with this talk.

# CHAPTER VII

# Comrade Eddie

RICK VISITED STIMSON during the first week in April 1943, with a suggestion that called for thought. No one denied that the United States had a powerful ally in Soviet Russia, especially when it came to battling German armies on Russian soil. But the old-fashioned fair-play American of the Forrestal or Stimson type instinctively distrusted the Russians and their leader, Marshal Josef Stalin. And, indeed, his record was not such as would cause any intelligent person to repose confidence in him. Rick shared these views, and his talk with Stimson suggested a way to get information out of Russia by having Rick play his visiting-fireman role and use the freemasonry of aviators to gain the confidence of Russian fliers and obtain some first-class military intelligence.

The problem was how to get Rick into the Soviet Union. There was no use asking President Roosevelt to appoint him special envoy, for he would not give Rick an errand to run in Nicaragua, let alone the Soviet Union. Stimson might ask General Marshall to attach Rick to a military mission of some kind, but there again the White House would call a halt, for General Marshall reported to the President. And when it came to intelligence, Roosevelt had Averell Harriman and Harry Hopkins talking to Stalin; there were State Department people going in and out of Russia; and the White House was eager not to make Stalin any more suspicious than he already was.

Stimson and Rick started their private plan by setting up a mission of extraordinary scope. The old man pulled aside a curtain and showed Rick a map. He pointed out how one went down to the Miami airfield and proceeded by way of South America, Africa, and India to a secret base among abandoned tea plantations in the Assam Valley, against the Himalayan wall. The air force was preparing to reveal that planes of the Air Transport Command had succeeded in flying cargo over the mountains from Assam to Kunming. These "Hump" flights were to keep the war going until American engineers connected an 1100-mile feeder to the Burma Road. But when Stimson and Eddie looked at the map, what they saw was a way by the back door of China into the Union of Soviet Socialist Republics.

Once in China, Rick thought, he might be able to get permission to enter Soviet territory more easily than he could in Washington. This left unanswered the question of how to get an official welcome from the Russians, but Rick believed in doing one thing at a time. Stimson understood and said he would speak to the Secretary of State at the Cabinet meeting next morning. Rick was to wait in his hotel room for a call. A little after eleven, he heard Stimson on the line. The news was bad: Cordell Hull had said nothing could be done.

As he continued to look for a way into Russia, Rick thought of the lend-lease program. The head of lend-lease was a recruit from the United States Steel Corporation named Edward R. Stettinius, another of Eddie's old and good friends. Things began to fall into line. Stettinius told Rick he would be glad to help, but they must keep the White House in ignorance, and Secretary Stimson also must remain in the dark until Rick was ready to go. Stettinius was to make appointments for Rick to see two men, the Soviet ambassador and the chief Russian lend-lease official in this country. Meanwhile, Rick's passport would go to the State Department for validation to all countries on the ATC line. Rick said he was sure Stettinius had useful contacts at State. Could he perhaps arrange for someone to "just casually happen to stamp Soviet Union on the passport too." Ed Stettinius said, "I can handle it."

The Russian lend-lease man was Major General Alexander Ivanovich Belyaev, and he did his best to put on a cordial smile when Rick came into his office. Rick said he might be able to help the Russians "get the most out of American machinery." Belyaev told Rick he would send a cable at once to clear the way. The staff was expecting Rick when he got to the Russian embassy on Sixteenth Street just north of the Statler Hotel. Ambassador Maxim Maximovich Litvinov had survived to the age of sixty-seven in the top levels of Russian communist bureaucracy. This may have accounted for Litvinov's preoccupied expression when he greeted Rick and congratulated him on his escape from death in the Pacific. Rick said he wanted to help Russia in the war against Hitler by visiting air installations and talking to pilots and commanders. Litvinov said he'd cable Molotov right away and let Rick know in about a week. Rick got the impression that everything was already settled. He thought he caught this message in the way Litvinov looked at him. A theory of testing truth by ocular expression had fascinated Rick. He said he would start out any new acquaintance by looking his man right in the eye as they shook hands. "His handshake may be firm and his greeting may be warm," said Rick, "but if his eyes look away, fail to meet mine or even flicker momentarily I know that there is something wrong somewhere."

When Rick went to the Pentagon for his parting interview with Stimson, the old man gave him honest looks. He also gave Rick an oral message for General Joseph W. Stilwell, wherever he could be found in China, Burma, or India. This was another message so sensitive that it couldn't be written down. Stimson then handed Rick a letter that appointed him Special Consultant to the Secretary of War in North Africa, Europe, the Middle East, China, Burma, and India, the instructions ending with words that Rick mentally italicized: ".  .  . *and any other areas he may deem necessary.*"

Rick was sure that "other areas" meant Russia. And he thought General Hap Arnold had this in mind when he said, "You're taking a hell of a long trip over a hell of a lot of big country." There was something special in the way Arnold looked at him. The trip was to start from Miami on April 27. This time Rick had for military aide a brigadier general named William P. Nuckols. The rank of this traveling companion showed Rick's importance. And the party included Dr. Alexander Dahl, an Atlanta osteopath who came along to keep Rick's joints and muscles comfortable on the cramped flights. At Adelaide's suggestion, Rick laid in a supply of nylon stockings for wives of foreign officials. He also carried several dozen compacts, with supplies of face powder and lipstick. Knowing that children like to be remembered, he added $50.00 worth of chewing gum to his baggage. He also bought three dozen cases of vodka. Using Arnold's seals and authority, Rick had this baggage shipped by ATC to Cairo, where he was to take possession of a plane assigned for his personal use. It was to be a C-87 Liberator, modified for transport service, and there would be room for vodka, chewing gum, and nylon stockings in wholesale lots. Rick left Miami in a C-47 on April 27, made the Puerto Rico stop, and on the following day found himself grinding along over some inhospitable-looking country.

Crashing in this jungle would be worse than a crash at sea, which was not a comforting thought to Rick as they passed above the headwaters of the great gray Amazon River. When they got in at Belém, he sent a radiogram to Hap Arnold, urging immediate action to improve navigation across the Brazilian jungles. This made Rick feel better, for the hours of anxiety had tightened his nerves. He continued the improvement with a massage by Dr. Dahl and several drinks with rum in them at the officers' bar.

Rick flew another 1500 miles across the Sahara, which seemed even more forbidding to look at than the Brazilian wastes. Rick decided if he had to choose between another three weeks lost on the Pacific and three weeks on the desert, he'd take the ocean. The C-47 told Rick in its somber droning that it needed rest. The long flight wore Rick down, but he recovered his spirits at Marrakech, where he got a warm welcome and a chance to talk to enlisted men and ask them their problems.

Rick had the respectful treatment he was entitled to at Marrakech, but when he got out at Algiers the atmosphere was unpleasant. No general met the party on the tarmac. Instead, a colonel, a captain, and a sergeant appeared and greeted Rick in a distant manner. On the way into town, they were uncommunicative, but made it plain that Rick was under a cloud. This kind of rudeness could come only from the top, and Rick knew that Ike Eisenhower had psychic radar for measuring disapproval from above and protecting his flanks and rear. When he got to the outer office, Rick found Ike's chief of staff, Major General Walter Bedell "Beetle" Smith. He asked Rick for his papers. When he saw Stimson's chop he became friendly and told Rick the Old Man was having a haircut but to go on in. Rick entered Ike's office; the barber finished and backed out, bowing low. The scene that followed was so entertaining that Rick remembered its details long after. Ike strode across the room, took a piece of paper from his desk, and shook it in Rick's face. He barked, "What in hell does this mean?"

Rick said he'd like to read it before venturing an explanation. As he read, he saw that he had been right about Litvinov. The eye signal Rick received from the little Russian in Washington had been correct, for this message, care of Eisenhower for

Rickenbacker, said that Foreign Minister Molotov had approved Rick's request to visit Russia. For final arrangements Rick was to consult the Russian ambassador in Chungking.

Ike knew that anything connected with Russia was "sensitive," bureaucratic language for matters best left alone. And in his years of desk soldiery Ike had learned that one can never spot trouble too far ahead. He also knew that in spite of his unpopularity at the White House, this Rickenbacker had weight, and had to be handled with care. And here he was in Algiers, clearing through Ike's bailiwick for a trip into Russia. Suppose some foul-up should ensue? Marshall might ask Ike why he hadn't prevented it. His mouth tightened as he glared at Rick. He was bullying the wrong man. Rick gazed into Ike's eyes, where he saw weakness and lack of sincerity. He touched his lips in the "don't talk" gesture, and said, "That's a military secret." He thus managed to insult Ike and turn off discussion at the same time, for anywhere that military secrets have to be dealt with, the rule of need-to-know is unbreakable. At the time, Eisenhower was bucking for Supreme Commander, Allied Forces in Europe, but some people thought Marshall might take the job. Ike now modified his tone and asked Rick if there was anything he could do for him. Rick said there was a major in the Cairo intelligence section named Alden Sherry, and he would like that man attached to his mission. Ike stabbed at pushbuttons, and an aide came running like a faithful dog. Orders rolled from the mimeo machine ten minutes later.

Before leaving Algiers, Rick offered to assist the brass by talking to men on the flight lines. One of the enlisted men wrote home:

> Eddie in a traditional blue suit and gray fedora seemed wobbly on his feet and supported himself on the arms of two officers. But when he started to speak he gathered strength and proved to be a pretty fine talker. He ended with a joke, the kind the typical GI would go for. Its punchline was "The navigator hasn't found that

damn place yet." Outwardly he doesn't appear to be too strong
but inwardly he must have the stuff that counts today. We waited
for him at the hangar from 10 to 11:15 when his plane landed.
He said he was over the age limit, "being 29," and also had a
busted fanny. That brought a little laugh from the boys. Another
little episode that sort of made the boys go for Rickenbacker was
this. When he walked in with the general we were all lined up the
entire length of the hangar but as soon as Rick stepped up on the
platform he immediately called to the fellows to break ranks and
close in around him and sit on the floor and get comfortable. The
fellows didn't have to be told twice and they liked the democratic
idea behind it.

Another GI wrote:

By the way, Captain Eddie visited our camp the other day and
told us all about his recent escape. I think he is a very good
speaker . . . He looks a lot older than he was when I was home
. . . He told a story, one day along the Burma Road a soldier was
walking. Suddenly he spied a WAAC looking up and down the
road. She appeared to be searching for something. Stepping up to
her he asked, "What are you looking for?" And she without turning round replied "Mandalay." It sounded funny when he told it.

Major Sherry, an old comrade from Squadron 94, joined the
Rickenbacker mission at Constantine Air Base, some forty miles
east of Cairo. He was delighted to see his old commander. But
Captain Rickenbacker had a much more impressive military
suite than he had been able to assemble in the old days; now he
had a major general, a major, an osteopath, two commissioned
pilots, a radioman, and a chief mechanic in his train. When this
company boarded Rick's Liberator in Cairo, along with his
baggage, which included the vodka, nylon stockings, chewing
gum, and lipsticks, the effect was sensational. Before leaving,
he dined with Ambassador "Pat" Hurley, an Oklahoma oil millionaire who had been Secretary of War for President Hoover.
Hurley tried to figure out what Rick was up to. After a few

drinks he thought he had it. He saw it all clearly: Rick intended to run for President in 1944. Rick said it was out of the question, but Hurley thought he was being coy. Then it came out that Hurley wanted to get on the ticket and become vice president. Rick made it clear that he could not take Pat Hurley seriously, and on this note, their meeting ended.

The Rickenbacker plane made its first stop at Abadan, on the Persian Gulf. Here was the assembly plant for lend-lease airplanes going into Russia. Temperature rose to 130° Fahrenheit at midday, no work was possible between 7:00 A.M, and 3:00 P.M., the plant was undermanned, and morale low. Rick reported the trouble to Washington and went on. He came down in Karachi on May 21.

Rick postponed his entry into China long enough to visit fighter squadrons in the Brahmaputra Valley. These men protected the new ATC airlift over the mountains into Kunming. Successors to the mercenary force known as the Flying Tigers, they were picturesque and were given to drinking Chinese gin and wearing Australian hats.

In a few days, Rick got to an airfield of the ATC's India-China Wing and put himself in the hands of a Hump pilot and crew. The Liberator stayed at Dum-Dum Airport, in Calcutta; it would come along later with Rick's special supplies. Before taking off for China, Rick visited the flight lines, as he always did at an air installation. He found pilots and mechanics in a discouraged frame of mind. Twenty-six planes had recently piled into the Hump; men were breaking down under the pressure of schedules that took crews from India to China and back on the same day. Living conditions were bad. Constant rain, mud, and heat made the Assam Valley unlivable except for creatures like the small, delicately colored krait, a poisonous snake that sometimes appeared underfoot. It was said that its venom killed as fast as a bullet. A cobra invaded a pilot's tent, and he killed it with a golf club. He had come directly from the

ZI, bringing his clubs, under the impression that he was going to pull duty like that of a pilot on the New York–Miami run. Rick saw a pile of dust in the road at Sookerating and then realized it was a dead jackal.

At that time there was a high road and low road by air from India to China. High-flying passengers and crews wore parachutes all the way over and hooked up oxygen masks half an hour out. The low road went down valleys, flying on the deck so that Japanese fighters would not have room to pull up after diving in their attack. Rick went the high way, and on the approach to Kunming thought the plane was going to ram a mud-walled village at the end of the airfield. This was standard procedure; the pilots skimmed roofs and touched ground. There appeared to be a number of fighter planes parked around the field, but on looking closely, Rick saw that they were wooden mockups, set out to deceive Japanese air raiders. Some of the mock fighters had begun to fall apart and looked like dead gamecocks. The atmosphere of Kunming was different from that of the Indian supply bases. Coolies chattered and laughed as they unloaded freight, and they appeared to have a wiry strength that Indian workmen did not possess. Kunming was a lively commercial city of 300,000, where illegitimate trading in war supplies went on. Rick saw what inflation could do to a medium of exchange. Rupee silver would buy Chinese banknotes in cartloads, and part of the freight the ATC brought in was paper money. The bulging canvas sacks of notes, engraved in Philadelphia, would carpet the decks so that many a passenger got a comfortable nap on a bed of them. It was not the first time Rick had watched the value of money disappear while the amount of it rose beyond calculation. He had seen the same thing destroy Germany. In each instance, Rick observed that the people were short of everything but money.

Rick had two men to see in China. One was the Russian ambassador, and the other was General Stilwell, both presumably to be found in Chungking, the wartime capital, 400 miles northwest of Kunming. Much of the wild mountainous terrain was unmapped, and the maps that existed were inaccurate. This was the sort of flight on which everyone was quiet and thoughtful. Rick watched the empty landscape or dozed while the engines droned. But when the plane lowered for Chungking, Rick was startled to see what it was supposed to land on. Nine Dragons Airport was sliced into a steep hillside at the juncture of the Kialing and Yangtze rivers, and it appeared that the pilot was flying sideways to get in. On the ground it was the least elaborate ATC installation that Rick had encountered. There was nothing but a corrugated-iron operations shack and a bamboo latrine that displayed a picture of Frank Sinatra.

As the jeep carried Rick into Chungking, he saw a sprawling, mud-colored city of cobblestone streets and narrow alleys. The population had increased from 300,000 to around a million because of the war, and blue-clad people crowded every corner. Rick saw many terraces cut into hillsides, like Nine Dragons Airport, with caves marked as air-raid shelters. He put up at the ATC visitors' hotel and began to make arrangements to wait on the Russian ambassador. Those people did business in such an extraordinary way that he might expect to see his man immediately, or in a week or a month, or not at all. Rick went first to sign in at the American embassy, and found out through eye language that the people there feared he would be an embarrassment and hoped he would soon leave Chungking. The alarm about Rick had sounded the week before, when the Russian ambassador had asked the Americans how soon he could expect Captain Rickenbacker. Rick now said, "Any time at his convenience." Next morning, he was seated at A. S. Paniushkin's desk.

These Russian bureaucrats might have been stamped out with cookie-cutter. Paniushkin was another Litvinov. He said

Rick was welcome to go on to Tehran, where Russian authorities would take care of the next step. Paniushkin signed the papers and bowed Rick out with compliments. Rick thought the Russians might intend to use him as a funnel for some kind of Muscovite deception aimed at Washington, and decided to be more than ever on his guard.

What Rick wanted to do now was visit General Stilwell and deliver the oral message. Stilwell had a vast territory under his command and was constantly on the move between Chungking, Delhi, Calcutta, and Kandy, on the island of Ceylon, where Admiral the Lord Louis Mountbatten led the British in frustrating American plans, as Stilwell saw it. Our other enemy, in addition to the Japanese, according to "Vinegar Joe" Stilwell, was Generalissimo Chiang Kai-shek. Having missed his man in Chungking, Rick learned the best chance of an interview would be at rear-echelon headquarters in New Delhi, where Stilwell sometimes put down as he went back and forth. Rick celebrated his departure from Chungking by taking tea with a famous lady, the widow of Dr. Sun Yat-sen, the revolutionary hero.

Madame Sun had been born Ch'ing-ling Soong, daughter of a rich Cantonese merchant. Her sister Mei-ling had married Chiang Kai-shek. At the time of Rick's visit, Chiang was piling up American supplies for war with Chinese communists after the defeat of the Japanese, and it was this policy that had earned Stilwell's disapproval. Those in a position to know said Madame Sun was more in sympathy with the communists, who had withdrawn to North China, than with her sister and brother-in-law, who ruled the rest of the country from Chungking. When Rick came to Madame Sun's residence, a sizable villa behind high walls, he found a guardhouse at the gate and a squad of Chinese policemen on duty. Madame Sun invited him to escort her to a cocktail party at the Russian embassy. Here the Russians made much of Rick and Ch'ing-ling Soong Sun. On the following day he boarded the plane for India, reflecting that he had enjoyed social success with the unpredictable Russians while completing his plans to enter their country.

On the flight back to India from Kunming, the air force carried Rick in an armed transport. The plane approached a Japanese airfield where the gorge of the Salween River forms the Burma frontier. As he passed over the enemy base, Rick went aft and hosed them down with a burst of .50-caliber bullets. Since Rick was a civilian, his firing broke the Geneva Convention, but nobody seemed to care. Perhaps Rick did some damage, for those heavy bullets would fall hard. He had dropped several pounds of lead from 19,000 feet.

Rick and General Stilwell shared an early breakfast in New Delhi and talked for two hours. Although Stilwell was an unforgettable character, Rick recorded little about him, for Russia occupied his mind and he wanted to be on his way. Stilwell was sixty years old, and certainly looked no younger, for his skin was yellow from Atabrine, which he took to hold the symptoms of malaria in abeyance, and his wiry frame carried no extra pounds. "Grim, gray, skeleton-thin," was the way *Time* had described Joseph Warren Stilwell when he marched out of Burma after his Chinese divisions failed to halt the Japanese. In style, he was the direct opposite of MacArthur. Rick delivered the secret message, of which the gravamen was that Stilwell should hold on and do his best to get along with Mountbatten and Chiang, and that an able officer named George E. Stratemeyer was on his way to take over the Tenth Air Force and act as Stilwell's deputy. And Vinegar Joe's promotion to four-star general was in the works. Then the bad news — a full-scale offensive against the Japanese was not in present plans. Stilwell wrote in his memoirs that "the War Department let me down on that."* They parted at Dum-Dum Airport, Stilwell leaving for China, Rick for Tehran.

The converted Liberator, which had flown in from Calcutta,

---

*Stilwell got his campaign in 1944, but was recalled before its conclusion and the reopening of the Burma Road.

got an early start from Karachi, crossed mountains to the northwest and trundled on over the ancient Persian plateau. Rick felt that he was again recognized as a person of importance, for General Don Connolly, of the Persian Gulf Command, welcomed him at Tehran Airport and insisted that he stay at the luxurious headquarters villa, where service in the bar began at breakfast time and continued as long as anyone felt the need of it. General Connolly was riding high, although the British disliked him and the spies of several nations did a continuing cash business with servants in his house.

Connolly behaved like a benevolent conqueror. The reason for his imperial attitude was that the Persian Gulf Command had achieved phenomenal success. It was a supply outfit and a triumph in the age of American know-how. They had built rail and motor roads from the Caspian Sea to the Persian Gulf, and Connolly had a right to be proud of what his 40,000 men had accomplished. It was all for the U.S.S.R., but who would count costs when Russians were chewing up German armies that might have fought Americans and British at a later date?

The atmosphere at Connolly's house was stimulating, with the gratifying excitement of objectives gained in spite of formidable handicaps. There were interesting people there. Rick met the eminent American writer Joel Sayre, representing *The New Yorker* on a visit to the Gulf Command. They had an immediate bond of sympathy, although they were meeting for the first time, because both were natives of Columbus. Also, Sayre had written *Gunga Din,* one of Rick's favorite movies. Joel Sayre recalled, "I found Rick immensely likable. He was an outstanding personality, but he handled himself so well that he was not in the least overbearing. Indeed, he was good company." Rick enjoyed several parties at Connolly's villa, and at one of them he fell into conversation with the Turkish ambassador, a squat, pillowy person who looked like a villain in an Alfred Hitchcock movie. The Turk said, "Captain Eddie, can you tell me what your country would like to have my country do?" Rick said, "We need airbases, how about it?" The ambassador asked if there was anything else. "Nothing you could furnish, Mr. Ambassador," Rick said, "but we also need bases in eastern Siberia. We could bomb hell out of Japan from there." The chancelleries of Tehran had reports of this talk by morning, and a version of it also went to Washington.

On that same morning, July 19, the Liberator left Tehran for Astrakhan, where the Volga flows into the Caspian Sea. Rick and his party were now proceeding under hazard. The pilot had an identifying code name and number, which he would announce if he saw Russian fighters in his path. Rick did not worry about that, for he had developed his theory that the Russians were going to try to make him a conduit for false information. So they weren't going to shoot him on the way in. The C-87 stayed on course and landed at Kuibyshev.

When the account of Rick's conversation with the Turkish ambassador reached Washington, it gave Mr. Stimson a shock. The report could have hurt him by weakening the air of infallibility with which he had kept Marshall in line and Roosevelt at bay. Stimson could well envision hostile empires springing up in the Pentagon itself, where Marshall had subordinates to do his bidding. Rick had committed a diplomatic crime. Also, there was one thing wrong with the report on Stimson's desk. It was partly untrue. Rick became aware of this when he read Stimson's Message Number 658, which was waiting for him at Kuibyshev: AMERICAN AMBASSADOR AT TEHRAN SAYS YOU AND BRITISH MINISTER CALLED AT TURK EMBASSY AND SAID YOU HAD MISSION FROM PRESIDENT UNITED STATES ASK TURKS MAKE AVAILABLE AIRBASES FOR USE AGAINST BALKAN BASES OF THE AXIS ALSO THAT YOU WOULD ASK STALIN TO SUPPLY BASES IN SIBERIA IS THIS CORRECT DONT GO TO RUSSIA OR TURKEY AND IF YOU ARE IN RUSSIA RETURN TO TEHRAN IMMEDIATELY AND WAIT INSTRUCTIONS THERE.

It looked to Rick as though Stimson had let him down. Could this be the man who had shown him the map and sent him on the mission? Eddie had it in writing: ". . . and any other areas he may deem necessary." Now it appeared that Stimson was trying to make Eddie look like an irresponsible fool. He immediately answered: HAVE FOLLOWED TO LETTER ALL INSTRUCTIONS ALL I WANT TO SEE IN RUSSIA IS THE DEPOT WHERE AMERICAN PLANES ARE BEING ASSEMBLED AND ENGINE PLANT WHERE AMERICAN ENGINES ARE BEING MANUFACTURED. This was Rick's Message Number 253, which drew Stimson's Number 664 in reply, still denunciatory in tone. After references to "possible complications" and "sensitive matters," Number 664 continued, STAY OUT OF TURKEY . . . DON'T TALK TO BRITISH TURKS OR RUSSIANS AND DON'T GET INTO POLITICS . . . I STILL SAY YOUR SERVICES ARE VALUABLE AND YOU HAVE STIMULATED MORALE OF AIR UNITS . . .

On the following day Stimson admonished Rick again. His message said, INSPECTION OF US ARMY ACTIVITIES ONLY WAS INCLUDED IN MISSION ENTRUSTED TO YOU SINCE I SPECIFICALLY REFUSED YOUR REQUEST TO VISIT RUSSIA I AM AT A LOSS TO UNDERSTAND WHY YOU WENT TO THAT COUNTRY. Stimson repeated the warnings about unauthorized talk, in words that made it appear he was addressing people other than Rick. Copies of the messages would go to Stimson's rivals in Washington and would also reach the Russians in Moscow. This meant that, although he was indignant at Rick's diplomatic indiscretion, Stimson had seized the chance to cover himself from flank and rear attacks at home while giving Rick stature with the Russians as a man in trouble with the American high command, their enemy. Rick ended the flurry of rebuke and reply by informing Stimson that he planned to visit the two or three Russian squadrons that were using American equipment, and then start home, about June 29.

He was a celebrity even in Moscow, where everybody took

pride in not being impressed by foreigners. The official news agency carried the story of his arrival, and the Stateside papers featured it. The American public took it as a gesture of friendship from the United States to our Soviet allies, but American communist publications were surly about Rick's trip. They had finally decided he was a capitalist oppressor. Litvinov had returned to Moscow, and he invited Rick to lunch with Foreign Minister Molotov and Marshal Georgi Zhukov, who was Army Chief of Staff.

Rick found himself at table in a splendid room large enough for 200 people. They had a great lunch, served on gold plates, but his three companions were grim until they got down a few shots of vodka. Rick could not understand why the top Russian officials weren't vodka-simple, the way they lapped the stuff. He made an effort not to relax as the potations he took, at the urging of his hosts, made themselves felt in his brain. What they didn't know at the lunch table was that Rick, as one of the leading drinkers of his generation, could take in a lot of alcohol and still control his tongue.

Litvinov acted as interpreter and opened serious conversation by saying to Rick, "The Foreign Minister would like to know what you wish to see during your visit." Rick's memory was that he asked to see "several different types of war production plants, including aviation, to see the defenses of Moscow and to talk with both the commanding officers and pilots flying the planes, and to visit the front — figuring that if I did only a percentage of these things I would be fortunate." Scribbling like a grocer, Litvinov put down Rick's reply on a pad, translating aloud for Zhukov and Molotov as he wrote. Rick was watching them all the time. They might try to veil their expressions, but they couldn't fool Rick. Molotov had one question: "Does the Captain have his own interpreter?" Rick said he would prefer to have the Russians supply the interpreter, and that a young man who was a pilot and also knew engineering would do nicely. Here was where Rick spotted a flash in Molotov's eyes. It meant he had made his sale. Molotov started to talk Russian, and Litvinov translated that the Foreign Minister saw possibilities in what Rick had asked, and would look into it. The meeting broke up then, and Rick was sure his willingness to let the Russians appoint his interpreter had turned the trick.

He felt so good about the outcome of the luncheon that he loaded a jeep with American cigarettes and four cases of vodka, and drove to the Metropole Hotel, where correspondents could always be found. They had a good time and the newsmen told Rick how hard it was to see anything in Russia other than official sights. He enjoyed the feeling that he could tell them something about this if he cared to, but the vodka had not started acting as truth serum, and he played dumb. When he went to his quarters he received a State Department message addressed to Tehran, telling him to stay there. As a general thing, people in the field paid no attention to State, for the department could not enforce military orders. Rick was a civilian anyhow, and the only way to get at him would be to have Arnold pull his transportation, which was not likely to happen. He therefore filed the department's message for his archives, and sat down to await word from the Foreign Office, which came later in the evening. They expected him at air force headquarters early on the following day.

At the appointed time Rick met his interpreter, a Captain Smolazov, who appeared to fulfill Rick's specifications to the letter. Rick also acquired an escort from the secret police, a colonel who looked like Mack Swain in the old Chaplin comedies — very large, with an expression so menacing it was hard to take him seriously. But Rick saw that other people were afraid of this uniformed ruffian. The police agent said he couldn't understand English, but Rick's ability to read eyes showed that the fellow needed no interpreter. Rick didn't let the colonel bother him; he asked to start the trip by visiting the command post of Moscow Air Command. It was far underground and they reached it through a winding tunnel. When they got to the operations room, Smolazov started to introduce Rick to the ranking officer on duty. But old and good friends of Eddie Rickenbacker turned up everywhere, even in the bowels of Russian earth. The Russian commander grasped Rick in a bear hug, crying, "Eddie! Where did you come from?" He had been one of the pilots of the Russian North Pole expedition in 1937 whom Rick had entertained at New York. Rick's note on the incredible meeting was "Now here was the commander of one of the most sensitive military operations in Russia, pounding me on the back and pumping my hand. I couldn't have asked for a better stamp of approval."

Rick's old friend Andrei Youmachev was now a general and seemed eager to show off the forces under his command. He pointed to a wall map so that Rick could see where the bases around Moscow were to be found, then called for a car. The air defense of Moscow was set up in three circles, and on the outer circle the pilots stood two-hour watches, sitting in their planes with engines running, ready to go. On the next circle they fired up the engines every hour, and the pilots sat in the planes. On the inner circle they fired engines every two hours, and the pilots waited in tents, drinking black tea and smoking cigarettes that smelled like trash burning on a city dump. They had never heard of Rick or his exploits in the first war, but took him to be a person of importance because he was with their general. On the whole, they seemed to have the intelligence of trained baboons, which was all they needed.

Next, Youmachev took Eddie to see a number of antiaircraft installations. There was no vodka in evidence, but the same gallons of black tea, drunk in glasses, and the fuming cigarettes that made American visitors look around for gas masks. Rick had no instructions to give the ground gunners, but he soon had Smolazov busy passing on advice to pilots. The men had mastered their American planes by the trial-and-error method. Rick noted that he "was able to give them a great deal of information that I had gathered in my previous missions, that would enable them to improve their handling of these planes." He thought both pilots and engineers could see these suggestions were valuable to the Russian air force.

Moscow summers are chilly, and Rick was glad to get lunch in the well-heated underground staff mess. The police colonel appeared and began to challenge Rick to empty his glass at each toast instead of taking only a sip. Rick saw that if he didn't drink bottoms-up, he would lose face; drinking hard, he might begin to talk too much and harm his prospects of seeing more of the air force attack and defense. He gathered mental and emotional forces to fight the alcohol. He thought he might keep it out of his bloodstream by psychic effort. They kept drinking until Rick was almost over the edge, but he clung to control, and on the completion of the seventh toast in full glasses the colonel slid under the table. The pilots surprised Rick with cheering and back-slapping; evidently they didn't like the colonel either. Rick walked to the car with Smolazov at his side; two girls came up and handed him bouquets of fresh flowers. He greeted the American ambassador, Admiral William H. Standley, at the American embassy with a bouquet in each hand.

Rick's powers of recuperation held up, so he started out with Smolazov on the following day and acquired an important item of military intelligence, which got quick delivery to Washington by diplomatic pouch. He heard Soviet fliers talking about the Germans in immediate opposition to them. The quality of these enemy pilots was falling off. They were not to be compared with the experienced fighters who had first invaded Russia. And it was known that these good fliers hadn't all been killed in battle; only a small percentage had been shot down. The only thing this could mean was that the Germans were withdrawing their most effective pilots to fight the British and Americans in Europe. Rick made a mental note to tell Hap Arnold to take immediate measures to make pilot training tougher, because our men would be dueling with Germans who had learned their trade in Poland and taken the graduate course in Russia. Any second-raters that Arnold sent up would soon be dead.

The question of Russian grand strategy was momentous. Lend-lease had to have a limit, and if the Germans started to break the Russians, and we found out in time that disaster was on the way, we could use those supplies elsewhere. The arming of Germans with captured American weapons was an unwelcome thought. It was worth finding out, if anyone could, where the Russians planned to fight. Rick put the question to Marshal Zhukov, asking if his people knew when the Germans were coming and what they intended doing about it. Zhukov answered, "They're coming soon, Comrade Eddie. They will circle and attack from the south." Rick concealed his excitement and asked again, "And what will you do?" Zhukov said in a matter-of-fact way, "We'll tear them to pieces." Rick could tell by the look in Zhukov's eyes that he wasn't lying.

Rick's charm was effective with most of the Russians he met. And he would reinforce his engaging qualities by handing out stockings or cigarettes. Rick also carried among his trade goods a few wrist watches of complicated design. They were the sort that had extra hands, dials, knobs, and warranties that they would continue to run while under water or frozen in ice. Watches of this kind had special fascination for airmen. It happened that Rick was grateful to an especially helpful captain in the Russian air force and wanted to make him a present. One of the watches would be right for this man. Rick would have to get the watch to him without anyone's becoming aware of the gift. But Rick's ingenuity was equal to the task. He waited until the captain left the plane after acting as pilot for the day's run, slipped the watch under the left-hand seat in the cockpit, and then said, "I think the pilot's seat needs adjusting." The captain went alone into the cockpit, and when he returned, he gave Rick a nod and an almost imperceptible wink. Rick's moment of satisfaction was as great as if he had outwitted the entire Soviet Union.

Shortly afterward, Rick had supper with some air force generals, who confirmed what Zhukov had said. Rick asked them why they confided in him. Their answer was simple: "We like you, Eddie." Next day, Rick got word that he would be welcome 200 miles south of Moscow in the sector around the city of Orel, an industrial center recently recaptured from the Germans, who had taken it in 1941. When Rick and Smolazov got to the airfield, the commander told him five Yak fighters would escort him to the front. Rick said they shouldn't burn gasoline just to give him an escort. The Russian said he had his orders, and if "anything happened" to Rick, bad things would also happen to the commander. On seeing the battered old Dakota (DC-3) they were to fly in, Rick thought enemy action was by no means the only danger he had to face, but was too polite to mention it. The pilot took off in the usual Russian manner, without warming up the engines. He simply turned them on and pushed throttle until the nose came up before he used the last of his runway. And he racked it up on one wing close to the ground as he turned to get on course. Rick gave a silent prayer of thanks for "the world's kindest and most forgiving airplane."

Like India-China pilots taking the low road from Chabua to Kunming, they flew on the deck and landed at a field where the Douglas A-20 was in use. Rick talked to maintenance men and pilots, then went to another field and, as he put it, repeated the performance. They then went to lunch, and Rick saw vodka bottles on the sideboard. It relieved his mind when he found that the hosts were not going to challenge him to a drinking contest. A friendly dram was fine with Rick, and an exchange of toasts always warmed the social atmosphere.

Soon the Russians began talking about the German enemy. They said the Germans had come against them with 2700 fighter planes when the battle began. This was close to the first figure Rick had heard, and he paid careful attention to the Russians as their liquor began taking hold of them. One of the generals made an extraordinary admission. He told Rick they had 3000 fighter planes on their side and were barely holding their own against fewer than 2000 Germans. The general tilted the vodka jug and said that even this second team of the enemy was good. His talk was far from the usual Russian boasting, for when a military man of this type praises the enemy, he may well be preparing the way to admit defeat. The conversation riveted itself in Rick's memory because of the alleged number of the enemy. And again Rick began mentally composing a message to General Arnold, to emphasize once more that serious combat training for young American pilots was a matter of their life and death.

Rick stayed at the front that night and enjoyed the singing and dancing of a Cossack troupe. They gave their last yells and leaps at two o'clock in the morning. Then Rick went with Smolazov to sleeping quarters in a barn, which was all that remained of a tidy farmstead in the path of war. But it was far from dreary or uncomfortable. There were two cots with fresh sheets, and a woman soldier served a late supper at a candlelit table.

Rick had received approval from the sector commander, Major General I. D. Antoshkin, who ordered that he should have access to ground troops as well as fliers. Accordingly, Rick spent the following day looking at tanks, artillery, and infantry. He got back to the cosy barn after dark and found his cot most welcome. Late at night he woke from a dream that an earthquake was taking place, to hear the thunder of guns. He peered out and saw the fireworks display of an artillery duel. Rick and Smolazov ran to the underground headquarters' bunker and found General Antoshkin in the war room. He told Rick the Germans had launched a serious attack. His plan was to hit back immediately, but the battle was less than five miles away. If the Germans got through, it would take them only a few minutes to reach Antoshkin's headquarters.

The danger stimulated Rick's great power of concentration. He needed concentration, for he saw in front of him one of the finest prizes an American intelligence agent could desire, the war map of the Russian line. It was under a plastic sheet on the wall, with bright lights above it. Staff officers were tracing current activities in grease pencil and moving the markers that indicated regiments, battalions, and guns. Rick "stood there, trying to look casual, and memorized the map." Antoshkin's army held.

Next day, Rick and his interpreter got back to Moscow, and he called on Ambassador Standley in his office. Rick said, "I have the Russian order of battle." Standley began yelling and secretaries answered on the jump. Rick walked up and down and dictated what he had seen on the situation map. When he had finished, Standley said, "This is the biggest intelligence coup we have ever scored on the Russians. Eddie, you must take off for Tehran right now and deliver it to Eisenhower." Rick asked him to hold hard. He said, "That would be suicide. I'd never get there." It was one thing for Russians to give toasts and bring out dancing Cossacks, but something entirely different for them to stop being suspicious of a foreigner.

Rick had experienced social success and had established sympathy through the common language of airmen. But out there at combat headquarters, General Antoshkin was probably smiting his forehead even now and asking himself why he had allowed Rickenbacker to stand in front of the map and read its military symbols. Attached to the general's command was a political commissar, who would be happy to report a breech of security. This was not sensationalism on Rick's part; it was his usual common sense. When it came to putting unlimited trust in strangers, Rick had a vein of old-country shrewdness not unlike that in his Russian hosts. Standley saw the point and gave orders that Rick's eyewitness report should go to Tehran at once in a diplomatic pouch that the Russians couldn't pry into. It would go on to Washington by the same method.

In a few days the remodeled Liberator took off, lighter by vodka, stockings, and chewing gum. The plane had a Soviet navigator, supposedly to keep it clear of antiaircraft batteries. But Rick knew that the Soviets would not hesitate to kill one navigator if they decided to blow up the plane. He had poked his nose into more military operations, he felt sure, than any foreigner had yet been allowed to see. If anyone thought better of it at the last moment, this airplane would never land in one piece.

Twenty miles from Moscow, Rick saw something that might mean his life was coming to a close. Number Three engine was throwing oil, which flowed like arterial blood along the wing. Rick shouted, "Head back!" The pilot racked up the heavy plane and pulled it on a line for Moscow. Things felt different on the ground, with smiling faces welcoming Comrade Eddie. "So you couldn't bear to leave us?" the officers asked at lunch, after mechanics had pronounced the engine totally ruined. Then Rick went to the American embassy, where he heard it would take a long time to get another engine — three months, perhaps six. Rick dispatched General Nuckols to Cairo for a replacement from the cannibal yards of broken planes that the U.S. Air Force maintained there. Before he could sit down to catch his breath, Rick got word that his clearance to visit the Stormovik aircraft factory had come through.

Rick's call at the Stormovik plant began with an incident similar to his meeting with Andrei Youmachev. This time it was the other Russian North Pole pilot who cried "Eddie!" for Mikhail Gromov also had enjoyed Rick's hospitality in 1937. Now he was chief test pilot of the Stormovik plant. As he whirled Rick around like the dancing Cossacks, underlings brought little tables, on which they set out vodka, biscuits, and caviar. Gromov introduced the plant superintendent, who explained that he had no trouble with absenteeism. Those who did not deliver enough work lost their jobs, and unemployed Russians had been known to starve. Rick understood him to say that working people went at it eleven hours a day, six days a week. What interested Rick most was the system of piecework, which rewarded the stronger ones with better food and lodgings. Rick asked himself, "What kind of Communism is that?" He noted also that "the Communists we had in America would have been most disagreeably surprised to realize the true state of affairs, and as for the Russians themselves the feeling was mutual. Many of those with whom I talked spoke in contemptuous terms of our party members."

Rick then went around the plant and saw them building the Stormovik monoplane, a low-winged armored machine that carried rockets and cannon which could penetrate the hide of a German Tiger tank. He learned the Russian technique of fighting tanks from the air. The secret was stopping them behind the lines, somewhat as he had hunted *Drachen* in France. Stormoviks would surprise their enemies while the tanks were still getting into formation like a hive of insects preparing to forage in a pantry. The Russian flying cannoneers would come on the deck, moving too fast for ground fire to track them, and disintegrate the tank swarm for that day.

On the following morning, General Nuckols announced that he had found a Liberator engine, and mechanics were installing it at the airport. Rick thought it would take several days. But the Russians wanted to impress him, and succeeded when they planted the engine on the wing by the next morning. They had worked all night, and Rick thanked them warmly. So once again the party took off, and this time kept flying. The navigator was cleared to take them over Stalingrad and show Rick the devastation of the place, where the shells of dead tanks looked especially horrible. Rick's note was "I could not help thinking that, if any of the cities of the United States had been destroyed to such an extent, there would be more interest in eliminating slowdowns, featherbedding, strikes, and absenteeism."

He was back at East End Avenue on August 7, 1943, and after a few days reported to Stimson's office. The Secretary was courteous to Rick, as he was to everyone. But the atmosphere was noticeably cool. They did not discuss the matter of whether Stimson had or had not instructed Rick to visit Russia. Rick knew that there would always be variances in what the parties to a difference of opinion might recall about oral agreements. Stimson said he wanted Rick to take a trip to the Aleutian Islands and see how things were getting on. As the site of a special mission, the treeless, fog-drenched Aleutians were Poverty Row, and asking Rick to go there was a polite way of saying his days as confidential agent to the Secretary were coming to an end. Rick said he would be pleased to carry out Stimson's instructions, but needed time to look into the condition of his airline before starting any more travels. Stimson said he understood, and they parted with expressions of esteem.

In the early fall, Rick paused to address a convention of retail credit managers and then left for the Aleutians. He put in an appearance at the island of Attu, the farthest point west on which one could find an American base. The duties were familiar by now: to inspect hangars, talk with officers and men, give assurances that they weren't forgotten. As far as the troops were concerned, letters home showed that his sincerity cleared Rick of suspicions attached to the average visiting fireman.

In talking to the soldiers, Rick kept to himself the greatest worry that he and other insiders entertained about the Aleutian bases. They feared treachery by the Russians, who were not at war with the Japanese. Hopkins and Harriman had brought the facts to Roosevelt, Marshall, and Stimson; and Rick shared the information, which was truly and seriously secret. His report about the Aleutians, therefore, was among the most valuable he brought to the leaders in Washington. And he said almost nothing about it. Nor did he ever have much to say about the boys out there on the Aleutians in subsequent public speeches. Rick knew how to handle matters when security was actually at stake. On his return to New York, he got a call from John Gilbert Winant, who had introduced him to the Spad and was now American ambassador to the Court of St. James's. He was in town for a short stay and asked Rick over to the Waldorf for a talk. Rick said it would be best for Winant to meet him at East End Avenue. When Winant asked why this was necessary, Rick said, "It's because your hotel rooms are bugged." Winant asked, "Are you sure?"

"I'm quite sure."

"But Rick, how do you know?"

"Don't ask me, Gil, just believe me — I know."

When Winant came to the apartment he said he planned to make an attempt at arranging for Rick to see President Roosevelt. But Rick persuaded Winant to give up the plan. He said it was useless to try, and even if Roosevelt gave him an invitation, he would not accept it at this late date.

Rick had traveled 55,000 miles, undergone hardship and danger, and had almost lost his life adrift in the Pacific. He had sent the War Department the Russian order of battle for the defense of Moscow. Under certain circumstances, this might have come in handy, and at the least it served to test statements of the inveterate Russian liars who fed our official contacts with official information. And Rick's personal impressions were those of a sensitive observer, unusually sympathetic to the personalities of others and experienced in the world. But Stimson had cooled because of Rick's visit to Russia, even though he apparently had approved it in advance. Consistency is not to be demanded of the great. As for the White House, there was no sign that anyone there appreciated what Rick had done, or cared to admit he existed. And now, at the end of his second war, Rick was higher in the world than he had been when his first war ended, yet he saw it as a world filled with enemies, a world that endangered his sort of man and challenged him to survive. Limping, battered, but still superbly self-confident, Rick prepared to face that world.

# CHAPTER VIII

# I Say to You Frankly

LIKE MOST of the other businessmen in the United States, Rick met prosperity in 1945 and 1946. At the middle of the latter year, when Eastern's accounting office sent up the figures on fiscal 1945, Rick saw that, for the first time, the airline had gone beyond $2 million in profits. And now that manufacturers could again make passenger airplanes, Eastern might expect to do even better than the $2,126,000 bookkeepers had written on the plus side. There must be good times at hand, forerunners of a future even more splendid than financial experts had predicted in the 1920s. Yet, although we had come together united to fight the war, now the country felt things begin to tear apart inside. Rick often spoke with foreboding, and touched a feeling that nearly everybody had, whether or not they shared his aversion to idlers on the assembly lines.

It is possible to follow the course of Rick's ideas as they developed. He was no more inconsistent than the next man, and his personal, word-as-bond integrity was impossible to deny. In considering Rick, one first acknowledged his unhesitating answer to the country's call in wartime, but along with this came his distrust of government and his belief that every man should be left to work out his own destiny. So he was pulled in two directions. The country was great and grand. In old times, semi-divine heroes had died to make it so. Now it was run for the benefit of loafers by a pack of greedy fools: such was Eddie's expressed belief. Still, he held that anyone who advocated tearing the whole thing down was a vicious plotter and should be stamped on. The result of his making his beliefs known was the constant necessity for this amiable man to maintain a belligerent front and be prepared for battle.

Rick felt that his family had the same indestructible qualities that sustained him in the turmoil of life as he lived it into the enigmatic present and forbidding future of 1946. He was right in this estimate, as far as David, William, and Adelaide were concerned. After distinguished service as a marine aviation gunner in the Pacific, David was preparing for Hamilton College. Bill was in the upper forms at the Asheville School. Adelaide had been occupied in doing war work, making a comfortable home for the family, and standing up to Rick in furious arguments when their personalities clashed.

But they were all surviving in good shape, for everyone close to Rick seemed durable and permanent — except for one member of his tribe. Rick's mother died at Los Angeles in her eighty-third year on March 31, 1946. And another person who had meant much to Rick went that year, when Damon Runyon died of throat cancer. For a while, Runyon had been able to appear at his favorite nightspots, even though he couldn't talk. He carried a pad and pencil, writing answers and comments for such friends as Steve Hannagan and Jimmy Cannon while he watched the crowds go by, and whenever Runyon saw Rick, his face would light up. Runyon made it known that he wished to have Rick scatter his ashes over Manhattan from an open plane. He soon died, and Rick scattered the ashes. Although it was against the law to do this, and Rick knew it, nobody tried to make trouble.

During Rick's absence on his later war missions, folk artists had continued to use him as their inspiration, and they produced a number of poems that resembled the ballads that had come down by oral tradition from old times in the southern mountains. This balladry about Rick found its audience through provincial newspapers and readings at local literary societies. Copies came into Rick's hands, and Miss Shepherd saved them, for eventual custody by the Library of Congress.

These American ballad-makers displayed the essentials of such verse — burning sincerity, and sticking to the narrative. The incident of the sea swallow, now identified forever as a seagull, had trapped the imagination of the balladeers just as Rick had trapped the bird. Before getting to the miraculous feeding of the castaways, one author opened with the briskness of a genuine folk song:

> I'm going to tell a story
>   Of Rickenbacker true and brave.
> Who with his brave companions
>   Fought the Pacific wave.

It happened that this author was a thirteen-year-old Iowa schoolgirl named Phyllis Beckman, but youth did not lessen her gift for getting to the heart of the matter. After expeditiously moving her characters from Los Angeles to the Pacific, Miss Beckman brought in the sea swallow episode:

> On the eighth day a seagull
>   Lit on Rickenbacker's head;
> It didn't take them very long,
>   To eat that bird, he said.
> They were so hungry,
>   They ate it bones and all,
> He said they wouldn't founder
>   If they ate another gull  . . .
> On the twenty-first day of hunger
>   An airplane reached them, then
> Rickenbacker said he never was so glad
>   To see an airplane and some men.

> So listen to me, my people.
>> Civilians and warriors alike
> It takes bonds and stamps and lots of money
>> To keep men like Rick battling the Reich.

These days Rick was more than the hero of ballads; he was probably the only living person to be portrayed in religious stained glass; professional artists notified him that they had used "the miracle of the seagull" in windows for churches of the Baptist and Methodist denominations, and at the naval hospital in Washington, D.C. In addition, Rick had become an expert on Russia. He expressed some unwilling admiration for their work habits while gradually veering to a stern anti-Russian doctrine that did not rule out the possibility of another war. He said on the radio:

> Russia, like China, has tremendous internal reconstruction jobs ahead of it in post-war years . . . At present the hours of employment are eight hours per day, six days per week, with an additional three hours per day with payment at time and a half. This is compulsory for everybody but married women with children. They have no absentee problem. If an employee is twenty minutes late, he is reprimanded. If he continues to appear late, he is tried by a court of employees and if found guilty, his wages are cut first, and then if there is continued abuse, his food ration is cut. In flagrant cases he is fired as unqualified to contribute to the war effort, which means the breadline.

Rick charged into a tautological peroration calling on the listeners

> to again re-establish the America that we inherited from our fathers with their sweat, tears, and blood . . . God knows, I say to you frankly, there is no one that detests to a greater degree than I the Communism that existed twenty to twenty-five years ago in Russia, and is still believed in by a few in America . . . Undying fame will be the reward of those who lend their energies and influence to bring about a new dispensation in world affairs — con-

tempt followed by complete oblivion will be the portion of the petty ones who will continue to play politics with this tremendous problem, or use for party purposes the tremendous forces involved.

On the same day Rick gave a news conference at which Lowell Thomas was present. Because of this, some of Rick's remarks reached the largest news audience in America. Thomas spoke of Rick in serious tones: "Captain Rickenbacker had still another striking thing to say — 'Russia may come out of this war the greatest democracy in the world, while if we continue to move to the left, as we are doing, we may easily be Bolshevik at the end of the war.' That would certainly be a strange reversal, to have Stalin uttering grave warnings against the red menace of the U.S.A. — that would be startling." Between them, Rick and Lowell Thomas created a stir.

One of the first results of this disturbance of public opinion came from the Louisville *Courier-Journal*. This famous newspaper attacked Eddie with an editorial headed, "The Captain Is All Mixed Up." The words constituted Rick's official removal from the lists of those who might expect courteous treatment from liberals and progressives in the United States. The paper used the term "labor-baiter" in describing Rick. Indeed, he was worse than that; he was a "veteran labor-baiter." To be drawn from this was the inference that Rick had spent years in persecuting workers. In fact, he had moved against them only on his return from the Pacific. But the *Courier-Journal* wanted to present Rick as a dangerous opponent, and its readers understood the use of hyperbole. The editorial writer lit into Rick by stating that if he was no better an observer of "things Russian" than he was of "things American," he was warning against the wrong danger. The trouble was "just the reverse of that which the Captain imagines, or says he imagines." With the time-honored hatchet technique of admitting one virtue to the victim, the paper said Rick was right in saying that a great deal of suspicion about Russia needed to be eliminated in America. Then came the imputation of disloyalty: "But after his little crack about this country going Bolshevik under its present leadership, we have to suggest it seems as much as anything else an American's duty to refrain from trying to create a lot of suspicion about his own President and Commander in Chief." The editorial dispensed with the customary salutes to Rick's fighting record in the First World War, and did not speak of his position in the public mind as a well-loved hero.

An event that showed the lighter side of Rick's activities took place on July 7, 1946, when he hit a golf ball at Sleepy Hollow and watched it fly from tee to green and into the cup, a hole in one. This called for drinks in the bar, and in a few weeks the Wheaties breakfast cereal makers sent Rick a certificate of membership in their Hole-in-One Club, with a letter that said, in part, "Yes, Captain Rickenbacker, when that little white pill bounced on the green and scampered into the cup, your name became emblazoned on the pages of sports history . . ." Rick answered that he was proud to accept membership.

Rick was good-humored about such honors and never failed to respond to decorations of the sort that the humorist Ellis Parker Butler called "goat feathers." Some of the goat feathers were militaristic, like the commission in the Confederate States Air Force of Tulsa, Oklahoma. Others were fraternal, like the honorary life membership in the Tall Cedars of Lebanon, Grove Number One; or mock-fraternal, as in the Historic Order of Owls, Tree Number 14; or the Ancient Order of Himalayas, Snowy Peak Number 562. And some were silly, like the diploma that an impertinent fellow conferred on Rick in behalf of the National Association of Screwballs. The citation made Rick Distinguished Screwball Number 1. The man said he had offered similar distinctions to Generals James Doolittle and Claire Chennault, but had heard nothing from them. Rick accepted a card of membership in the Love 'Em All Club, made out to Casanova Eddie Rickenbacker, "by virtue of his sincere interest and efforts in behalf of 'Loving 'Em All.' " Rick also allowed himself to be listed in the Royal Order of Ground Hogs, with the slogan "He's Glad He's a Ground Hog Instead of a Ghost." A press agent named Carl Byoir was running an organization called the Society of Arts and Sciences, supposedly founded by Herbert Spencer in 1883. This Byoir added a goat feather to the collection by conferring on Rick a Regency in the Field of Transportation. Rick wrote a formal letter of acceptance, ending, "Be assured that I will cooperate with the Society to the best of my ability at all times."

Numerous goat feathers also began adhering to Rick in the form of militia colonelcies, and honorary memberships in police departments and state highway patrols. Rick accepted them all, and when the certificates of membership were handsomely engrossed, he put them into four large leather-bound albums, which the student may inspect today at the Air Force Museum at Wright-Patterson Air Force Base, in Dayton. He also received recognition by an organization that made him a member of an inner circle that did not seek publicity, existed only for fun, and counted no more than eighteen or twenty members. This was something that called itself the Skeeters, and held meetings whenever a few of its members happened to enter the bar of the restaurant whose full name was Jack & Charlie's 21 Club, a Manhattan institution usually referred to as "21." The Skeeters were a roster of New York celebrities. In addition to Rick, one found among them such men as C. R. Smith, president of American Airlines, a Texan who had some resemblance to Rick; Bernard "Toots" Shor, proprietor of a well-known bar and grill; Ted Husing, leading sports broadcaster of the time; Jack Blan van Urk, historian of fox hunting; Sonny Werblin, talent agent; Bob Considine and Bill Corum, stars of the Hearst newspapers; Frank Hunter, wine agent, big-game hunter, and former Davis Cup star; Ned De Pinnet, president of R.K.O. Pictures; Abel Green, editor of *Variety;* and Charles Berns, co-owner of "21." Besides drinking at the bar, the Skeeters liked to hire as many limousines as necessary and go to the races at Belmont Park.

Membership in that group was a distinction in the eyes of many successful New Yorkers. The informality of it did not lessen its importance to those who valued such things. Rick belonged to two other masculine groups that required the highest commercial rank for admittance. One was called the 29 Club, which had 29 members, mostly corporation heads, including the president of U.S. Steel. They took over an East Side town house, where they met for lunch. This was the sort of thing that sociologists believed to be part of an apparatus they called the "power elite." Rick also belonged to the Question Club, which got together about twenty automobile executives for dinners and luncheon meetings. The organization had started in Detroit in 1912 and would have been a great hunting ground for historians of the motor industry, had they penetrated it.

Clothes entered into Rick's presentation of himself to the importance world. His dark, double-breasted business suits and faultless evening clothes came from tailors in London and New York who were masters of the craft.* He always wore a soft hat of medium gray in the fedora shape. This was a descendant of the lucky hat Rick wore in the Pacific, which had escaped years of effort by Adelaide to put it in the dust bin.** The postwar hat appeared to be much like any hat. However, when those who had eyes for detail looked at Eddie's hat, they perceived that it had a certain individuality, something slightly at variance from the norm, which gave it a jaunty air, for all its gray smoothness. The individual touch came from two unvarying

* Rick finally settled on Stadler & Stadler, of New York.
** The original hat, which survived disaster in the Pacific, may be seen in the Smithsonian Institution.

dimples in the center of the crown, which would trace a figure eight in the felt if viewed from above. How came this complicated crease never to alter, the top never to flatten, no matter how often Rick tossed the hat on a chair? His son David secretly examined the hat and found the answer — two large paper clips anchored the felt beneath.

A remarkable thing about the tall and distinguished-looking E. V. Rickenbacker was his resemblance to Ring Lardner. After Lardner's death, in 1933, men would stop in astonishment when they saw Rick coming along the street, and say, "I could swear that was Ring." Both came from the Midwest, and each was close to the heart of the American folk. And each had an undeniable, Indian-chief dignity that went with height, prominent facial bones, and a noble nose.

Some members of the Links Club, on East Sixty-second Street, had asked Rick in 1944 if he would like to join them. Two years later his name passed the committee, and he had the use of a beautiful little clubhouse between Madison and Park avenues. Rick's entrance here meant that he had received approval in a group of socially established New Yorkers. Another sign of Rick's acceptance and influence among carriage folk came when he himself wrote a letter to help David Rockefeller get into the Sleepy Hollow Country Club, at the request of Laurance Rockefeller. So the shabby hungry kid from East Livingstone Avenue had arrived at a place where he could do a social favor for a Rockefeller. And the terrible shoes, the fatigue of child labor, had receded an incalculable distance in some other dimension than time.

Rick's Christmas letter for 1946 was the most foreboding he had yet composed. It ran to a page and a half, and asked its recipients to "make the effort to forget the petty selfishness and greed that have always kindled the fires of hate, and resolve, individually and collectively, to perpetuate this land of ours — America — for generations to come as it was perpetuated for us by generations past."

There was to be no more question of where Rick stood in relation to the voices of progressive thought. He took a position, from which there could be no retreat, by tossing the accusation of disloyalty he had received from the *Courier-Journal* back into the camp of Stalinist intellectuals and journalists. Rick opened by calling these people "American Quislings." He could never gain forgiveness for that, because Vidkun Quisling was a fascist. He continued by paying his respects to "Tumbleweed-Thinkers, Screwball-Sociologists, or liberals who are suffering from softening of the brain as well as the heart." These people had much to answer for. Rick said, "The vapor of decadence, in American literature, thought, and education, is all part of their poison brew."

Although he traveled much and made speeches, Rick gave attention to the airline and its employees. It occurred to him that in most corporations the phase "board of directors" has an awe-inspiring sound. To say that the board has decided something is to close debate: *Roma locuta est, causa finita est.* Into Rick's brain now came the idea to "make a lot of people directors." In 1946, Eastern had 6700 employees, the number having risen from 3400 in 1944, when many were away in military service. It was obvious that the company would take on thousands more as business improved. Rick didn't need a course at college to know that the feeling of going unnoticed in a huge, impersonal company would discourage his brighter employees as the airline grew larger. Rick put it this way: "The bigger the army, the farther the generals are from the doughboys and the more chances there are of error."

He drew up a plan that divided Eastern into three echelons. At the top was what Rick named the advisory board, comprising all the vice presidents of the company. Then came the principal department heads, in a second echelon. Next was Rick's contribution to the science of airline management, and it was a good one. He took the minor officials, the sales managers, station chiefs, and traffic engineers from the stops along the Eastern line, the field men, and put them into what he called the third echelon, or field board of directors. In the spring of 1946 he started to bring them twice a year to New York or Miami for a week of meetings. These field men numbered about 400 when the plan went into operation, and Rick ordered each one to produce a written report, including suggestions for improving matters in his part of the system. The men took this seriously, because each had to file his report with Captain Eddie before the meeting, in which he would be called on to get up and read it to the other men, all under the boss's eye. Some of the men would be visibly shaking when they rose to speak.

Rick schooled his pupils from a dais on which no furniture appeared except a stool brought in from the hotel bar.* Rick would stand throughout the day and evening, occasionally perching on the stool for a few minutes to rest his aching leg. He had started reading reports at three o'clock that morning and had prepared traps for men he judged to be in need of prodding. Rick was a veteran crowd-handler from his days on the lecture platform, and he had seen the best of them since his earliest years as a traveling salesman and a racing man on the cornstalk circuit — the evangelists, pitchmen, medicine-show professors, and carny barkers — all the practical psychologists who worked directly with people before the days of radio and television. And he had discovered the way to exhort subordinates without losing their respect at racing pits in America and hangars of Squadron 94 in France. Therefore he felt completely in control when he ran these meetings, seldom wasted a word, and used only spare, forceful hand movements. The impression he gave was one of concentrated attention on his audience and the matters before it; and like all fine actors, Rick made his performance seem natural, never giving a hint that he knew it was a performance, and a good one.

*The Commodore in New York; the Columbus in Miami.

At the start of each meeting Rick said everything was under seal of confidence, and no arguments were to continue outside the hall. He then opened the proceedings with a prayer, after which he increased the tension "by making a couple of recommendations that would not work, letting myself be proved wrong and accepting it in good grace. As far as I know, no one ever realized that I was deliberately setting up straw men so that they could be knocked down."

The first series of field meetings ran for a week on a hard schedule, starting at eight in the morning, and recessing for one hour, with another session after dinner. There was value in letting men feel that they shared an ordeal, which is recognized by folk wisdom in many tribal rites of passage. When they reached the end of the week, the field men had a grand convivial evening with Rick in the chair. This, too, had value in making the field men take pride in their jobs. Rick found it gratifying to hear them talk of the past week like battle comrades. They went home convinced that their jobs were safe and their boss aware of their existence. In all this, Rick was a pioneer of the encounter group and the mental-therapy meeting.

As to the pilots, the first thing Rick had done when he got hold of the line was to pay them more. He said that a man with financial problems would not be able to concentrate on his work as an airline pilot should. Rick had not only increased their salaries; he put stock options at their disposal that offered the possibility of substantial net personal worth. But those who were not pilots complained that Eastern paid the lowest wages in the business. One executive said, "Rick doesn't squeeze pennies. He squeezes mils." And customers felt the pinch when sitting on cushions worn flat as the metal of the seats beneath. It was like sitting on a dish towel spread on a stove lid. But Rick was right when he said that there were only two things that airline passengers really wanted — to get where they were going safely, and on time. This was what the advertising men called "Eastern's double dependability." Rick liked that sales message and gave orders to stress it. Contrary to most airline advertising, the slogan had some connection with reality. It held good up to the late 1940s, during which time Eastern experienced no bad accident after the Atlanta crash. Rick didn't like art work in airline advertisements, but he did approve of one picture that drew admiring comment in the trade. Painted in the style of Norman Rockwell, the picture showed a grandmother sleeping in her seat on an EAL plane, with a little girl asleep in her lap. "That's advertising," Rick said to Brad Walker, his account man at the Fletcher Richards Agency.

Before the war, Rick felt that he had done away with women as cabin attendants. He said that someday women might be pilots, but had convinced himself that female passengers preferred to have men looking after their comfort in flight. He said to interviewers, "Women don't like to be served by women, contrary to what you may think. They don't like a sweet, smirky young girl coming up and smiling at them and offering them a can if they are sick as hell. They would rather have a man who is businesslike and practical, gracious, but not familiar, to tend them. Furthermore, women can't stand air travel like men can — just normally they can't." Rick concluded that "with ships getting bigger all the time, the girls were unable to handle the work. The men would get up and help them when they should have been served by them. I've done it myself, helped make up berths, and so forth. The customer didn't get the maximum service. The boys could do more work, and you could ask a boy to do things you couldn't ask a girl, and therefore the customer is better served . . ."

Rick developed his philosophy of women as cabin attendants, and went on to record a few thoughts on women in general. He said, "Whereas the boys looked ahead to a career, the girls had the bulkhead — marriage, the only thing. They married all the pilots, and then they started marrying the customers and are still marrying the customers, and making damned good wives . . ." Rick was putting down these thoughts during the war, and he remarked that there were women pilots ferrying aircraft around the United States, and "before this war is over, women are going to learn things they never knew existed before . . . They will find lots of places for usefulness that they never knew existed before, and justifiably so. After all, it's their world as much as it is ours. And it is not only the young and the able, the physically and mentally fit who have a place in it, but the old and decrepit, the halt and the blind, as well. It's their world too." Nevertheless, he thought men would make better cabin attendants, and clung to the crotchet, although he was not able to put it in force.

When Rick got warmed up to it, he could foresee women in jobs that his personal feeling would not be likely to assign them. But when it came to Negroes, Rick did not give evidence that he thought they had any important achievement ahead. He fondly recalled "good old darkies," who had behaved in a proper manner at some former time. But he replied with marked coolness when Walter White, the Negro leader, protested against his speaking of "darkies" in a public address. Rick also acquired a reputation in some quarters for holding a low opinion of Jews. It went so far that one began to hear that Eastern Airlines discouraged Jewish patrons. This was not what one would wish to have said if one wanted to carry people to and from Miami, Florida.

Trouble had developed because of a publicist named Merwin K. Hart, who conducted an organization called the National Economic Council. The NEC dedicated its efforts to classical economics, and in so doing gave less than enthusiastic support to various causes that were dear to the official organizations of American Jewry. Mr. Hart was a tackling dummy for the Anti-Defamation League of the B'nai B'rith; they found him useful when appealing for funds, and Hart in turn used their enmity to good effect when he himself passed the hat. It was a sham battle, beneficial to both sides. The unsophisticated didn't know this, and there was indignation when Walter Winchell reported in his gossip column that Eastern Airlines had given $5500 to Merwin K. Hart and his Council. Letters of high emotional content began to flood Rick, and he found them offensive. He didn't like the righteous, belligerent tone in the threats of boycotting his airline. To each complainer Rick sent a letter stating that the gift to NEC was four years old, but in any event Eastern reserved the right to do as it pleased with its own money. The letter concluded, "If, after reading the above, you do not agree with me, then I say to you frankly, I will have lost nothing and neither will Eastern Airlines if you continue to refuse to use our services, which are for the benefit of all."

It was seldom that Rick went so far as to give any potential customer the idea he was unwelcome. But he did land hard on a drunk who made a nuisance of himself in flight. It was in behalf of the reign of stewardesses in airline cabins, which Rick had been forced to recognize after the war. Routed through Atlanta, he found one of the women crying because the drunk wouldn't keep his hands to himself. The drunk became aware of a tall man standing in the aisle, and then peered up into a face that seemed to be made of some hard kind of wood. It was Rick, who said, "Get the hell off this plane in Atlanta."

Rick behaved in a different way to another trying customer, and took pains to make sure he was a customer for life. It happened that some kind of mix-up at Newark delayed a lot of passengers to Florida, and one of them, a Jewish businessman, said in strong language and at length that this was an outrage. One of the staff people reported that a customer had raised hell over the delay, and the complaint got up to Rick. Then Rick discovered that the man's name had not been entered on the manifest. Rick decided he had to have that name, and put detectives on the trail. When they located the man, Rick went to see him and gave what the disgruntled passenger later called "the greatest sales talk I ever heard." For the rest of his life this man used Eastern planes when going to any place they served, and everywhere sang Eddie's praises. That was the way Rick preferred to have things go in public relations.

Rick might have come closer to the mark in the matter of trusting one class of people over another if he had announced no confidence in Bolivian airplane pilots. Private and military flying instructors had long been terrified by Latin American pupils. Their handling of planes in flight reminded spectators of gauchos dashing over the pampas on spirited horses, which made for moments of excitement at races and exhibitions while decreasing the factor of safety for miles around. A dreadful price for this psychological shortcoming was exacted at the National Airport on November 1, 1949, and a shipload of Rick's customers had to pay it. Late in the afternoon, an Eastern DC-4 from New York came trudging down in the haze to make its landing. A Bolivian military plane flashed out of nowhere and rammed the liner. Fifty-five lives ended, including that of the cartoonist Helen Hokinson. The gaucho was piloting a P-38, the plane Rick had helped develop during the war.

A gratification came to Rick on April 14, 1950, when *Time* magazine featured him on him on its cover. Rick might have been prepared for this journalistic honor by a letter he had received from the advertising manager of a Hearst paper, who was moved to write *"You are America's greatest American."* Rick offered no argument and put the letter in his files. The magazine was not quite so fulsome, but if Rick's life up to then had been a play, the cover piece could be called a rave notice, the kind that lines up ticket buyers. After describing him as "a scarred and wilful old warbird," *Time* saluted Rick as "one of America's most famous and successful men — not only a kind of Buffalo Bill of the gasoline age, but an intimate of rulers, and a self-made captain of industry as well." The magazine noted that

Rick "had been ferociously damned by some, but was the only living human soul who had ever been able to wring consistent profits from that debt-ridden peacock of modern transport, the airline industry." The news-peg for the story was that "fortnight ago" Rick had announced Eastern's 1949 profit of almost $2 million, "the airline's 15th consecutive year in the black."

Rick had a concern beyond politics. His business was to hurl enormous weights of metal from one gravitational field into another and then reverse the process. And he had grasped the principle of the used car as applied to the aircraft industry. The real purpose of the trade was to keep airplane manufacturers working. There must be, therefore, a continuous flow of metal from the mines through the factories and out into the national economy in the form of assembled machines. And what Rick knew without looking at ledgers was that every time he took delivery of a transport plane it became a piece of used machinery and he had the responsibility of finding money to replace it.

He had to do this in the face of competition from other big airlines — and there was at least one too many in business — and under the burden of taxation. In 1952, to give an example, Rick reported that he had paid $3631 in taxes per employee, or 187 percent of net profit after taxes. But the march of used aircraft to the grave must continue. Indeed, Rick had to speed up this inexorable march. The reason for acceleration was simple: the new commercial jets were almost ready to fly. Among other things, this meant farewell to travel on ocean liners from New York to London. It was hard to believe in 1957, when forty steamships on regular runs carried 1,010,146 passengers between the United States and Europe. This was the greatest number on record, but Rick knew there would be a sudden change. Although his was not a transatlantic carrier, Rick in 1957 had already ordered a fleet of jets to be delivered as soon as possible. The price was $425 million.

This business of jet aircraft gave Rick a demonstration that his luck still ran good, when all he had been looking for was a demonstration of the new British de Haviland Comet. Rick took "a bunch of his boys" to England for test rides on British jets. At bottom, the airline business was still at the livery-stable level. Buyers were expected to beware, and sellers were none too scrupulous about samples on view. The first day Rick and his boys went up for a run, they knew that de Haviland had already lost a test ship. Still, the odds were pretty good that this sample flight would not endanger anyone. The plane took off, and Rick felt the engines' undeniable thrust. They flew around for a couple of hours at 40,000 feet, "all over England," which looked like any other country at that height. Rick told about it a few years later when he was dictating material for his archives:

> I finally sauntered back into the tail, to the galley department. There I noticed that the fuselage was acting like an accordion. I couldn't believe my eyes. I finally put my finger against it. And it was moving about three quarters of an inch, out and in. Out and in. It scared the living life out of me, because I said, sooner or later, that metal will fatigue and crack, and boom — because of the pressurization of the airplane at over 20,000 feet. . . . We got down and I told the boys about it, and they were all shocked and surprised, and I said, "Never again will I fly this type of airplane, because we could have lost our top management in one accident, completely." I then went over and talked to the engineers, and even talked to the directors of the company, and they belittled it, said it couldn't happen. Well, it did happen again. It killed a lot of people when it blew up over the Mediterranean, but it showed that my judgment or supposition was correct . . . It was a simple matter of the pressure inside against the lack of pressure outside, you see.

That sight and feel of breathing movement on the Comet's metal skin stayed in Rick's mind for a long time. Technicians talked about metal fatigue, which had supposedly plagued the

Comet. But it wasn't easy to understand how inanimate matter could get tired. So far as the Comet's manufacturers were concerned, if Rick and his friends fell from the sky on a test flight, bad show; the next generation of Comets would profit by their example.

Rick settled down to running the airline, and the days of these years, at East End Avenue, had a pattern during the periods Rick was home, off the road. When he got back from the office, he always gave the same whistle at the door, a sound that Bill remembered as simply two notes, a descending minor third, like a cuckoo's whistle, saying, "I'm here!" and asking, "Anybody home?" The next sequence of events was unvarying, for Rick had three radio programs he never missed if he could help it, and they came during supper, as he called the third meal of the day. He brought a portable radio to the table, and in spite of "Eddie — really, now!" from Adelaide, he heard the Mutual Network commentator Fulton Lewis, then "The Lone Ranger," and a fifteen-minute news program. Lewis was unabashed in a conservatism that some didn't like and called reactionary, but Eddie liked it; and the Ranger's simple but effective storytelling also left no doubts in his mind. While listening, Rick ate neatly with the manners Elizabeth had implanted in him long ago in Columbus. As he lifted and laid down the table silver, Adelaide couldn't help admiring his hands, vexed though she might be at the radio. The hands were the sort supposedly found in surgeons and artists, strong and graceful with long, well-turned fingers. Such hands did indeed usually indicate artistic ability, which Rick had felt fermenting within him as a boy, when he carved stone angels for churchyards and created graceful floral watercolors. The hands also showed that Rick might have become one of those ornaments to humanity, now apparently extinct, a first-class cabinetmaker and carpenter.

The family routine allowed for pleasant Christmases and

Thanksgivings, with generous hospitality and excellent dinners from the range of Mrs. Perry, a fine cook. Christmas brought punch bowls and a tall fir tree. Rick was sound in the faith on Christmas tree decorations. He liked plenty of red and green, shiny ornaments hung in recesses of greenery, and a sparkling star at the top.

For all the heavy silver, the English china, and the servants, there was plain eating on East End Avenue, as the description of Rick's uncomplicated appetite must make clear. On Sunday evenings, when Mrs. Perry was off duty, Rick found satisfaction in supping almost invariably on frankfurters and beans. No matter how humble the fare might be, Rick was never known to prepare a meal himself or to wash a dish. The Sundays would begin with another high-caloric treat, fried cornmeal mush. Rick ate this with butter and syrup, and vowed that nothing in the world tasted better. After Sunday breakfast, he would read the papers until noon and then go to the office.

Like millions of others, Rick would try to follow a diet from time to time. One such was known as the Gaylord Hauser regime, said to be the secret of Greta Garbo's durable good looks. It was believed that if you kept to this diet, which was mostly lettuce, clear soup, and skimmed milk, you would be purified and generally toned up, with years added to your allotment of threescore and ten. Once a year Rick would try it. He would start taking a vacuum bottle of vegetable broth to the office for lunch. No cocktails at Café Louis XIV or "21." When this went on, men saw that there was no afterlunch period of benignity when bad news could be safely brought in. Along about the second week, the Captain would order a lamb chop, and the people around him would begin smiling again.

During his youth, Rick had paid tribute to the boy-and-his-dog line in the breviary of American customs. The fact was that he didn't care for pets, except for a lucky kitten at the race-track, and seldom bothered with them. But as sometimes happened with Rick, there were exceptions to the rule. One was a doe named Queenie, who would accept food from Rick's hands at the Texas ranch.* Queenie wasn't entirely tame and wouldn't bring her fawn to the house, but kept it hidden in the woods. The other pet was a bird named Sir Oliver Cromwell, who lived in a cage when he wasn't flying around the house. This little creature was a budgerigar, the Australian parakeet also known as the lovebird. It appeared that Sir Oliver's love was concentrated on Captain Eddie, to whom he invariably flew if uncaged when Eddie was around. At bedtime Sir Oliver liked to tuck himself under Eddie's silk pajama collar. No one knew why Sir Oliver chose that refuge or why Rick tolerated the bird. He not only indulged Sir Oliver but worried if he failed to eat, and gave him tonic. Adelaide once discovered Rick and a newspaperman in the study with their heads together in serious discussion. It turned out they were talking about Sir Oliver's health, which was poor at the time. The newspaperman said, "I raise canaries, and I'll tell you what to do. Mix a lightly boiled egg with gruel and offer that to Sir Oliver." The two men went to the kitchen, a maid prepared the bolus, Sir Oliver took a few pecks at it, and next day was himself again, diving to Rick's shoulder and uttering his usual self-confident cries.

As the record has shown, studies of Rick's life must include his fearless use of the cliché. When Rick found a phrase useful, he would never retire it on grounds of its having worn out its welcome. This saved him happily from the use of trendy neologisms and rancid journalese. Still, one was never far from a familiar phrase in Rick's conversation. In one day, Rick could be heard to say that someone was *crooked as a dog's hind leg,* but perhaps for all that *quick as greased lightening.* Ill-advised attempts at humor might be *funny as a crutch,* but a hilarious evening *as much fun as a barrel of monkeys.* An honest man would impress Rick for being *straight as a die,* and could be trusted

*Rick owned this 2700 acre spread near Hunt, Texas, from 1949 to 1954.

*from here to Kingdom come.* You could *talk till you were blue in the face* trying to speed some people up, but they would remain *slow as molasses.* Others would start quickly and *run like Billy-be-damned;* these might be independent spirits who *didn't give a tinker's damn* about anything. But when it came to running, those who *ran like scared jackrabbits* were unworthy of respect. Those men straight as dies were also *honest as the day is long,* and Rick could count on them to face the enemy and *hit him like a ton of bricks.* They would go after him *hammer and tongs,* fighting *tooth and nail.* Speaking for himself, it made Rick *madder than a wet hen* to be subjected to unfair criticism, because he knew that his dealings were *cleaner than a hound's tooth.* For this reason, Rick usually *slept like a log,* but when not feeling well, he might *toss and turn all night.* He *wouldn't give a plug* (not plugged) *nickel* for schemes proposed by charlatans, but would *fight like a wild-cat* in defense of a sound idea. When he saw something handsome, it was *pretty as a picture,* even if the weather was *hotter than the hinges of hell,* or it was *raining cats and dogs.* And generally speaking, if things went well, Rick could be *happy as a lark.* He had some personal turns of speech, repeated so often he was no longer aware of them: there was the touch of Columbus "Dutch" in *didn't I told you* and *I tolded you,* and he invariably said *morning, night, and, noon,* instead of putting those words in their usual order.

At the office, Rick's orderly ways resembled his domestic doings. Here also everything revolved around his personality and his method of handling the details of living. Rick said he could judge a man's caliber by whether or not he was addicted to meetings. The gatherings of the echelons didn't count, for these meetings were Rick's idea. Otherwise, he had no enthusiasm for committees and thought that office work was no way for a man to pass his time. As one who had raced for prize money, fought with guns in the air, and trouped the provinces, Eddie knew what it meant to survive by his wits. But beyond the cunning of the brain there had to be the strength and skill of hands if it ever came to a question of survival. You must know how to use your hands. Rick's public speeches revealed that this maxim had started in a nightmare haunting his mind, the same vision that others had experienced, but usually did not like to mention — *the war wasn't over.* And there was no way to guarantee that there'd be no fighting within the States, and no way of knowing what form the enemy might take or where his base might be.

Rick made five big speeches during April 1951, and in perhaps the most impressive one told his hearers:

> We are now living in a garrison state, or a state of armed neutrality — although few of you realize it. I doubt very much whether any of us present here tonight will ever again see and enjoy those peacetime periods in this land of ours, as we have known them during our life up to now. For one thing, we are going to get taxes on top of taxes, resulting in a lower and lower standard of living as time goes on. With those taxes will come controls on top of controls, which means the loss of more and more of those liberties we cherish so dearly . . . I say these things as a realist, which I have always been throughout my life — and the American people must become realistic too, and face the facts. World War Three will conscript us all and ruin us all.

Rick then added Lenin's question, "What is to be done?" He suggested that we ask ourselves, first, whether we are preserving the freedom established by the Fathers. Second, considering ourselves a generation responsible for certain years of time, whether we have renewed our national faith during this time. This echoed the message in the Gettysburg Address. And third, "Knowing that the life of man is pledged to higher levels here than it is elsewhere, are we striving to hold aloft the standards of liberty and hope? Or are we disillusioned and defeated — feeling the disgrace of having had a free field in which to do new things in the cause of freedom and not having done them?"

On March 12, 1952, Rick had a concrete problem to discuss when he appeared before the Civil Aeronautics Board and the House Interstate and Foreign Commerce Committee. The subject was the closing of Newark Airport, which had been ordered on February 11 after the third terrifying crash in fifty-seven days. Aircraft had crashed in streets and backyards, which made people anxious about showers of engines, wings, gasoline, and corpses from the sky.

Rick was functioning as an attorney for the airlines. The National Air Transport Association had appointed him spokesman because he was the most attractive and trustworthy figure they could put forward. Rick knew he was in a battle for favorable publicity, against powerful enemies. Besides the Congressmen, an air force staff delegation and a House subcommittee were on hand. All these men would like to see Eddie and his industry in trouble, and yet they had to approach him cautiously. Although he had cultivated the reputation of being impulsive in speech, he had a cool fighting brain, and, as he said many times, he did not believe in attacking an impregnable position.

The first thing Rick felt he could do was to lighten the fear of aviation that the three wrecks had caused. Rick said there was always a possibility anything moving might run into something else moving or at rest. There was no way in the universe for two bodies to occupy the same space at the same time. But look at the figures for the past year: in 1951, there had been sixteen million landings and takeoffs in the United States without even one fatal mishap. This was the classic defense by statistics against human instinct. The way Rick put it, the possibility of any more trouble at Newark was mathematically out of the question. Rick then took up the business aspect of things. He said that because of the Newark shutdown, everyone had to use Idlewild Airport, and this was going to be bad. The public was paying a price in all the confusion: there were 5000 people every day looking for air transport in and out of New York City and not finding it. Nobody questioned Rick's figures, but the politicians kept Newark Airport shut down long enough to deal it a blow from which it has not yet recovered.

Rick felt that he was on aviation business when he traveled around the country to fill speaking engagements, because in his person he represented commercial flying, not only that part of it which Eastern carried on, but the whole system of planes and ports that the industry promoted. He tried also to represent the quality of being reputable, of being the good American in whom we all believed. For even while Eddie was predicting permanent international war and the end of liberty, he had moments in which he saw the old values held in respect and the basic tenets observed, and the United States distributing benefits to all nations that cared to receive them in a friendly way.

This also was the vision of Henry R. Luce, which his editors set forth in the Mid-Century Number of *Life* magazine. Rick would have been happy to think he'd contributed some ideas, but was never able to get Harry Luce to stop talking on the occasions when they met. Since Eddie liked to get in a word himself, their friendship never amounted to much. Even after the election of Richard Nixon to the presidency, Rick continued to repeat predictions of disaster. "One day what we call the Cold War will pass," said Rick in North Carolina. "One day, in our own way, we shall deal with it. In righteous wrath we shall wipe off the face of the earth this loathsome tyranny that is distracting honest men from honest work. When that ugly chore is finished, we Americans can return to our ways of peace and work." Rick made it clear what he believed the ugly chore would call for, as he added, "We must fight for our American way of life . . . but dollars and *bullets* are not enough." (Emphasis added.)

In those words, Rick mentioned the third big war that he had previously said would draft us all, wipe out our liberties, and corrupt what was left of the country. He faced this conviction with his usual coolness, and kept on running his airline with an eye to sound operation and profit. Rick's associates said he insisted on approving every expenditure of more than $100. Although this is hard to believe about a company as large as Eastern Airlines, it is documented that, on one occasion, the office managers ordered new filing cases in New York, Rick said, "Hold on there. We have four empty cases in Miami," and he was right.

From the time of Elbert Hubbard and the *American* magazine, down to the present, journalists writing up corporation bosses have quoted unnamed associates reciting a familiar litany about the big man's steel-trap mind, his phenomenal memory for detail, and how he is tough but fair. But some of Rick's associates were not always so complimentary. They made complaint only over cocktails in dark barrooms or to their wives. The complainers said Rick didn't delegate authority, that he became unhappy when not the center of attention, and that he inhabited a world populated by only one person — Captain E. V. Rickenbacker. The critics would charge that Rick's kindly interest in junior employees was only for the gratification of his ego. They said that his help to young men in trouble, which consisted of advice and sometimes a loan or gift of money, was the expression of a desire to run other people's lives.

It was true that Rick wasn't the first sympathetic and generous man who could also be something of a busybody. But his legendary toughness usually softened before the end of a bawling-out. At such times, those outside the closed office door would hear measured tones from Rick, presumably in admonishment for some fault; but, before long, Rick's hearty laughter would be heard, and soon the culprit would leave smiling and apparently walking on air. A man who could administer a rebuke without causing resentment obviously had a human touch and the ability to think of someone other than himself. Rick was no bully, and he took no pleasure in other men's psychic discomfort. Most especially, he disliked having to order the firing of an aide. When a man wasn't performing satisfactorily, Rick would say, "We'll have to find something for him," and would take pains to get another job for the failing employee. The critics said Eastern paid such poor salaries that it was hard to find replacements. But it was held in the airline business that your job was safe at Eastern, though you wouldn't get rich. And the arrangements for employees to acquire Eastern stock made the jobs more attractive for those who wanted to finance investments from their pay.

In administering the airline, Rick got to his office early on the days when he was in New York, hoping to clear up all details before noon. He had Miss Shepherd as confidential aide in doing this, and Miss Shepherd deployed her secretaries according to the work on hand. Rick's catlike neatness showed in the way he had them keep his desk clean; he usually handled paper as fast as it came to him, and cut off the flow of it for the day when he went to lunch, leaving the afternoon clear.

The tidings of great joy, that Ike was in the White House, soon lost their glittering promise for Rick's American Way. Although Ike might throw down a bridge hand or miss a putt in annoyance when he thought of them, federal employees continued to breed like maggots. The older ones dozed in their cubicles, but others took to the field and began looking over the shoulders of people trying to work. Although Eastern Airlines had been growing at a good rate, there was no doubt that the central government, in Washington, and the governments in the state capitals were growing even faster. Nevertheless, Rick approved plans for Eastern to order 100 new airplanes, to be finished and delivered in 1954 through 1957, for which he promised to pay $200 million.

At the time, such an amount was almost unthinkable in the finances of a private company. Fortunately for Rick's peace of mind, he didn't know that even bigger bills from manufacturers would land on his desk during the years ahead. In spite of the increasing swarms of federal agents, Rick could go to Washington in 1954 and plead the cause of aviation in general, presenting himself as a man who had come out of the First World War with that mission, and that alone. Now, Eddie was predicting that soon we would have supertransports flying from coast to coast in six hours, and, speaking for Eastern, he pointed to an increase in plane miles from 2000 to 250,000 per day. And for nineteen consecutive years, Rick said, in spite of all difficulties, Eastern had earned a profit. In thirteen of those years, he "had not taken a single penny of the taxpayers' money in subsidy." Rick later maintained that while under his control Eastern had never received a government bonus.

There were several reasons to make 1954 as a year to remember. With the boys out of college, Rick and Adelaide felt that the East End Avenue apartment was too big for them. Perhaps they were starting to feel lonely. The ranch in Texas was too far away. Before long, almost all of its 2700 acres went to the Boy Scouts of America in a princely gift. Rick had put down no roots there; he was a city man. He talked with Adelaide about the advantages of living in hotels. Why not have a suite, which would amount to a moderate-sized apartment, but with no need for servants? They moved to the Park Lane, but the place had turned "too commercial," Rick said, and they went to the Carlyle, on Madison Avenue. The hotel was fashionable, and there were many foreigners chattering in the lobby and elevators. Rick told Adelaide, "They cater to a bad crowd here." The hotel even rented facilities for dinners in honor of Khrushchev and Castro. As if this weren't enough to drive civilized people away, President Harry Truman stayed at the Carlyle when he was in town. This meant that Secret Service gunmen would infest the place, with the same effect on tenants as a gang leader's bodyguard. When Rick couldn't stand it any longer, they moved to the Stanhope, on Fifth Avenue near the Metropolitan Museum, a pleasant neighborhood in those days. The Stanhope was a quiet, agreeable place, and Rick said later, "We had a beautiful apartment and enjoyed it for two years." Then the owners sold to a greedy speculator, who raised the rent by 15 percent when Rick wouldn't buy the apartment on a cooperative basis. Rick moved out and "found an ideal penthouse at the Regency Hotel on the 21st floor overlooking Park Avenue." The management gave Rick a fair lease, and he and Adelaide lived there in contentment until moving to their last New York home, at the quiet and elegant Dorset, in the Fifties between Fifth and Sixth Avenues.

As a polemicist, as a man who demonstrated theories of engineering and transportation in practical fields, and as a public character, Rick had made his years go by so fast he found it hard to believe when he became sixty-five years old. He decided he had ten years of heavy duty left in him, and the directors of Eastern agreed. Announcement came two months after Rick's sixty-fifth birthday that he had signed a contract to serve for ten years as Eastern's president, chief executive officer, and chairman of the board. The directors touched on the question of Rick's age by saying the traditional retirement at sixty-five was "out of keeping with the needs of the time." Those needs, said the directors, were for "mature and experienced judgment." In that year and the next, Eastern Airlines registered a profit of $28 million.

And this year former President Hoover asked Rick to go to Europe and inspect the American intelligence activities there. The trip produced a report that went into the Hoover Commission files, and perhaps had the effect of all such documents, which is probably not much. But there was one unquestionably good result from the trip. After Rick had reported to Hoover, a staff assistant in Washington sent Rick a note couched in language so stiff that it came within the definition of impertinence. The bureaucrat ordered Rick to bring in the special passport he had received for use in Europe. He had no intention of keeping the document, but there was an implication that Rick stood somehow in the wrong and out of order. Miss Shepherd's note on this letter reads, "Captain took this personally." It would have done one's heart good to hear him on the telephone to Washington, giving a sincere account of how bad manners affected him. Petty officials scattered for shelter like cockroaches when a light goes on. Then a person of higher rank wrote an apology, and a polite man, walking very softly, called at Rick's office for the passport. They picked the wrong citizen to be rude to that time.

To receive an invitation to join a select company, one that everybody can't associate with, has the stimulation of champagne with none of its bad effects. Rick was conscious of this pleasant benefit when he read a letter that arrived in July 1958, asking him to attend the Bohemian Grove Festival as a guest in one of its most desirable lodges, the Caveman Camp. The forty or fifty lodges at the Grove were clubs within a club, and some stood higher than others on an invisible ladder. Members of the camps all belonged to the Bohemian Club itself, which inhabited a handsome building on Taylor Street in San Francisco. The Bohemians were impressed with each other, and they believed that those who gathered each summer at their Grove festival were the managers of America. This did no harm, and Eddie's hosts at Caveman Camp stood second to none on the ladder of Bohemian prestige.

When Eddie got there early in August, he found Caveman Camp the reverse of primitive. It was a sylvan lodge with a rustic atmosphere created by stone fireplaces and Navaho blankets, everything comfortable in an unostentatious way. Woods were superb and trails inviting, but there would be no criticism of a guest who did nothing but sit on the wide verandah and soak up the peaceful atmosphere of the camp. And when the sun went down, you would stroll to the mess hall for dinner, then return for an evening around the fire. There was whiskey in abundance, and by some miraculous process the hangover element had been left out, or so it seemed to the guests and members who woke up breathing pure mountain air.

The great thing was that when you talked and got things off your chest, you were confiding in *leaders,* for losers couldn't have passed the men at the gates, respectful club servants and grim-faced county cops with big guns in their harnesses. Here you were with the most important men in the country. That thought never left you at Caveman Camp, where you could see those men around you, cheek by jowl. First there was one whom they called "the Chief" — none other than former President Herbert Hoover. Then there was Lowell Thomas, celebrated for his daily newscasts on the radio. And there was Allan Hoover, the Chief's son, greatly admired by his friends. There were Henry S. Sturgis and Jeremiah Milbank, men of such great influence downtown that they might be called insiders' insiders. There was Dr. E. Wallace Sterling, president of Stanford University, along with a famous member of its hospital staff, L. R. "Yank" Chandler, M.D. There was General Al Wedemeyer, who had been the American commander in China, and De Witt Wallace, publisher of *Reader's Digest,* side by side with Senator Barry Goldwater. You could see Clarence Budington Kelland, the famous writer of serials in the *Saturday Evening Post,* adjusting a jaunty bow tie of the same material as his shirt. There was Eugene Pulliam, the Arizona publisher; Roy W. Howard, of the Scripps-Howard chain; and Rick's host, Albert C. Mattei, a San Francisco oilman.

By August 18, Rick's Bohemian Grove vacation was over, and he returned to New York — "back to the salt mines," as he expressed it when he wrote to his friends in appreciation of the stay at Caveman Camp. Cordial letters went both ways, and those coming back to Eddie showed that in his performances at the campfire he had made a hit. He could savor it now as he remembered each of those wonderful evenings, including the one when the Chief recalled the cold day on which he had given Eddie the Congressional Medal. Rick knew he had carried his liquor well, letting it release the charm of his personality, but not betraying him into maudlin buttonhole-grabbing or the telling of jokes that people laugh at to cover their embarrassment. He had carried everything off beautifully. How sweet it was to realize that he had not been wasting himself in this center of power. It was good to know that the president of Stanford was just a friendly man called "Wally," and to consult with shrewd-faced "Bud" Kelland about a contribution to the Goldwater campaign chest. Friends helped each other out. That's what friends were for. And how satisfactory it was to hail the capitalists Milbank and Sturgis as "Jerry" and "Hank" and to see Bert Mattei's eyes glow with pride at the impression his guest was making.

All this good will had been intensely gratifying because Rick had a critically important business objective in mind when he went to California. He had completed plans for the expansion of Eastern Airlines all the way to the Coast, to make the greatest system of aerial transportation under one management the country had ever known. He had told his friends the Cavemen all about it. And now here was a letter from one of them, saying, "Never in all my experience have I seen a man put together so huge a corporation in so short a time, and I am still proud of the fact that I have — was it one or two million in stock?" They could make fun of it if they liked and Rick himself had sent a post card showing a United Airlines plane in flight and bearing his message, "This is a wonderful airline — have two stewardesses lined up for merger with Eastern." Rick wrote to Bud Kelland, enclosing his Goldwater check, and said the Grove now seemed "as though it was more or less of a dream, to wax free from telephones, meetings, confusion and frustrations . . ."

Rick's letters of thanks usually contained a reference to "the grand old Chief" and expressed satisfaction that his son also was there. He wrote to Pulliam that "hopes at Eastern are high." Everyone at camp had told him he had a good idea. He had listed the cities where his planes would go: Oakland, San Francisco, San Diego, Las Vegas, Phoenix, Tucson, Albuquerque, El Paso, San Antonio, Houston, and Dallas — all to be linked with New Orleans, Jacksonville, Tampa, Miami, Atlanta, and New York. Government hearings on the route applications would start in January 1959; therefore now was the time to rally the magnates of the redwoods and clear the way for Captain Eddie.

Alas for theories of sociologists about the power elite. There was no help forthcoming for the transcontinental plan. Apparently the man to see about this was Lewis K. Gough, a former national commander of the American Legion. Rick had reason to believe Allan Hoover or his brother could influence this man. He said he hoped the Hoovers could get to Gough before the hearings, for he was "hard to sell." Nothing came of it. The Chief had no suggestion to make. Hank and Jerry made no references to the plan in their letters. And when at last he thought it over, Rick saw that he might as well have stayed in New York or gone to Europe that August, for all he had accomplished in enlisting business support. Business was done in offices, not in the Forest of Arden.

There was a consolation prize, and a rich one, if good fellowship, the beauty of redwoods, and pride in belonging to a famous club have value. Rick had sounded an additional note in his letters to the Cavemen, candidly expressing his desire to be one of them. In sending "kindest personal regards" to all his "new friends," Eddie had not hesitated to add phrases about how "the privilege of knowing and being with you" had left "a mark of friendship" that appeared to be indelible. He had continued, "There is nothing I would rather do than be a member of some kind of Caveman Camp, and if it is possible I would appreciate your advising me on the proper procedure . . ." Cordial answers came back. Those who had pulled away in some alarm from the airline-expansion scheme made all the more haste to show Eddie they liked him very much as a person. Bud Kelland assured him, "Your presence did so much to make this encampment memorable to us all." Bert Mattei wrote, "The Caveman group are all for you." But before they could take him in, Eddie must be elected to the parent club. The Cavemen supplied the necessary supporting letters, though they had not all known Eddie for the required length of time. One recommender wrote to Rick, "I informed the Bohemian Club that I have known you for three years, and this perjury is justified on the basis that the time spent with you at the Grove dragged on so that it seemed like three years." Rick's election to the Bohemian Club went through, and he then became a member of Caveman Camp.

Having made this last sale on the personality market, Rick settled into harness with his airline and prepared to fight for the southern transcontinental route. The hearings in January 1959 were unproductive. Lewis Gough couldn't think of any reason to help, and American and Continental carried enough weight to keep Eddie out when good things were distributed. He had to accept defeat on his entire proposal, just as he had lost his battle, a few years before, when he tried to merge Eastern with Colonial Airways.

One source of trouble was that when Rick appeared before a political board, he looked too good. And he made political job-holders look too bad. He would stroll in with his commanding appearance, making nothing of his limp, walking with a controlled stride. He looked battered but absolutely undefeated, and he used his lower-register voice on them. The contrast between Captain Eddie and the officials and politicians was obvious, inescapable, and much to their detriment. Furthermore, he believed in what he was proposing or defending, and thus spoke with what William S. White called "blazing sincerity." The only answer politicians and bureaucrats could give was to refuse whatever Rickenbacker wanted. This made Eddie the victim of triumphs by small minds.

Nevertheless, Eastern continued to earn profits while other airlines found the going rough indeed, and moaned like dinosaurs dying in a swamp. An odd thing in connection with Rick's administration was the attitude of the traveling public toward Eastern. It was unfavorable to an almost comic degree. A kind of shabbiness pervaded the cabins of Rick's aircraft; it was hard to define, except when one sat in a worn-out seat, but made an impression on too many people to be put aside as merely another product of a whispering campaign. Some of the people who flew regularly between Atlanta and New York went to the trouble of having celluloid lapel buttons made up with the inscription "WHEAL," for "We Hate Eastern Airlines." Similar hatred boiled up against the Pennsylvania Railroad when it began to lose its tone in the late 1950s. The best a common carrier can hope for from its public is lack of outright malevolence; people will love their automobiles, but never machines they hire, buses or taxicabs. This was something Rick had learned to live with.

When he thought it important, Rick told the truth about airplanes, as when he wrote to his son Bill, "To become a good pilot and remain one never forget that an airplane is like a rattlesnake, you must keep your mind and eye on it constantly or it will bite you when you least expect it which could prove fatal." And so he could understand lack of affection for an airline fleet. He disliked what he considered public greed for "free" meals and drinks. Rick had to serve meals aloft because all airlines offered them, but the passengers paid in the price of tickets. Why they didn't see this was more than Rick could understand, and he thought it led to false advertising and gave competitors a chance to tell lies about the banquets they claimed to supply.

With all his troubles, Rick kept things going so well that Eastern showed a profit of $7,078,000 for 1958, the year of his visit to the Grove; and he took delivery of forty propjet Lockheed Electras in that summer.* By the end of the following year, he had entered the era of modern commercial flight, when Eastern insignia went up on forty new Douglas DC-8s, each with four straight-jet engines.

Rick entered his seventieth year in October 1959 and remarked that he was not paying any attention to aches and pains, and would hold off "the old man with the knife on the stick" as long as he could. He added that there was no use kidding oneself; that old man could not be indefinitely kept at bay. With this in mind, and perhaps influenced by the arrival of jets, Rick began to look for someone to succeed him at Eastern Airlines. He also had to deal with a strike by machinists and engineers, which lasted thirty-nine and a half days. But the problem that never went away was selecting the company's next president. Rick would sit at the corner table in the bar at "21" and discuss the problem with such friends as Peter Grimm, a real estate magnate who belonged to the Cavemen and was widely respected. One man would come under consideration, then Rick would discard his name and bring up another. Some thought that Rick put off making a final decision because it would mean retirement and having no occupation, but they did not know their man. Rick had found plenty to do for years before he entered the airline business, and he could fill his days acting as a polemicist any time he wished to. He knew by experience in the world that hard days were coming, and he wanted Eastern to have a young man running it, a man who could hang on and keep things going through bad times.

On September 9, 1959, Rick announced that his man was Malcolm A. MacIntyre, the former Undersecretary of the Air Force, who had resigned that post in July. Now the directors of

---

*Eastern's profit for 1957 was $9,378,000. This brought the combined profits for 1957 and 1958 to more than $16 million.

Eastern made him president and chief executive officer. But Captain Eddie was not going to disappear. He would continue as chairman of the board of directors. And he would be chairman of an executive committee, to deal with policy matters. "Besides heading the executive committee," reported the *Journal of Commerce,* "Captain Rickenbacker will head the operations committee, whose membership is made up of the executive heads of all the airline's departments." Malcolm MacIntyre had come aboard at the end of an auspicious year, even without the western domain that Eddie had coveted. When they went over the books, they found a profit of $11,403,000.

That was the last profit the line was to enjoy for quite a while. MacIntyre gave over to Floyd D. Hall in 1964, and the four years 1960 through 1963 showed losses totaling $64,329,000. During that time, pilots had gone on strike for eleven days, and flight engineers for a total of eighty-eight days in two strikes. However, the greatest loss for one year — $37,760,000 — came in 1963, when no Eastern employees were on strike. Too many airlines, too much money locked in aircraft and unproductive land, rising labor costs — all were there to torment Rick and his friends. The reason for most of the bad things happening came under one word: inflation.

In his memoirs, Rick said that the appointing of a man to take over was partly due to his disgust at "a trend toward socialism" and at the way the government permitted "other airlines to duplicate routes we had pioneered, particularly when they had to be subsidized by taxpayers' money." He gave an example that had been rankling from as far back as 1949, when National Airlines collected $3.97 per ton-mile to haul mail between New York and Miami, whereas Eastern got "only 66 cents a mile — one-fifth as much." Psychologically scarred but personally undefeated, Rick made it his custom to behave toward government as a hedgehog does with a farmer's cur —roll up in a ball and present spikes, but make no attack. He therefore found it alarming when his son Bill defied the law of the land.

Bill Rickenbacker and the government had collided over the question of privacy. In connection with the 1960 census, there went out a decree that in every fourth household, citizens must answer under threat of imprisonment a questionnaire for the Department of Commerce. This questionnaire struck Bill as "unconscionably long, uncivilly inquisitorial, and absolutely unconstitutional." Bill Rickenbacker tore it up and wrote in a magazine article that when "the Satrap of the Snooper State comes to ask me why I refuse to contribute my share of statistics to the national numbers game, I shall call for my lawyer." The government haled Bill into court. Rick's policy had been never to go into a fight you knew you couldn't win. But there was no question where Rick's loyalty lay. After Bill put the facts before him, he offered to pay the legal expenses. Bill declined the offer but treasured his father's parting remark: "Give the bastards hell!"*

Although he knew it would draw fire from many respectable sources, Rick did not hesitate to offer himself as a figurehead for the national conservative political movement. Braving the accusation that they were archreactionary Republicans under a light disguise, conservative writers and speakers had begun to promulgate the doctrine that Rick had been working on for years. He brought his principles together in a speech called "Conservatism Must Face Up to Liberalism," which he delivered at a meeting of the Chicago Economic Club early in 1961. The weather was vile, but more than a thousand men and women came through snow and sleet to the Palmer House and packed the hall. Lasting more than an hour, the speech halted twenty-four times for prolonged applause, and the ovation at the end lasted four minutes. Rick summed it up:

* For a detailed account of the case, see William F. Rickenbacker, *The Fourth House* (New York, 1971).

I began by declaring that the liberals were no longer firmly in the saddle, that the winds had shifted, that conservatives were rising up across the land, finding new strength in their old convictions, making their voices heard and winning at the polls. Modern liberals had forsaken the original meaning of the word. I said to them frankly, instead of advocating freedom they were striving to pile up the power of government in Washington. It was the conservatives who must take individual freedom as their battle cry and resist the steady encroachment of Federal power. I delivered an all-out attack on the Federal income tax, recommending that we take the government out of competition with private enterprise and eliminate the billions of dollars in expenditures annually being poured down a rathole. I suggested a national lottery to increase revenue without taxation.

At this time Rick came across a humorous novelty of the sort one can buy at hotel newsstands. It was a piece of paper representing "One Kennedy Dollar," measuring one inch by two. Rick sent out a number of them, and one reached the office of Senator Stephen M. Young, of Ohio, who reacted in a manner satisfactory to those who derived amusement from such people. Young sent a newsletter to the folks at home, telling of his achievements in Washington and denouncing enemies of the people. And he led off his December 1961 newsletter by noting that "Eddie Rickenbacker, president of Eastern Airlines, and a Republican who has not yet recovered from the election, is distributing 'One Kennedy Dollar.'" Young went on to say that "if our government had not been subsidizing the operation of Eastern Airlines over the years, Rickenbacker, instead of being a frustrated executive now become a 'statesman,' would probably be an ex-automobile racer."

The venom in this attack showed that the shrunken little dollar struck some nerves. Rick could have overlooked the contemptuous tone, but the statement about government subsidy went against one of the basic tenets of his career in aviation. He sent the letter to his lawyers, who prepared a reply. Their point was that until the Civil Aeronautics Board first established rates for Eastern Airlines under the Civil Aeronautics Act of 1938, Eastern's mail pay was set by competitive bidding and provided for in contracts with the government. Eastern at no time requested subsidy from the CAB, that agency never found that Eastern required subsidy, and no mail rate was ever established for the purpose of funding Eastern's operations. The lawyers reminded Young that Rick was from Ohio, and added that Eastern served five Ohio cities. There was a lot of competition, "image" was important, and the newsletter had done harm that thousands of employers and stockholders had reason to resent.

Young was legally safe in his senatorial robes, but they got heat to him. He had found it an unpleasant surprise to hear that he was kicking around Ohio constituents by slurring Rick and his airline. Men spoke to men in cloakrooms and over telephones, and the thought occurred to the senator that campaign contributions might wither away. And so Young backed down, although he made amends as grudgingly as he could. After some pettifoggery about "the subsidy element in mail costs" twenty and thirty years before, he said that "the writer regrets any inference* and withdraws any statement that either Captain Rickenbacker or Eastern Airlines is or has been dependent on government funds." Then he tried to repair some Ohio damage by noting that Rick had been decorated for valiant war service. But Young said he was still angry about Rick's distributing the midget dollar.

This affair of Senator Young made the old urge commence again, a desire to be far from the United States for a while. Rick decided to make a trip to the Orient. But he wouldn't be going to Vietnam, though Robert McNamara, the Secretary of Defense, stated that "by every quantitative measure, we're winning the war." Off Rick went, bearing up under the fatigue of a

* He meant "implication."

30,000-mile journey in his seventy-third year. Adelaide went along, and she was two years older than Rick. They followed the route of the Pacific mission for much of the way, and Rick had the satisfaction of seeing at last the island that Captain Cherry had been looking for when they got lost.

Rick and Adelaide visited Alaska, Japan, Okinawa, Korea, Taiwan, Hong Kong, Bangkok, Sydney, Melbourne, Wellington in New Zealand, the Fiji Islands, Honolulu, and Seattle. He offered a conclusion about the South Pacific and the Orient which continued to keep the lid tight on any possibility that he would receive the grateful thanks of organized labor. Rick let out the underslung voice a notch and told newsmen in Seattle: "One thing about those people out there. They aren't plagued with union regulations and hours of labor as we are. Most of them work fifty to sixty hours a week."

Back in the United States, Rick ran into trouble that showed him one could never be sure of the press, no matter how experienced in its manipulation one might be. Rick might well have supposed that he was safe from attacks in Nashville, Tennessee, where he had pleased a select audience at the *Banner* anniversary party in the previous year. It was the other paper in town that tried to lay him low. Having digested the Chicago speech and subsequent remarks by Eddie, including a talk in Nashville, an editorial writer on the *Tennessean* attacked Eddie in the Sunday paper of October 7, 1962. The headline MR. RICKENBACKER RANTS appeared over a piece that began, "For an aging public figure who has enjoyed a glamorous and successful career, Mr. Eddie Rickenbacker seems to be a most unhappy gentleman." And when Rick called for the abolishing of the income tax, he had the same effect on the editorial writer as if he had called for the skies to fall. The editors concluded: "Rickenbacker ought to be ashamed. Wherever his airplanes fly, they are subsidized by government cargo. Wherever they land they roll on government concrete, guided into the airport by government

employees and aided by governmental technical equipment
. . . This country's institutions and policies have developed by
necessity for the benefit of the people. They are not perfect,
but until Mr. Rickenbacker can replace them with something
better, we should work to improve upon them rather than destroy them."

This was a poisonous attack, for it withheld Eddie's accepted
title of captain, made no mention of his fighting record, and
passed over his service in the Second World War. Rick could
shrug that off, but the accusation about Eastern surviving on
public money he could not let pass. He wrote to the publisher,
Silliman Evans, Jr., who had inherited the paper from his father. Rick's letter refuted the editorial charges in detail but did
no good. And this attack had come from the heart of Tennessee, the Volunteer State. Rick could infer from that how he
must stand with liberal circles in his beloved second home
town, New York City. But he had known since returning from
the Pacific mission that New York wasn't any longer his terrain.

Rick settled to his task of speech-making, and also became
sponsor of the Committee to Support the Monroe Doctrine. To
advance this cause, he addressed a college in Fort Wayne on
April 25, 1963, and said that "since Franklin Roosevelt recognized the Soviets we have been living a diplomatic lie. If we
continue to do this, we cannot survive as a free people . . . I
say to you today, in Cuba we have lost to Communism the most
decisive battle of the Cold War. Instead of winning, we have
been siphoned still deeper into the whirlpool of global Marx-
ism . . ." Rick was entitled to speak as one having authority.
This he demonstrated by reviewing his accomplishments in a
field that had always claimed his interest, the prediction of
things to come. But he did not claim absolute prescience, saying, "Thirty years ago I made predictions, and some fell far
short of what has taken place. Now we are to have aircraft flying twenty-five hundred to three thousand miles per hour, and

cruising fifty to two hundred and fifty miles above the earth. They will have range to circle the globe twice without refueling." From such aircraft we could form "a perpetual peace patrol." Then Rick went on to say that we could have "atomic power" for aircraft, and that spaceships, within fifty years, would be "self-sustaining planets in themselves." Therefore, he begged his hearers, let us keep America strong and "hold close the candle of life."

If Rick had believed it, he would have taken comfort from the statement by Arthur Sylvester, Assistant Secretary of Defense, in early 1963, that "the corner definitely has been turned toward victory in Vietnam." Such words only deepened Rick's melancholy. Bad things kept happening in New York.

The city planners battered down the Pennsylvania Station, an architectural masterpiece by Charles Follen McKim, of McKim, Mead, and White. Rick was partly responsible, as one who promoted air travel, but this "monumental act of vandalism," as the *New York Times* called it, was more than Rick had bargained for. Without the station, Manhattan seemed to sag on one side like a cripple. They kept up Rockefeller Center pretty well, and Eastern was a favored tenant in the building that bore its name. But the Civil Aeronautics Board did nothing to improve matters, in June 1963, by refusing permission for Eastern and American Airlines to merge. Railroads all over the country were beginning to do so, but, for some inscrutable reason, Eastern and American couldn't get a merger through the bureaucratic mill.

There came November 22, a hazy day in the northeastern states, like the day of Pearl Harbor. Suddenly President Kennedy was dead. The shock hit people in various ways. Rick heard early reports that this was the work of "extreme rightists." There were those who would put the label on Rick, no matter how monstrous it was to think of him in connection with violent disloyalty and shots from ambush. Like Browning's Asolando, Eddie was "One who never turned his back but marched breast forward," and he expected others to do the same. His personal reaction to the Kennedy family had always been that they were nuisances to Eastern Airlines, constantly asking special favors when going to Palm Beach on the Florida run, and Rick endured his share of indirect calumny during the confused hours after the crime.

In his 1963 Christmas letter, Rick disregarded Dallas and the investigation. If Dallas was a hinge of history, Rick wrote as though he had already swung its door, to face the future. And then on December 31, Rick stepped clear of the aviation business. His archives put it, "I retired from active management and the board of directors. I was 73 years old. There were many more things in the world that I wished to do and see, and I could not do them while putting in seven days a week running an airline."

# CHAPTER IX

# The Reckoning

THE BLACKOUT on the night of November 9, 1965, was a challenge to Captain Eddie. He had been walking from a nearby appointment to the office he now occupied on Rockefeller Plaza, one block north of the Eastern Airlines Building, when the lights went out and he found himself part of a murmuring, shuffling crowd whose members made their way along in the illumination that automobiles provided. Rick walked up eighteen flights to his office, where he found Miss Shepherd and a secretary looking from the windows and wondering how long the city would remain in darkness. He then walked downstairs with Miss Shepherd and the young lady, found his chauffeur waiting on the sidewalk, and took all three to dinner at an Italian restaurant that was operating with its usual lighting of candles on red-checked tablecloths.

Rick and Miss Shepherd took the secretary home to Queens and stopped for a brief call, after which he had the chauffeur drive Miss Shepherd to 27 West Fifty-fifth Street, where he walked up six flights to make sure his associate safely reached her own door. The limousine then took Eddie to the Regency, on Park Avenue, where he walked up twenty-one flights to the penthouse, which was his current home. He had not done this stair climbing and traveling around a blacked-out city in any spirit of bravado. It simply hadn't occurred to Rick that he was in his seventy-sixth year and presumably not capable of such feats.

In that year Rick had returned to Manhattan from a trip abroad, and as always in those years when he felt the urge to travel, Adelaide had been at his side. The pace was easier now, but Rick did not spare himself or Adelaide, when the impulse to be in movement came over him. In his notes covering this trip, Rick had written that he found it "unbelievable that the Russians can still claim to be a peaceloving people," and that "we should have handled Cuba the way they did Hungary and there would be no further trouble." In East Berlin he had asked for directions to the graveyard where Richthofen and Udet lay buried. The officials didn't want him there, but Rick insisted on it. At the cemetery gates stood a communist guard with a vicious dog. Rick's archives state: "I had told the East Germans I wanted to pay my respects to some fallen enemies. Then, at the gates, I told the sentry who I was, and that I intended to get in. The guard telephoned his boss, there was conversation, and somebody on the telephone gave his approval. We found that the lock on the iron gate had rusted, and the guard had to force it. The Richthofen monument was massive and just had the name RICHTHOFEN. Unfortunately our photographs turned out no good." Rick added that the East Berliners appeared to be in good health, but were "a frustrated-looking lot of people."

Rick also visited Africa, where he drew disturbing conclusions about the future of that continent in relation to the rest of the world. He had come back to a country about to lose a trusted elder citizen, Herbert Hoover, who died in his apartment at the Waldorf Towers on October 20, 1964. The loss was painful to Rick because in recent months he had so often answered the call of Hoover's secretary, who would say on the telephone, "Captain, the Chief is really very lonely this evening." Rick and Adelaide would go to the apartment and spend an evening with the old man. Adelaide recalled that their visits to Hoover were sad, for the Captain and the Chief had no one to talk to but each other. They were Model T Americans, and if the America they looked back to so fondly was to some extent a myth, it was built on faith and loyalty and a belief in basic virtues. The Captain and the Chief were among the handful of symbolic citizens whom everybody knew, who still personified the good American, so that you felt proud to claim some kinship with them.

In the first three quarters of 1965, before the lights went out, Rick had been able to weigh his opinions and strike a balance that told him his immediate personal world was not so bad. He took a limited view of his beloved New York City, often having himself driven in a hired limousine, and making "21" a port of call. The office on Rockefeller Plaza was an almost exact copy of his room in the Eastern Airlines Building down the street. He had the same desk, the same signed photographs of Ike, Nixon, and Herbert C. Hoover.

Rick's new office was a workshop where he managed personal holdings, handled an enormous correspondence, and turned his attention to the next large task that confronted him, the writing of his autobiography. For the master salesman proposed to sell himself as a figure in American history, and also to show his fellow citizens the meaning of the history he had lived through. Rick had an invaluable coadjutor in Miss Shepherd, whose years of careful supervision over the files of Rick the man of action now stood Rick the historian in good stead.

His tentative titles included:

*The Indestructible Captain Eddie Rickenbacker*
*The Man Who Has Lived Many Lives in One*
*The Autobiography of a Great American*
*The Man Who Is Alive Today Because of His Faith*
  *in God's America*

*The Man Who Has Cheated the Old Grim Reaper Many Times*
*The Man Who Wants to Live Forever*
*I Had to Fight to Live So Long*
*The Indestructible American*

These suggested titles show how Rick's thoughts tended toward the fighting of death. He "wasn't getting into the box yet," and he would "fight like a wildcat" to stay out of that box. Rick knew the old adversary was circling nearer all the time, but he gave him no welcome and no suggestion of surrendering in advance. There was a kind of symbolism in the lights going out just as Rick had settled to telling his life story.

The labor of writing such a book as Eddie embarked on can be compared to digging a ditch. And during the time his piles of transcribed pages were growing, Rick continued his usual ways of relaxing. Unless he was on the wagon, he could enjoy his prelunch cocktails, and unless he had recently sworn off, two or more packs of cigarettes a day. Rick maintained he didn't smoke cigarettes all the way down, and said, "I light three to get one." He had a favorite comic strip, "Little Orphan Annie," which he never missed, and a favorite TV serial, "Bonanza." Rick identified himself with the character portrayed in this story by Lorne Greene, who played a wise, elderly rancher in such convincing style that he had become a symbol of kind paternalism. One day Rick encountered Lorne Greene by chance in an elevator at the Regency. They revealed that each was an admirer of the other, exchanged autographs, and parted with compliments on both sides. Rick treasured his Lorne Greene autograph, and never missed an episode of "Bonanza."

At this time Rick said income tax collectors had "made a C.P.A. out of every businessman in the country. I'm saving deliberately, now that I need it, and I'm not going to let the government racketeers take it away from me." And in the material Rick left behind to mark the blackout year was the list of men whom he said he admired and in whom he saw traits worthy of imitation. They were Herbert C. Hoover, Churchill, Lee Frayer, Admiral Dewey, Robert Wolfe (a Columbus banker), William C. Durant, Henry Ford, Alfred P. Sloan, Jr., Ralph Mulford, Walter P. Chrysler, Washington, Jefferson, Lincoln, McKinley, and Generals Pershing, Patton, Doolittle, Mitchell, LeMay, Marshall, and, perhaps surprisingly, MacArthur. When Rick gave out the list, a questioner asked about former President Truman. Rick answered, "Well, he knew how to swear. He knew how to drink bourbon. He knew how to make up his mind, and unfortunately made it up in the wrong direction. But on the whole, he wasn't too bad." "What about J. F. Kennedy?" "Overrated." "Nixon?" "A better man than people give him credit for, in my opinion."

Rick followed the news in his stronghold on Rockefeller Plaza and could not bring himself to agree with Walt W. Rostow, a White House adviser, who said, "The Viet Cong are going to collapse within weeks. Not months, but weeks." The truth looked simple to Rick: don't let the enemy lay down rules for the fight. He had learned this from fighting in the air. But Eddie's friends Stimson and Arnold had died in 1950; no one of comparable rank and influence asked for his advice now. Academicians were disdainful when they heard Rick's voice, for it was a voice of experience they had not shared.

But Rick crowned all his work of scorning intellectual fashions in 1965, when answering questions about his view of international affairs. "Captain, what do you think of the United Nations?" He replied, "I have no confidence in it as it has worked out. The original charter was good. The basic concept is good if you lived up to it. I've said it privately, the problems of the world today are no more than racial. Dark folks don't like white supervision." "Captain, do you consider American colored people as honorary members of the white race of America, or do you consider that their allegiance lies with people of color overseas?" Rick replied, "We are fortunate in that we number around ten to one. But the rate that the blacks breed and multiply, that will constantly go down, because we have birth control in America because of intelligence on the part of whites. It benefits the colored people not to have it, in order to multiply to the point where they are a greater influence than the whites. It's that simple, and that is true of any minority." "How are you going to sell birth control?" "Gradually. Even the Pope has decided to consider it. Whether or not it will go fast enough I don't know." "But specifically, what about American Negroes?" Rick answered, "To start with, they'll consider themselves Americans, and if the time ever comes when they outnumber the Americans, then they will ally themselves with colored peoples in all parts of the world."

Those who didn't like Eddie or his ideas couldn't find a weak spot in his remark that birth control was the key to the world's progress. He had spent enough time in the Orient and in Africa to know what he was talking about. Bringing babies into a world where they had no chance to survive wasn't his idea of encouraging the spread of civilization. But his tone offended liberal supporters of birth control, who had a tendency to cry "Rickenbacker, get off our side!" This showed the complications of ideology. Rick's endorsement of birth control, for example, put him at odds with Catholics, who thought that he was fine on the subject of communism. At heart, he didn't trust the Roman Catholic Church, as he had shown when he was near death in Atlanta; this went back to Livingstone Avenue and Pastor Pister. And when talking of birth control, Rick also maintained that hard, noninflatable money would raise the standard of living for Asiatic people. To liberal ears, talk of hard money meant placing financial concerns above human needs.

Rick did not overlook the plans that came along for the improvement of the human race. He wrote to one of his publishers that "Utopias will not be realized until the good Lord permits a change in the basic structure of human nature." And he pounced on an item that came through the Associated Press, reporting that there were twenty-four billion rats in India and that the creatures ate twenty-six million tons of wheat per year, out of the supplies sent by America for the people of India. Rick said that common sense would have us spend some of our money killing rats so that the grain would go to starving wretches in the cities and countryside of India. Rick had been there, too, and had seen the miseries he spoke of.

Then he turned his attention to the Office of Economic Opportunity in Washington. Although the value of this office might come under question, there was no doubt that it provided economic opportunity for sinecurists whose pay ran from $18,935 to $35,000 per year in the 1960s. Rick had noticed that government service in itself had become a lucrative trade, and correctly predicted that the numbers of placemen and their salaries would increase in the next ten years. Lovers of government jobs and pay were furious in their resentment of Rick. Since these job-holders numbered millions, Rick thus acquired a formidable army of enemies. He found their hatred bracing and stimulating, and finished 1965 with a Christmas letter that ran to only one page: "Since crossing the three quarter century milestone on October 8, 1965, I have been thinking of my countless blessings. The good Lord had been kind to me . . ." Rick quoted "The American's Creed," by William Tyler Page, and added, "Yes the Lord has been kind to me and I am very grateful!" He ended with conventional holiday greetings, leading to his time-honored close, "Sincerely, Eddie."

Rick concluded his life story by repeating his view of world politics: "It is my firm opinion that the rivalry of color will supplant the current rivalry of ideology. It will pit the whites against the non-whites . . . I realize that this picture of world-wide strife is a forbidding picture indeed, but I can only repeat that I am not advocating it. I am merely projecting the situation in the world today . . ." Reviewers had good things to say about Rick's autobiography but complained that he did not reveal himself. He belonged to a generation that didn't do that. An understanding critic was Stanley Walker, who had been city editor of the *Herald Tribune.* He called Rick "a rough and ready fellow," and one you would like to have beside you in a fight. But Walker made it clear that Rick was better than his book.

Throughout 1968 Eddie continued to feel the emotional weight of the war in Vietnam. It was depressing, and Rick restored his spirits by a trip to Cincinnati, the city he had left for the first war. He sat on the main floor at Shillito's department store, with its iron-railed balconies rising around a splendid central court. Here he autographed more than 400 books, and the buyer sent an order for 1000 more.

The publication of Rick's version of his life story, in 1968, showed that he intended to give value to anyone who asked him to sign his long name. His son Bill noted that "a full ceremonial signature took about 30 seconds of his time. Maybe he released and satisfied in this way some of his artistic urge. Captain Eddie sat down, hunched over, worked hard, and in the silence of concentration produced this unmistakabe mark — while the petitioner drank in the silence and observed the man's energy and honesty pouring in his direction."

Eddie was beginning to feel the strain of those promotion trips. The delight of being a center of attention was a strong stimulant, and good for a man of his temperament, but now energy ran low, and he came down with pneumonia. Before he got out of the hospital, where the doctors thought he had a collapsed lung, Rick had come close to death. But he was sending his Christmas letter as usual at the end of 1968: "Another year has passed and what a year! Many things have happened, but the most important of all is that early in 1969, we will have Richard M. Nixon as our new President and a new administration." Rick added that we must join hands and help the leaders of our government, but he didn't give the impression that his heart was in it, for the letter was brief, almost perfunctory in comparison with the thundering two-pagers of the past.

The Christmas letter that went out at the end of 1969 echoed the gloomy tone of the one before. Rick wrote, "There never has been a period when so many problems have faced us as a Nation." He thought it "almost too late to correct the many false steps." But the old vehement hortatory voice was muted, and after this, Rick wrote no more of the Christmas letters that had grown into serious essays from the one-paragraph greeting of years before. He had reached a point where he began to put aside things that he had once thought he must do at all costs as part of a system of self-imposed obligations. Like Stevenson's Weir of Hermiston, he had long been marching up the great bare staircase of his duty, and he lightened his load as the top of it came near.

# Home to Ohio

RICK LIVED BRAVELY ON, with Adelaide at his side. Soon there arrived a startling date — October 8, 1970. His ninth decade had begun. So far as contemporaries were concerned, Rick was almost alone now; he had funerals to attend, eulogies to deliver, and letters of condolence to write. Rick's friends did not die; they "passed on to the Great Beyond." But his sincerity shone through the conventional words. Miss Shepherd said, "We fear to see the newspaper — it is always someone else gone."

Bill saw his father as one who kept on under this emotional battering, "sturdy, husky, happy to be alive." Sturdy and husky he was, and doctors said he had muscles like those of a man in his forties. But the muscles held up an ailing, creaking frame. His back was straight, but his face could not keep secret the rough mileage in his life. He had seen them come and he had seen them go. Now he was like the Duke of Wellington, who also lived to old age as a public landmark, growing deaf and at times irritable, but keeping the edges of his personality crisp and clean. And like the great duke, Eddie experienced opprobrium in spite of heroic military service. The duke heard the hoots and hisses of a London mob on the anniversary of Waterloo in his eighty-first year. Rick could have heard the same by appearing at almost any union meeting, and he was now editorial game from the center to the left of the journalistic spectrum.

Not so distressing was the resemblance of the two old gentlemen in looking after large amounts of correspondence. The duke had complained, "It is quite curious with what a number of Insane persons I am in relation. Mad retired Officers, Mad Women . . ." In the same way, Eddie dealt patiently with cranks and the writers of begging letters, and with people who wrote to tell him he was wrong about this or that. Only the most abusive failed to get a reply. Again like the duke, Eddie was careful to answer letters from children, and he got them by the hundreds. Rick would reply gravely, in the same tone he used toward adults, and if the child presented a problem, he gave it thought. He incised the long signature on countless autograph cards, with an extra one for an eight-year-old who asked it for her little sister: "She's a good little sister but she cannot write yet."

Rick also put himself sincerely into the answering of adults who seemed to think he could cast light on their problems. A man wrote to say that he was agnostic but was trying to regain faith. Could Captain Eddie make a helpful comment? Rick replied: "Quite frankly, if there was not a God in Heaven, and if I had not had faith in that Power Above, which I was taught to understand and believe as a child at my mother's knee, I would not be here today." Rick had also worked out a closing for his standard speech, which said he wanted "nothing further in material value or personal prestige — no power, no wealth, no political plums. But I do pray that this exhortation in the name of freedom and liberty will spread into every nook and cranny of this land of ours for the benefit of future generations . . . Then, and only then, can we say when the candle of life burns low — thank God, I have given my best to the land which has given so much to me."

The elegiac tone was noticeable, but Rick in his daily pursuits remained cheerful, though he let people know when something aroused his temper. He liked to visit his sons' families. Dave and Patty Rickenbacker in New Jersey found him a delightful guest, although Patty couldn't help noticing that he seemed to think no serious conversation could be attempted if ladies were present. He seldom appeared without his ample, well-worn briefcase, but refused to disclose its contents. Someone had said that Rick had a million dollars in cash always readily available. Patty suggested that this million might be what made the briefcase bulge. But Rick only smiled. Another crotchet was conserving liquor. Once, at Dave's house, he mistook the contents of a martini pitcher for water, and poured some on top of his bourbon. Dave said, "Dad, throw it out." Rick replied, "There's no sense in wasting good liquor," and drank the mixture, which seemed to do him no harm. Rick drank his last alcoholic drink around 1970. He didn't swear off; whiskey just didn't seem to do anything for him, so he stopped drinking it. At about the same time, he stopped smoking.

In those closing years, Eddie and Adelaide lived in their last hotel suite in New York, at the Dorset, on Fifty-fourth Street between Fifth and Sixth avenues.* The small paneled lobby, courteous attendants, rich-looking clients rising to their quarters in swift silent elevators — it was all dignified and gilt-edged, just what Rick wanted. The David Rickenbackers recall going into town for dinner with Rick at the University Club one evening when Adelaide was in Florida. Patty and David were delayed in traffic and arrived so late that Rick had given up waiting. They found him in the great top-floor dining room. Lunchers crowd this room at the middle of the day, but in the evening it is, "quite frankly," as Rick would say, gloomy — even though an acknowledged masterpiece of McKim, Mead, and

* A New Yorker to the end, Rick would never call Sixth Avenue the Avenue of the Americas.

White. Patty and David found Rick alone at a small table. The atmosphere was almost funereal and Patty thought it sad, but Rick smiled happily when he saw them, and he hauled himself to his feet.

It wasn't long before Rick gave up on New York, closed the Dorset suite, and joined Adelaide in Florida. They had a fine house in Coral Gables; but now they sold it and moved across the Rickenbacker Causeway to a place as agreeable in its way as the Caveman Camp. This was the Key Biscayne Hotel, which concealed its grounds and villas down a narrow road off Ocean Drive. The private park reached to a sea wall, with palm trees, a swimming pool, and a small golf course landscaped in an unassuming way. The hotel part of the establishment had a dining room and bar where the atmosphere was timeless and serene. Adelaide and Rick moved into Villa 68, and later into Villa 74. This was a two-story house on the sea wall, with a broad window in its ground-floor living room, overlooking the ocean.

Rick was a commodore of the Florida Navy, and he liked to look over blue water. Sometimes a freighter would come by, a mile out and surprisingly fast, and there were always small boats with sails of red, yellow, or blue, each a silhouette the shape of an Indian tepee. And as he looked about him on land, he liked to watch the young women, and they would always wave and say, "Hi, Captain Eddie!" He would see them on the little golf course as he pitched and putted around — "Captain Eddie! Hi there!" This was the best of Florida, but the Key Biscayne Hotel was expensive. That aspect of it did not bother Rick, and he worked contentedly at his correspondence when he wasn't simply basking and allowing his nerves to relax. He frequently put on his favorite phonograph records, music of the toe-tapping variety, polkas and such ballads as "Mac-Namara's Band." You would often hear this music among the palms as you walked up the path to the villa. Rick said, "I'd give my shirt if I could play the piano."

Rick's kinship to the characters of Ring Lardner continued, for Lardner's story "The Golden Honeymoon" took place in Florida, and here was Rick, about to celebrate his fiftieth wedding anniversary at Key Biscayne, in September 1972. Like Lardner's old man, Rick appreciated his helpmate, and they had a nice celebration. Then, on October 12, Rick was sitting with Adelaide and his niece when the haymaker stroke caught up with him. Adelaide and the niece thought he would die right there. The ambulance rushed to the mainland over the Rickenbacker Causeway to Mercy Hospital. This was a long, tan building with dwarf Australian pines around it, on South Miami Avenue. Eddie could see the causeway and the ocean from his bed, but it would be a long time before he took interest in scenery. Nevertheless, the Associated Press moved a story out of Miami on October 20 that he was getting better.

In fact, he was going through a dreadful ordeal. For a while Rick was in a low state of consciousness, almost in a coma. Then he had to undergo surgery for relieving the pressure of fluid on the brain. Although some patients die from it, Rick survived this operation, and the doctors called his prospects good. But the prescribed treatment seemed to be destroying Rick's ability to live, and he kept getting worse, even though two orderlies tended him night and day. Next, pneumonia attacked him, and the doctors thought he couldn't last. He fought it off and survived a kidney failure. But he did not improve afterward, and lost the ability to talk.

Adelaide decided it was time for a change and had Eddie taken to a cheerful nursing home, where he rapidly improved and recovered his powers of speech. After a short stay he returned to Villa 74, and a friend described him as being "serene." This was in January 1973. In February Miss Shepherd was writing that Rick had amazed everybody, including the doctors, by a recovery that appeared to be complete. These months, he told Adelaide, were the happiest of his life.

And late in June the old thing commenced again — the desire to make a long trip. Perhaps Rick's north European ancestral roots were pulling at him. At any rate, he asked Adelaide if she would make the journey with him to Switzerland so that he could see where his parents had been born. Adelaide said she'd go with him. There was something heroic in this, not because of her age, although she was in her eighty-sixth year, but because of her health, which had been in a precarious state for some time. One of the worst troubles besetting Adelaide was failing eyesight, and she had other miseries. Nevertheless, she agreed to go if that was what Rick wanted.

Rick made a public appearance in the Miami Fourth of July parade, and they went to New York shortly afterward, to take plane for Zürich. The David Rickenbackers came to their hotel rooms and with sympathetic eyes saw some significant details. For one thing, Rick was solicitous of Adelaide and tried to do everything for her, even though he was shaky on his legs. Because of Adelaide's waning eyesight, the housekeeper had put bulbs of extra power into every socket. In this light, Eddie and Adelaide looked old but undaunted. They seemed to combine to help each other, sometimes without having to speak. Adelaide had dropped a wallet containing her passport and traveler's checks between the seats of the plane coming up from Florida. There was telephoning about this, and Adelaide asked Rick why he didn't call some bigwig about it, someone like a senator. He replied, "The day when I had influence is long gone."

The impulse to be in Switzerland landed Captain Eddie, his wife, Miss Shepherd, and an American medical orderly at the Hotel Barlach, in Zürich, on July 12. This was to be base camp for Eddie's trip into the countryside to see the ancestral home of the Rickenbackers. But now Adelaide took a bad turn with pleurisy, and the expedition slowed down. Next day Rick had a spell of irregular breathing, and on the following day they asked Adelaide's doctor to advise them about what they should do. The doctor listened to Rick's heart; then he spoke to Adelaide privately. He'd like to have Rick go to the hospital for some x-ray pictures. Adelaide told Miss Shepherd she feared to repeat this to Rick, but when she did, he surprised her by saying, "All right, that may be a good idea."

When Rick got into the hospital bed, he leaned back against the pillows and seemed to be at peace, free from anxiety and strain, calmly facing the inevitable. On the following day the doctors diagnosed pneumonia. Perhaps he could return to the States as a stretcher case. But Rick preferred to stay where he was. Then his heart began beating out of rhythm. On Thursday, the hospital staff thought he was dying, but he revived.

Dave took plane in New York, arriving in Zürich on a damp, gray Saturday morning. He telephoned from the airport, and the nurses put Rick on. He had always called Dave "pal." And now he was able to say, "Hello — pal." It was the same jaunty voice, but weak. Dave was glad he had telephoned, because when he got to the hospital, Rick didn't know him. Rick remained mostly unconscious for the next two days and died about 4:15 in the morning of Monday, July 23. The doctors said it was heart failure. Whatever it was, he had seen it coming and had accepted the fact that Rickenbacker's luck had finally turned bad. But perhaps it wasn't so bad at that. For an American of the Rickenbacker make, 1973 was a good time to die.

Eddie received three memorial services, which put one in mind of last appearances by a great theatrical star. The first service, on July 27, took place in the Presbyterian Church on Key Biscayne. The second service took place at the Marble Collegiate Church on Fifth Avenue, on August 7. At the third service, on August 10 in Columbus, they put Rick's ashes into the ground at Green Lawn Cemetery beside his parents. After the committal, as the family and other mourners stood by, four jets from Squadron 94 shot into view. Just before they came overhead, the first ship pulled straight up while the other three raced on in the missing leader formation, the air force equivalent of the riderless horse. David said later that when he saw the single plane disappear and heard the sound of the motors fade, the effect was shattering. Bill said, "The family gathered afterwards for refreshment; and before long we were saying good-bye and doing what Dad would have urged us to do — get on back to work." They went their ways, and left Captain Eddie to his rest.

# Notes    Index

# Notes

Aside from the author's research by letter (LAU) and conversation (CAU), the main sources of this biography are in the deposits of Rickenbacker papers, diaries kept by Captain Rickenbacker in 1918, 1919, and 1922, and the master script, unpublished, of Rickenbacker's autobiography, *Life Story of Edward V. Rickenbacker* (LSEVR), which runs to some 8000 typewritten pages. Rickenbacker distributed his papers, letters, manuscripts, and memorabilia as follows:

To the Air Force Museum on the Wright-Patterson Air Force Base at Dayton (AFM) went drawings; paintings; plaques; medals; china; captured German aircraft equipment; eight albums containing news clippings, certificates of honorary membership in various organizations, citations of merit, and honorary degrees; four typescripts totaling 1237 pages from LSEVR; a number of Rickenbacker's decorations, including his Congressional Medal of Honor; sixteen captured German medals and aviation badges; a German cigarette case; the diaries of March 2 to December 31, 1918 (D1); and March 22 to November 4, 1919 (D2).

The Manuscript Room at the Library of Congress has the largest collection of Rickenbacker material, consisting of some 36,000 items. Rickenbacker's correspondence (CLC) is here, in 262 file boxes. Material other than correspondence in this collection is designated MLC and includes albums of congratulatory letters and telegrams on various occasions; six volumes of his magazine articles; the uncut first-draft typescript of his autobiography; a volume of Christmas letters; a

6537-page typed extract from the master script of Rick's LSEVR; and two hampers of miscellaneous telegrams, notes for speeches, and office memoranda.

At the Library of The Ohio State University in Columbus are fourteen bound volumes containing Rickenbacker's public speeches, beginning with prophecies at Banff in 1919; broadcasts, talks, and public statements; and the complete master script for LSEVR.

The National Air and Space Museum at the Smithsonian Institution contains plaques, photographs, volumes of news clippings, all medals not at the AFM, and an album covering the Atlanta accident.

The Indianapolis Motor Speedway Museum has photographs of Rickenbacker during his career as an auto racer; typewritten notes and news clippings relating to his ownership of the speedway; records of prize money paid for the 500-mile races; the American Automobile Association's statistics establishing Rick's standing as a competitive driver; extracts from *Motor Age* and from manuscripts by trade journalists describing his races; and miscellaneous models, racing trophies, pictures, and souvenirs.

The third diary, covering the wedding trip from September 16 to November 28, 1919 (D3), is in possession of the family.

## Prologue. One Summer in Columbus (*pages 1–9*)

Columbus during the years of Rick's boyhood, before he took to the road, is preserved for the student in the Ohioana Room at the Ohio State (not University) Library, and microfilms in the Newspaper Room at the Columbus Public Library. The Captain told the episode of the ludicrous shoes to Hans Christian Adamson after the wreck in the Pacific for Adamson's book, *Eddie Rickenbacker*. The accounts of other school episodes and early jobs at child labor are found in LSEVR. Daily weather reports in the newspapers tell of the suffocating quality of a central Ohio summer and mention the temperature above 90° before noon on the last day of William Rickenbacker's life. Captain Rickenbacker in his reminiscent years said that his father had died as the result of an industrial accident. The story of what actually occurred took up front-page space in the newspapers, which identified William's assailant as a drifter from the South.

## Chapter I. The New Noise (*pages 10–39*)

The account of Rick's career as salesman in Omaha and Texas is based on LSEVR and items in Columbus newspapers. Automobile racing in the period 1910–1915 is described in Sioux City and Indianapolis newspapers and in *Motor Age*. The activities of Charles Erbstein were covered in the Chicago *Herald*. Rickenbacker's talk at the Sioux City Commercial Club banquet is based on local newspapers and on manuscripts in the Indianapolis Motor Speedway Museum. The von Rickenbacher hoax may be read in the Los Angeles *Times*. Background material on racing at Sheepshead Bay was found in *Motor Age*, the New York newspapers, and the Federal Writers' Project guide to New York. Rick's telephone calls at Cincinnati are given in LSEVR, and his training for the race is covered in the Cincinnati *Enquirer* and the Cincinnati *Commercial Tribune*.

## Chapter II. To Make the World Safe (*pages 40–75*)

Background material on the American participation in the war is drawn from memoirs by Generals Harbord and Pershing; Sir Philip Gibbs, *Now It Can Be Told;* and Laurence Stallings, *The Doughboys*. My accounts of training and combat are based mainly on D1 and LSEVR, with some corroborative detail from my own experiences in the air. Rick told in D1 how he felt about the collegians at Issoudun, and further light is thrown on this by John Davies, in *The Legend of Hobey Baker*. The facts concerning Major Lufbery's death come from a collection of contemporary documents at AFM, which also confirms Rickenbacker's list of combats and victories from the *Records of the American Expeditionary Force, 94th Aero Squadron* (RG 120).

## Chapter III. The Personality Market (*pages 76–121*)

Rickenbacker gave, in D2, a painstakingly detailed account of his first days back in the States, banquets and public ceremonies, hardships on the lecture tour, and efforts to find a job. He made many references to the technical side of public speaking in LSEVR, CLC, and MLC. A daily and hourly record of job hunting is in D2, along with Rick's thoughts on proper business aims for a war hero and the possibility that lack of formal education might be an insuperable handicap. The triumphant parades at Chicago, Columbus, and Los Angeles are described in MLC and the local newspapers. The many certificates of membership, AFM, show Rick's remarkable popularity wherever he went.

## Chapter IV. Assembly Line (*pages 122–160*)

The business meetings preceding the formation of Rickenbacker Motors are described at the end of D2. From then on, the fortunes of the company can be traced in CLC, and the various models of the car worthy of its name, which included an eight-cylinder sport roadster, may be studied in MLC. In LSEVR, Rickenbacker enlarged on the tactics of organizing the company, and the trade and regular press also followed it. The business climate of the mid-1920s as it affected automobile making was analyzed in *Motor Age* and the metropolitan press. Alfred P. Sloan, Jr., furnished additional background in *My Years with General Motors*. The account of Rick's last days with the company is based on CAU. The story of Rick's wedding trip, as he related it with Lardnerian irony, was found in D3.

## Chapter V. Common Carrier (*pages 161–210*)

An immense amount of documentation is available for Rickenbacker's activity as an airline developer. Rick's own publicity men filled hundreds of newspaper columns and magazine pages with accounts of his career as manager of the General Motors aviation interests, and later as an independent promoter controlling Eastern Airlines. The stories are accurate, but additional facts are in LSEVR and CLC, where Rickenbacker describes his resentment of John Hertz and Ernest Breech, in addition to his work as factor for Harriman and Lehman in the airline holding company. Sources for the Atlanta wreck are LSEVR, LAU, CAU, and the Atlanta and New York newspapers. The Southern railway wreck was described in CAU, and the doctor's letter about drinking came to me through a confidential source.

Chapter VI. Peril on the Sea (*pages 211–255*)

Rick's interviews with Secretary Stimson are described in LSEVR. For the first ten days of disappearance in the Pacific, all newspapers carried accounts of the search for the missing men. The story then subsided, to burst out again in front-page headlines with news of the rescues. My account of the ordeal is based on Rickenbacker's report to Stimson, which was carried in full by the wire services, interviews with the survivors (AFM), Adamson's *Eddie Rickenbacker,* Lieutenant James Whittaker's *We Thought We Heard the Angels Sing,* and Rickenbacker's descriptions in LSEVR and CLC. The numerous ballads and homilies that Rick's ordeal inspired are in MLC.

Chapter VII. Comrade Eddie (*pages 256–283*)

Rick describes his confidential interviews with Stimson in LSEVR. The theory of eye language is in the same document, and the State Department cables about Rick's entering Russia are in CLC. Material on the Persian Gulf Command originated in CAU. Rick gave an account of the mission to Russia in LSEVR and went into more detail in the dictated reports (MLC).

Chapter VIII. I Say to You Frankly (*pages 284–327*)

Rick's public speeches here and throughout the book are taken from the manuscripts of his talks. His troubles with newspapers in Louisville and Nashville were told in the papers involved, and further light is thrown on these matters in CLC and notes in MLC. A full account of the dispute with Congressman Young, and the lawyers' letters, can be found in CLC.

Chapter IX. The Reckoning (*pages 328–336*)

Rick's adventures in the blackout come from CAU and LAU. His labors in dictating the autobiography, an addition to LSEVR, can be assayed in MLC, where the bills for transcribing are on file. Rick's opinions about New York City are set forth in CLC, and the description of his manner of life at East End Avenue and in the Manhattan hotels is based largely on CAU.

### Epilogue. Home to Ohio (*pages 337–344*)

Aside from the newspaper reports, which are on file in MLC and AFM, my own conversations with persons involved are the principal sources of the account of Captain Rickenbacker's last days. The news clippings in AFM show that the air force installation near Columbus was named Rickenbacker Air Base a year after Rick's death. Its call name is Rick Tower.

# Index